The Postapocalyptic Black Female Imagination

The Postapocalyptic Black Female Imagination

Maxine Lavon Montgomery

BLOOMSBURY ACADEMIC
LONDON • NEW YORK • OXFORD • NEW DELHI • SYDNEY

BLOOMSBURY ACADEMIC
Bloomsbury Publishing Plc
50 Bedford Square, London, WC1B 3DP, UK
1385 Broadway, New York, NY 10018, USA
29 Earlsfort Terrace, Dublin 2, Ireland

BLOOMSBURY, BLOOMSBURY ACADEMIC and the Diana logo
are trademarks of Bloomsbury Publishing Plc

First published in Great Britain 2021
This paperback edition published 2023

Copyright © Maxine Lavon Montgomery, 2021

Maxine Lavon Montgomery has asserted her right under the Copyright,
Designs and Patents Act, 1988, to be identified as Author of this work.

For legal purposes the Acknowledgments on p. vi constitute
an extension of this copyright page.

Cover design by Eleanor Rose
Cover image © Yuliia Blazhuk / iStock / Getty Images Plus

All rights reserved. No part of this publication may be reproduced or
transmitted in any form or by any means, electronic or mechanical, including
photocopying, recording, or any information storage or retrieval system,
without prior permission in writing from the publishers.

Bloomsbury Publishing Plc does not have any control over, or responsibility for,
any third-party websites referred to or in this book. All internet addresses given
in this book were correct at the time of going to press. The author and publisher
regret any inconvenience caused if addresses have changed or sites have
ceased to exist, but can accept no responsibility for any such changes.

A catalogue record for this book is available from the British Library.

A catalog record for this book is available from the Library of Congress.

ISBN: HB: 978-1-3501-2450-9
PB: 978-1-3502-4855-7
ePDF: 978-1-3501-2451-6
eBook: 978-1-3501-2452-3

Typeset by Integra Software Services Pvt. Ltd.,

To find out more about our authors and books visit www.bloomsbury.com
and sign up for our newsletters.

Contents

Acknowledgments — vi

1. Beyond the End of History: Race, Gender, Sexuality, and a Postapocalyptic Imaginary — 1
2. Coming of Age on the Dark Side: Speculative Fictions of Black Girlhood in Octavia E. Butler's *Fledgling*, Nalo Hopkinson's *Brown Girl in the Ring*, and Edwidge Danticat's *Claire of the Sea Light* — 17
3. "Queering" the New World Order in Michelle Cliff's *Abeng* and *No Telephone to Heaven* — 65
4. Un-zombifying Blackness in Erna Brodber's *Myal* and Gloria Naylor's *Bailey's Café* — 91
5. Romance after the Ruin: Looking for Love in the Era of the "Post" in Toni Morrison's *Tar Baby*, Jesmyn Ward's *Salvage the Bones*, and Beyonce's *Lemonade* — 117

Notes — 151
References — 169
Index — 177

Acknowledgments

In the completion of any enterprise, especially one involving the production of a book-length monograph, there are individuals who labor behind the scenes—invisible, silent, often unacknowledged—but without whose assistance the project would not have come to fruition. I would be remiss if I did not pay homage to those who played a key role in the research, writing, and revision of this book.

First, I want to thank my research intern, Sabine Nemours, for her role in locating scholarly resources on Octavia E. Butler and for invigorating lunchtime conversations about Afro-futurist feminism, Black women's fiction and cultural production, and current social and political events. I learned from you as much as you gleaned knowledge from me. I also wish to acknowledge graduate scholars in my Postapocalyptic Black Female Imagination seminar who not only shared my enthusiasm for Afro-futurism but also challenged me in ways that prompted me to refine my arguments early on. Through lively debate and robust conversation, these scholars helped to push the project's geographic and disciplinary boundaries beyond its initial construct.

A one-semester sabbatical and summer research grant allowed focused attention to research and writing. Along with scholarly audiences at Ethno-futurist, Afro-futurist, and African-American Literary and Cultural Studies conferences nationwide, colleagues Chester J. Fontenot, II, Ronald Baxter Miller, and Candace Ward offered helpful insights along the way. My sister, Juanita Montgomery Hale, was a source of inspiration when I needed the extra push that would get me to the finish line.

Last but not least, I owe a debt of gratitude to my husband, Nathaniel Crawford, my partner in love and life, and our daughter, Samantha Natalya Crawford, a talented, up-and-coming literary scholar in her own right. Thanks for allowing me a room of my own to get my work done.

For each of you, the future is as unbounded as your imagination and willingness to move beyond the limits that confront us all.

1

Beyond the End of History

Race, Gender, Sexuality, and a Postapocalyptic Imaginary

Hack this: Why do so few African-Americans write science fiction, a genre whose close encounters with the Other—the stranger in a strange land—would seem uniquely suited to the concerns of African-American novelists? Yet, to this writer's knowledge, only Samuel R. Delany, Octavia Butler, Steve Barnes, and Charles Saunders have chosen to write within the genre conventions of SF. This is especially perplexing in light of the fact that African-Americans are, in a very real sense, the descendants of alien abductees. They inhabit a sci-fi nightmare in which unseen but no less impassable force fields of intolerance frustrate their movements; official histories undo what has been done to them; and technology, be it branding, forced sterilization, the Tuskegee experiment, or tasers, is too often brought to bear on black bodies.

Mark Dery, "Black to the Future"

They say Armageddon been in effect. But let me tell you how this business began ...

Reginald Dwayne Betts, "The Countdown to Armageddon"

Write the things which thou hast seen, and the things which are, and the things which shall be hereafter ...

Revelation 1:19

If evocative song titles such as "Mystery Babylon" and "New World Blues" from Ebony Bones's genre-crossing album *Behold a Pale Horse* hint at the British Queen of Afro-Punk's fascination with future-oriented concerns, then the spectacular portrait of the artist on the album cover gestures openly toward the use of otherworldly and alien iconography in announcing her 2013 musical release. The cover features Bones sporting a blonde Afro, wearing a black cape and stilettos, riding an upside-down white horse, and holding a crystal ball in her hands.[1] Bones is the Brixton-born daughter of Caribbean immigrants, and the artist's critically acclaimed second album represents a fusion of eclectic musical genres including afro-beat, classical, and post-punk. Drawn from Revelation, the trope of the pale horse signals a pandemic spawning widespread death and destruction accompanying the biblical end-of-times while the fantastic cover heralds an avant-garde style that traverses established musical boundaries.

To what extent, though, is it possible to account for the current preoccupation with the end-time events not only with the talented songster, but also among other musicians, authors, visual artists, filmmakers, moviegoers, superhero comic book fans, as well as literary and cultural critics worldwide? Now that society has witnessed the *fin de siècle* without an apocalyptic finale, why does the specter of a cataclysmic end of the world and its uncertain eschatological aftermath continue to exert a powerful influence on a late-twentieth and early-twenty-first-century imagination? What are the implications of an indigenous cultural past in envisioning a utopian social order? Can members of marginalized cultures intent on recovering a lost, fragmented heritage envisage possible futures? Questions about the existence of extraterrestrial figures, aliens, and post-human creatures, ethical issues surrounding genetically engineered or technologically enhanced beings, theories surrounding deadly plagues, and matters concerning the role of biotechnology in the realms of medicine and science have been the focus of considerable debate in recent times. Such efforts prompt literary theorists, cultural critics, scientists, and ordinary citizens to re-think customary boundaries between art and science, technology and the body, and, most important for this project, history and the future. *The Postapocalyptic Black Female Imagination* not only interrogates Black women's postapocalyptic imaginaries; it also breaks scholarly ground by attending to the manner in which a non-hegemonic positioning transforms representations of futurity in distinctive ways.

Mark Dery's catalog of Black science fiction writers betrays a US and masculinist bias with pioneering novelist Octavia E. Butler as the lone female named as a contributor to the trendy genre.[2] Rather than serving as a coda, a final pronouncement regarding the Black literary engagement with science fiction, his essay offers a starting point for recovery in a scholarly reappraisal of Black fantasy culture. Since the publication of his landmark essay announcing the beginnings of a formal study of Afro-futurism as a literary and cultural phenomenon, scholars have undertaken the challenging task of mapping the field in innovative ways.[3] Not only have Black women made significant contributions to fantasy culture through literature, film, art, music, and other forms of expressivity, including hip-hop, they also reveal a broad, albeit unacknowledged commitment to futuristic concerns as writers and artists across the diaspora create worlds that confront us with utopian visions of a society where humanity can be transformed, often dramatically, making space for a reappraisal of Afrofuturist canon formation.

The last few decades have observed a proliferation of criticism on Black fantasy culture, but much scholarly work remains in an investigation of Black women's interventions into science fiction.[4] Current scholarship underscores the importance of historical recuperation in the project of reevaluating the work of marginalized or forgotten Black women authors and the manner in which writers have created an identifiable tradition apart from a masculinist literary lineage. Mae Gwendolyn Henderson describes a tradition of authors who investigate gendered and racial decodings of Black women in literature in order to offer "strong revisionary methods of reading, focusing as they do on literary discourses regarded as marginal to the dominant literary-critical tradition."[5] Representative texts often entail disruption and revision, she rightly observes. "Disruption—the initial response to hegemonic and ambiguously (non)hegemonic discourse—and revision (rewriting or rereading)," Henderson points out, "together suggest a model for reading black and female literary expression."[6] Hortense Spillers situates her reading of Black literary and cultural production within a context involving recovery of the long-suppressed feminine as a critical linkage in the project of Black Atlantic identity construction.[7] Central to national debates surrounding social justice issues, policing practices, and identity politics, Kimberlé Crenshaw's concept of intersectionality, which refers to the interlocking influences of race, class, gender, and sexuality, offers a useful, if not problematic, paradigm for approaching literature and expressive culture by and about women of color.[8]

Unlike writers and performers whose futuristic imaginaries serve a private and individualized function, Black women deploy fantasy and the fantastic as a means of social critique and in a manner reflecting the cultural history of the group as a whole. With women of color, images of a transformed social order emerging in the not-too-distant future offer a basis for reexamining social and political issues of the present moment, and those visions announce a reclamation of a gendered Africanist past. In other words, for Black women, the future is Black and female, and representations of an otherworldly existence summon a diasporic heritage, but with gendered inflection that prompts a reappraisal of core themes in contemporary Black feminist thought.

Implicit within remarks on the part of celebrated novelist Octavia E. Butler is her reliance upon the genre conventions of science fiction as a method of cultural criticism. "I was attracted to science fiction because it was so wide open," Butler reveals.[9] "I was able to do anything and there were no walls to hem you in and there was no human condition that you were stopped from examining."[10] Butler's fictionalization of a postapocalyptic culture where aliens, vampires, and other extraterrestrial beings are commonplace disrupts a temporal history that insists upon a separation between past, present, and future, between ordinary experience and a fanciful world peopled by ethereal figures. In the futuristic realm Butler envisions, not only do cyborgs, bionic women, and vampires appear routinely as a part of everyday life; those figures also embody an intersectionality that challenges received notions of race, class, gender, and sexuality. These otherworldly beings can happily coexist with folkloric personae such as the soucouyants of Afro-Caribbean fame, known for their shape-shifting abilities. By challenging science fiction's reliance upon tropes of whiteness and maleness, she opens up the genre to a wider reader-audience, encouraging a reassessment of established identity constructs and the temporal spaces where such identities are forged.

The Postapocalyptic Black Female Imagination employs a theoretical methodology informed by the latest scholarship in gender and cultural studies as a means of examining moments of catastrophe and disaster and the futuristic imaginaries that follow. This project juxtaposes works widely considered as mainstays in Afro-futurism alongside those not previously included within fantasy culture in revealing the utility of reading Black women's postapocalypticism as an unacknowledged subgenre of science fiction. Works under investigation envision a cataclysmic upheaval that portends the end of an old era and the beginning of an altogether new reality existing as a part of, yet separate from, temporal history. The cataclysm could be either a past occurrence or one taking place in time-present of narrative action. It might consist of a rendering of an actual incident, or a visualization of one transpiring in the not-too-distant future. A natural or human-made disruption may also signal an apocalypse with Edwidge Danticat's fictionalization of the 2010 Haiti earthquake. Jesmyn Ward and Beyonce attend to the post-Katrina Southeastern US Gulf region in the wake of a category five hurricane that upended the area's social, environmental, and cultural life. Incidents of social unrest or a pandemic likewise signify a postapocalyptic sensibility prompting Nalo Hopkinson's account of urban chaos following Toronto's 1992 Yonge Street Riot in *Brown Girl in the Ring* or Erna Brodber's rendering of sickness and disease in *Myal*.

The prevalence of sexual dysfunction, psychological distress, physical impairment, or infection attests to the lingering consequences of the past. Those conditions also demonstrate the persistence of trauma in the lives of Black Atlantic subjects. Frantz Fanon posits the notion that slavery and colonization constitute an originary trauma marking the lives of a raced population.[11] Much of the postcolonial condition involves efforts to address the residual psychic or physical wounds of oppressive colonial and neocolonial influences. Tropes of illness and healing assume paramount importance in the fantastic worlds Black women seek to construct, signaling the lasting results of an unsettled trans-Atlantic history that refuses to release its stranglehold on the present. Although science, technology, and medicine present themselves as solutions to physical, emotional, or psychological ailments, traditional institutional structures and modern medicine fail to displace enduring folk remedies involving Obeah, Myal, herbal cures, and homeopathic practices.

Recent scholarship attends to the traumatic moments of the trans-Atlantic journey in relation to the dislocating nature of the Middle Passage and the implications of that journey for emerging identity constructions in a New World setting.[12] Such insights are resonant with James Berger's assertion that "the study of post-apocalypse is a study of what disappears and what remains, and of how the remainder has been transformed."[13] Berger focuses on the Black experience as characteristically apocalyptic and traumatic; he is concerned with end-time events not just as a means of protest and empowerment, but also as an instrument of revolutionary change. One is reminded of James Baldwin's theorizing about moments of secular catastrophe in biblical terms and as an instance of seismic rupture involving "historical vengeance, a cosmic vengeance" issuing from unresolved racial tensions.[14] Keith Byerman's discussion of the apocalyptic visions of John Edgar Wideman, Toni Morrison, and Charles Johnson leads to an investigation of how artistic representations of end-time events are "linked not only to contemporary obsessions with technological and political disorder and religious and media images of Armageddon but also with historical recurrences of such concerns at end moments of centuries."[15] As Byerman remarks, "By exploring the sources of the crises and meaning of transformative moments, the writers imply the truth of our moment. In this sense, the 'end of time' becomes an opportunity to consider the ends of history. In each case, the end that concerns them is race."[16]

Morrison asserts that "matters of race and matters of home are priorities in [her] work."[17] The act of writing is similar to an excavation process enabling the historical reclamation crucial to healing on the part of Black Atlantic subjects and contemporary readers who, like the ghostly figures that people the pages of her fiction, bear witness to a turbulent past. Her observations regarding the historical distortions resulting in the systematic removal of "the presence and the heartbeat of black people" direct attention to the "writerly" imperative at the center of her fictional canon.[18] As the Pulitzer and Nobel Prize-winning author reveals,

> You have to stake it out and identify those who have preceded you—re-summoning them, acknowledging them is just one step in that process of reclamation—so that they are always there as the confirmation and the affirmation of the life that I personally have not lived but is the life of that organism to which I belong which is black people in this country.[19]

Morrison's comments point to historical recovery as a guiding impulse in her narrative project as she seeks to excavate the buried chronicle of Blacks in a global historiography where the boundaries demarcating the body and outer world, art and science, past and future, nation and diaspora are increasingly blurred. For Morrison, history and historic events are part of a reality that refuses to disassociate itself from time-present or the potentiality of a future with its claims to bio-technical and scientific innovation. Her portrait of a post-catastrophe Eden in her fourth novel, *Tar Baby*, directs attention to the contemporaneous nature of historical events in a late-twentieth-century African-Caribbean setting. Son emerges as a liminal figure whose mysterious arrival at the Street home summons a history of slavery and forced migration along with inter-galactic time-travel involving a cosmic alien influx, including insinuations of an extraterrestrial plague subjecting islanders to involuntary blindness. Isle de Chevaliers, a magically real island paradise resonant with myth and legend, lends itself to the border-crossing that points to a destabilizing mash-up linking trans-Atlantic slavery with stories of an extraterrestrial invasion and biblically inspired accounts of an Armageddon-like rescue featuring a legion of blind horsemen. Morrison's decision to situate Son's journey within a cultural context recalling the trans-Atlantic journey offers a commentary on a range of contemporary issues and an opportunity to explore multiple lines of possible futures apart from colonial inscriptions.

This project therefore pursues two interrelated lines of inquiry: first, it explores the implications of Black Atlantic literary and cultural criticism for an Afro-futurist epistemology in a manner that refuses to position works by Black women as appendages to mainstream science fiction or a largely masculinist speculative tradition; and, second, the study interrogates the role of vernacular culture in the creation of futuristic imaginaries that betray a postapocalyptic sensibility. While postapocalypticism shares Afro-futurism's concern with the intersections between an African diasporic heritage and the realms of science and technology, its uniqueness lies in its attention to the aftermath of biblical and media images signifying a cataclysmic end of the world, and, in terms of this study's gendered emphasis, the implications of a new social arrangement for gender roles and sexuality. Dystopian/utopian fiction and apocalyptic fiction surface as related concepts with Susanna Morris's Afro-futurist feminism offering a similar theoretical construct.[20] Morris attends to matters of Afro-futurist critique as they interconnect with gender and sexuality in Black women's fiction. In the Black woman's narrative tradition, postapocalypticism signals an investment in the imaginative archives of Black Atlantic history in a manner resonant with catastrophe as a catalyst for futuristic realms featuring erased hierarchal designations where Black women reach their full potential.[21] Postapocalypticism intervenes in theories surrounding Black Atlantic identity construction with cataclysm, moments of crisis, and disaster figuring as rupturing moments along a nonlinear, a-temporal continuum. The outcome of moments of crisis is a radically transformed social landscape with reimagined race, gender, and sexual configurations.

Black identity construction entails a subsuming and reemergence of the feminine as a marker for dynamic subjectivity in the service of utopian realities. Figurations of Africa as a cultural metaphor are thus essential to an appraisal of the futuristic imaginaries in Black women's literary and cultural production, with the Middle Passage as a fluid space of semiotic uncertainty giving way to multilayered significations involving a new social order where dialectical tensions of masculine and feminine, Blackness and whiteness, self and "other" cease.[22] Even though strategies involving vernacular lore, diasporic rituals and beliefs, and a reclamation of a maternal past are constituent aspects of Black women's literary and expressive culture, they assume new meaning within a postapocalyptic imaginary in the project of mending a ruptured historical continuum, healing the social and psychic wounds issuing from slavery and colonization, and exploring innovative avenues of Black female agency.

Black and Indigenous Studies posit the notion that colonization and imperialism constitute an unrecognized apocalypse through genocide, slavery, and the compulsory displacement of an indigenous population. Theorizing the Middle Passage in relation to speculative genre conventions liberates the trans-Atlantic voyage from temporal constraints and prompts a rethinking of history, identity, and the linguistic structures seeking to inscribe the perilous journey from Africa to the Americas. Drawing upon the work of Gregory Tate, Calvin Warren, and Eshun Kodwo, Kristen Lillvis attends to post-human identity constructions in relation to Blackness as a site of semiotic indeterminacy.[23] Her assertions regarding the disordering effects of the Middle Passage encourage a consideration of the trans-Atlantic voyage as a passage through a fluid dialectical site given to evolutionary shifts manifesting themselves in altered identities. Transitional in nature, the Middle Passage figures as an interstitial space that is neither linguistically coded nor geographically demarcated; it is an unscripted, unmapped site of infinite linguistic, temporal, and corporeal possibility. In its implications for a new social setting, the trans-Atlantic journey therefore holds the potential for an original subjectivity unencumbered by existing locational or identity formulations, a redefined communal landscape emerging in opposition to the limitations of past inscriptions.

Recent scholarly interventions into the intersection between apocalypticism/postapocalypticism and hip-hop point to the ways in which vernacular structures implying futurity trouble Mark Dery's prescriptive critical framework in his framing of an Afro-futurist literary canon.[24] The unconventional temporalities that figure in Black women's literary and cultural production beckon us to abandon received ways of seeing and being seen, to cross over into an original social and psychic space. What is at stake in an appraisal of Black women's futuristic worlds is a critical methodology that takes its discursive cue from an unwritten body of expression marked by nuance, complexity, and contradiction, one evolving from and leading to an enriching multiplicity of meaning.

The inclusion of works representing the United States and Anglo-Caribbean underscores this study's investment in African diasporic cultures as a locus for the dialogic relation between writers and artists whose creations reveal an engagement with crisis and disaster and the utopian worlds that ensue. Lisa Yasek offers a reading of *Invisible Man* in terms of Ellison's use of the techniques and conventions of science fiction, and she appropriately concludes that "the fantastic tropes of the encounter with the alien other and travel through time and space suggest how Afro-futurism holds the potential to bring the Afro-diaspora experience to life in new ways."[25] Sofia Samatar makes a persuasive case for the inclusion of African artists in the discourses on Afro-futurism through a Pan-African geopolitical framework in interrogating texts by Nnedi Okorafor, Tendai Huchu, Tomi Adeyemi, Wanuri Kahiu, and Wangechi Mutu.[26] *Binti*, part of a trilogy by award-winning Nigerian-American Okorafor, locates itself in a trans-Atlantic history featuring time travel, cultural clashes with the alien "other," and the ambivalent relation with home. The novel's titular heroine is a poor, Himba young girl, guided by an ancient astrolabe, "on the threshold ... between home and my future."[27] Binti's journey to Oomza Uni aboard a genetically enhanced fish serving as a space ship is at once both a coming of age and a voyage cross cultures, nations, and worlds resonant with the immigrant experience. If an encounter with the genocidal, war-like Meduse prompts Binti to summon the indigenous cultural practices of her remote village, that moment also occasions her role as a master harmonizer whose mathematical and scientific aptitude allows her to reimagine gender norms. Recent "Black to the Future" conferences within and outside of the continental United States advance the project of expanding the geographic and scholarly boundaries of Black fantasy culture to include Okorafor and an emerging group of Black female authors. It is important to note as well that the 2018 box-office phenomenon *Black Panther* holds the distinction of being the first mainstream science fiction movie to be set in Africa and feature a predominantly Black cast.

Language plays a central role in an appraisal of Black women's postapocalyptic imaginaries with the construction of what bell hooks fittingly describes as a reimagined social space as a site for framing "new, alternative, oppositional aesthetic acts."[28] Encoded within the unwritten lore constituting Black expressive culture, the passage to fanciful worlds entails a dismantling of established social arrangements embedded in the objectifying discourses of the dominant culture. Jacques Derrida's concept of "free play" as a disruption of presence has implications for postapocalypticism in terms of the multifaceted identities and alternative realities writers and artists envision and the role of catastrophe as a signing event marking a disassociation between the signifier and the signified, an instance of narrative rupture prompting a re-centering of meaning outside established semiotic structures.[29] Lamonda Horton Stallings situates her critique of female sexuality in vernacular structures and modes of cultural production often excluded from mainstream critical interventions. In her reading of narrative moments involving the wild woman, Horton Stallings deploys a critical methodology involving what she labels "trickster-troping" as "a metaphor for futuristic possibilities of identity."[30] "The binaries that women in the West are confronted with," Horton Stallings asserts, "seek to create a utopia by erasing difference or subordinating difference. Trickster-troping captures Black female writers' and performers' deliberate narrative intersection of folklore, vernacular, myth, and queerness within their texts to interrupt social binaries and express sexual desire."[31]

Like the duplicitous, shape-shifting Papa Legba or Eshu Elegbara of Yoruba folklore fame, postapocalypticism functions as a mediating figurative presence by situating itself at the metaphoric crossroads, a liminal site involving connections between erased and re-constituted identities, presiding over crossings in the risky journey to imaginary worlds existing within yet apart from prevailing social arrangements. Its dialectical method is to translate the dislocating experience of trans-Atlantic passage into tangible form by unveiling the source of controlling influences or charting the move outside the often-invisible forces of hegemonic control in a manner that maps efforts to negate the destructive effects of colonial and neocolonial powers. The urge toward recuperating a diasporic heritage bound with the feminine emerges as a predominant concern in a postapocalyptic culture. But the utopian imaginaries in Black women's literary and cultural production do not merely emanate from the tension between a diasporic past and alternative futures; they instigate that tension in attending to cataclysm and disaster as symbolic acts of individual and communal emancipation central to the literary or cultural artifact as a whole. Moments of catastrophe summon Blackness in the nihilistic terms Calvin L. Warren deploys in describing race as a destabilizing presence and a force against which whiteness makes itself known.[32] As a fluid construct, race lends itself to theorizing the ways in which an estrangement between the signifier and the signified tends toward new signs heralding a reconfigured self and society, a New World Order arising out of prevailing linguistic systems. What comes to mind is George Lipsitz's theorizing about the crossroads as a site for transformative social, political, and cultural possibilities, or bell hooks's imagining the margins as a locus of empowerment outside white, male structures.[33]

The idea of the "post," which summons figurations of the interstitial space between clearly defined periods of time as well as cultural, aesthetic, or social movements, has implications for the current study in terms of artistic efforts to critique present-day realities through the deployment of a postapocalyptic imaginary. In my understanding of intermediacy, I am indebted to, among other intellectuals, Kwame Anthony Appiah whose meditation on the commodification of African art prompts his claim that "many areas of contemporary African cultural life—what has come to be theorized as popular culture in particular—are not in this way concerned with transcending, with going beyond coloniality."[34] Appiah makes a convincing case for an interrogation of present-day African art and artifacts, and, by extension, Black Atlantic cultural production, using a model involving a syncretistic exchange of international commodities and ideas in mediating against notions of the "post" as "a space-clearing gesture."[35] In a similar manner, Homi Bhabha theorizes temporality in relation to the cultural legacy of colonialism and imperialism. Postcolonialism, as he conceives it, interrupts popular conceptualizations of temporality and spatiality in critiquing efforts to hypothesize "the Beyond" as a site divorced from the present moment or the here-and-now.[36] Among raced subjects in a postcolonial setting, the era known as the "post" is resonant with an in-between site that defies hierarchal social constructions evolving from efforts to pose a distinction between self and "other," Blackness and whiteness, male and female, as well as strict notions of temporal history.

Although George Lipsitz situates his interrogation of urban youth traditions and contemporary social justice movements within popular culture, his insights shed light on the synergy present in Black women's literature and expressivity in terms of the intersection between cultural traditions from the past and the construction of alternate, more democratic futures. For him, the 1992 Los Angeles race riots following the acquittal of police officers after the beating of Rodney King constitute a moment rife with apocalyptic significance—a time that marks the figurative crossroads between ideologies rooted in neo-conservatism and new paradigms for race, class, and culture.[37] Lipsitz's criticism of what he appropriately labels "apocalypse on the installment plan" is useful as he puts forth a heuristic reading of twentieth- and twenty-first-century urban life grounded in figurations of history as a dynamic process involving a contemporaneous interplay between various cultural traditions.[38] Elsewhere, he employs a white spatial imaginary in an interrogation of the racial and locational politics of post-Katrina New Orleans, a city struggling to redefine itself in the wake of natural disaster as well as decades of economic disparities, social tensions, and political strife.[39]

Postapocalypticism functions in a Derridian sense as the always-already of cultural production in a world given to unexpected social, political, and environmental shifts of catastrophic proportions—a world teetering on the brink of disaster and ruin.[40] In reinscribing discourses surrounding the "post"—postcolonial, postmodern, post-civil rights, postfeminist, postracial, and, most recently, post-Covid-19—language becomes a means of framing compound lines of possible futures, of opening up previously uncharted spaces of literary and cultural critique, a medium for theorizing not only what's next, but also what if?

The postapocalyptic worlds Black women imagine point to wide-ranging concerns—from environmental issues to state-sponsored violence in Black and brown urban communities to the ambivalent role of science and technology in relation to Black bodies. Matters relevant to changing sexual identities and gender roles in the face of cosmopolitanism are a recurring consideration in signaling core concerns of contemporary Black feminisms. Border-crossing and its insinuations for inter-galactic time-travel, self-reflexive encounters with the alien "other," and efforts to recover a gendered diasporic heritage emerge as predominant features of a postapocalyptic cultural landscape. Chapter discussions return to these concerns as organizational principles that ground this project within a feminist and Black Atlantic historical and cultural nexus. In each instance, the move toward futuristic worlds occurs in terms of symbolic encounters with newness as writers and artists refigure the past as "a contingent, in-between moment" that "interrupts the performance of the present," encouraging a rethinking of temporal history and the possibilities that await.[41]

Works under investigation take place against a backdrop of social and political instability in the mid to late twentieth and early twenty-first centuries, and Black women attend to the pressing problems that challenge world stability amidst unprecedented globalism. At the time of the writing of the present study, the world faces the uncertainties of a global pandemic fueled by the coronavirus (Covid-19) along with an increased attention to the role of technology in response to the exigencies of remote instruction and telework. The prospect of a contact tracing system designed to monitor the spread of the deadly virus is nothing short of an Orwellian vision of governmental surveillance that skirts the boundaries of science fiction and Revelation's account of end-time events. New York Governor Andrew Cuomo's remarks during an April 19, 2020 press conference underscore the postapocalyptic insinuations of the current moment as he casts a forward glance into the period following the pandemic. Suggestions that the public should engage in "Re-imagining New York" and "Learn the Lessons [and] Build Back Better" speak futuristically of the time *after* recovery from the coronavirus, the era of the "post," as an opportunity to begin anew, to look back and forward simultaneously, to improve infrastructure, address health and socioeconomic disparities placing communities of color at increased risk for the deadly disease, and enhance the interface between federal, state, and local governments and the realms of science and technology.[42] In other words, rather than serving as an uncritical extension of the past, the future as he envisions it is a cautiously optimistic one that reflects upon the past while marking a departure from the failed practices and policies that have contributed to the turmoil of the present.

The dangers of uncontained pandemics, police violence against communities of color, anti-immigrant social practices, debates surrounding climate change, and a despotic national policy directed toward policing America's southern border imply our current moment and point to the turbulence that threatens to plunge the contemporary world into further chaos. Prevalent throughout Black women's literature and expressive culture is a firm belief that Black women do not just survive the apocalypse; they also play a pivotal role in ushering in a more environmentally sound, health-conscious, humane, and socially just world.

Moments of catastrophe are as varied as the artistic visions from which they issue, and with every calamity—whether it is a natural disaster, genocidal society, tyrannical government, unbridled technological intrusion, or a combination of factors—linear history is under assault, subject to manipulation in the service of a transmuted social landscape. In each instance, catastrophic upheavals are not discrete occurrences along a chronological or diachronic continuum; they figure as symbolic instants interwoven with the language structures of the artifact as a whole. Edwidge Danticat's framing of *Claire of the Sea Light* around the 2010 Haitian earthquake locates futurity within linguistic structures outlining a turbulent African-Caribbean history.[43] The earthquake, or, rather, Danticat's fictionalizing of that event, serves as a reminder of Haiti's entrapment within a tragic cosmology involving a succession of environmental, social, and political disasters. That Danticat situates the novel's unresolved closure within legend and lore surrounding the revenant, a spirit-child fated to repeat a cycle of departure and return, discloses the synthesis between Judeo-Christian eschatology and Haitian-Creole vernacular in reinscribing the account of Claire Limye Lanme's anticipated homecoming, an event that speaks futuristically of the possibilities for recovery, renewal, and healing, not just for the motherless young girl, but also on the part of a dislocated Haitian-immigrant community.

Chapter 2, "Coming of Age on the Dark Side: Speculative Fictions of Black Girlhood in Octavia E. Butler's *Fledgling*, Nalo Hopkinson's *Brown Girl in the Ring*, and Edwidge Danticat's *Claire of the Sea Light*," attends to Black girlhood in relation to the "post" with the figure of the woman-child as a signifier for the worried border space between childhood and adulthood, girlhood and womanhood, innocence and a transgressive sexual expressivity. Relying upon theoretical insights drawn from Toni Morrison's *Playing in the Dark*, the chapter lays the foundation for a reappraisal of the temporal stakes involved in the Black female bildungsroman by framing the journey from girlhood to womanhood within aspects of vernacular culture involving erased and reconstructed identities. Tropes of fantastic encounters with the alien "other" offer insight into the self-reflexive interactions leading to a reconstituted self and society. Rather than reading the "other" as an expression of Black female pathology or deviant sexualized behavior, the chapter argues for the utility of a shadowy female persona as a locus for critiquing conventional gendered and sexual roles.

Chapter 3, "Queering the New World Order: Michelle Cliff's *Abeng* and *No Telephone to Heaven*," situates the discussion of erased and reconstructed identities within a space involving the intersection between Black Atlantic cultural criticism and recent scholarship in Black queer studies. Building upon Omise'eke Natasha Tinsley's spirited critique of Paul Gilroy's celebrated trope of the ship in motion as a symbol for trans-cultural exchange, the chapter directs attention to recovered and reinvented identities as a constituent aspect of a Black female narrative project. A reading of Cliff's first two novels as companion texts offers a basis for reexamining queerness as a locus for reembodying an emergent Black subjectivity existing apart from a white, male, middle-class, cis-gendered norm. The chapter thus argues for queerness or trans-ness as an essential aspect of a postapocalyptic landscape featuring reimagined sexualities.

Zombies in Black women's literature and expressive culture merit sustained critical investigation beyond the scope of the present study. Apart from their popular culture manifestation in productions such as the 2010 television series *The Walking Dead*, based on Robert Kirkman's ongoing comic book series, or the 1954 novel-turned-postapocalyptic science fiction thriller *I Am Legend*, zombies assume a raced, gendered dimension in relation to a futuristic imaginary with Black women whose resistant subjectivity heralds a new era of autonomy and self-actualization. The figure has US connections with slavery and plantation life, but its roots are in African-Caribbean folklore and Voudoun rituals. Reanimated corpses or virally infected beings join the vampire, revenant, and soucouyant in wandering a postapocalyptic wasteland, entrapped between Guinea, a metaphor for a decolonized African past where the benighted slave finds release from earthly toil, and a confinement within the interlocking influences of race, class, gender, and sexual domination, between the world of the living and the realm of the (un)dead.

Chapter 4 therefore derives its impetus from intersections between Black feminist and postcolonial theory in an interrogation of what Mark Dery famously refers to as the invisible forces of dominance frustrating the movement on the part of a raced population, but in relation to a zombie apocalypse where Black women assume control over governmental and institutional structures in a postcatastrophe world.[44] Relying upon scholarship surrounding the in-between-ness marking the postcolonial condition, the chapter relates border subjectivity to fictional representations of zombies or zombie-ism as a cultural metaphor with implications for a postapocalyptic civilization. Together, *Myal* and *Bailey's*

Café revisit notions of a zombie apocalypse by seizing upon the zombie as a tropological representation of an entrapment within hegemonic whiteness and patriarchal authority. By translating the unseen influences of race and gender dominance into a tangible, New World form, the novels seek to liberate Black female subjects from white, male supremacy in a restructuring of social and institutional systems. "Un-zombifying Blackness in Erna Brodber's *Myal* and Gloria Naylor's *Bailey's Café*" not only relies upon a postapocalyptic imaginary in attributing such an entrapment to linguistic structures signifying whiteness and Blackness, the chapter also attends to the role of oppositional strategies of resistance in framing decolonized sites of self-actualization.

The closing chapter returns discursively to issues of historical erasure, but in a manner attendant to male–female liaisons and the potentiality of romantic love as a mode of resistance against hegemonic authority. Whereas Toni Morrison relies upon the myth of the blind horsemen in an account of Son's affair with Jadine Childs and Jesmyn Ward turns to classical mythology in a retelling of Esch Batiste's stormy love relationship with Manny, Beyonce situates the storied account of the journey from betrayal to healing within vernacular structures involving mythoi of female personae whose complex subjectivities defy essentialist identity configurations. "Romance after the Ruin: Looking for Love in the Era of the "Post" in Toni Morrison's *Tar Baby*, Jesmyn Ward's *Salvage the Bones*, and Beyonce's *Lemonade*" relies upon Naomi Klein's theory of disaster capitalism's Shock Doctrine in a critique of the resistance strategies on the part of catastrophe survivors in the wake of natural or human-made disaster.

A meditation on Ebony Bones's innovative album cover offers a starting point for a scholarly investigation of Black women's futuristic visions and a launching pad propelling the conversation surrounding postapocalypticism forward into previously uncharted critical and intellectual territory. If the world of Black science fiction constitutes a viable area of inquiry, then *The Postapocalyptic Black Female Imagination* endeavors to bring Black women writers and artists into the academic exchange surrounding fantasy culture in ways that position Black women, not as satellites hovering eternally on the edge of an academic cosmos, but as conscious contributors whose works merit placement at the center of an ever-expanding Afro-futurist galaxy.

2

Coming of Age on the Dark Side

Speculative Fictions of Black Girlhood in Octavia E. Butler's *Fledgling*, Nalo Hopkinson's *Brown Girl in the Ring*, and Edwidge Danticat's *Claire of the Sea Light*

> *Anxiety and xenophobia fueled by a sense of cultural loss, the very real deprivation of displaced populations, anger emanating from a permanent austerity economy, and the surveillance and suppression necessary for the perpetuation of privilege provide preconditions for explosions everywhere. The interconnectedness of cultures displayed by world music is not without utopian possibilities, but the ravages of unimpeded capital accumulation create grave dangers as well. These crossroads are dangerous for all of us; how well we negotiate them may determine what kind of future we will face—or whether we will face any future at all. Dangers await at the crossroads, but never with more peril than when we refuse to face them.*
>
> George Lipsitz, *Dangerous Crossroads*

> *Children can play a part in emergent world literatures because in cultures seeking independence, children enjoy a natural, if precarious, enfranchisement. They provide a fresh point of view as Gullivers without fantasy, sojourners of the present, exploring the islands of manhood and womanhood, remaking the maps.*
>
> Geta LeSeur, *Ten Is the Age of Darkness*

With their transformative potentiality, the crossroads have compelling implications for the journey from childhood to adulthood, a move occurring in relation to the passage from time-present to a futuristic existence, from here, in terms of diasporic locations and relocations, to nowhere. George Lipsitz's observations about perilous crossroads relate not only to world music as a locus for cultural confluence in an increasingly global setting, those assertions also insinuate the challenges and possibilities associated with the coming of age narrative in a geopolitical space defining Black female sexuality in oppositional terms and in relation to models of pathology. Postapocalypticism opens new lines of scholarly inquiry in a reappraisal of the bildungsroman in terms of intersectionality and the creation of futuristic imaginaries evolving out of the spaces between discourses of whiteness, maleness, and hetero-normativity. Works under discussion in this chapter attend to how Black girlhood is constructed and the ways in which the youthful protagonist unsettles dominant paradigms of race and gender resulting in an adultification of Black girls.[1]

Through a reliance upon a youthful figure as a signifier for unsettled temporalities, Black women writers gesture toward the utility of a mysterious woman-child whose complex subjectivity critiques prevailing models of womanhood and femininity so as to propel the scholarly conversation about young female subjects forward into relatively unknown discursive terrain. One thinks of the eponymous ghost-child in Toni Morrison's award-winning *Beloved*, Lula Ann Bridewell or Bride in *God Help the Child*, Indigo in Ntozake Shange's *Sassafrass, Cypress, and Indigo*, Binti in Nnendi Okorafor's *Binti*, Zelie in Tomi Adeyemi's *Children of Blood and Bone*, Lena McPherson in Tina McElroy Ansa's *Baby of the Family*, and Avatara "Avey" Johnson in Paule Marshall's *Praisesong for the Widow*, among other fictional personae. Such a figure defies a strict allegiance to postcolonial discourses of cultural hybridity, psychoanalytical principles involving a Jungian connection with the subconscious, or the realm of laboratory-inspired genetic engineering.

Notions of womanish girls, which evolve from insinuations surrounding a transgression of culturally ascribed behavior separating youth from an assortment of manners, attitudes, and conduct accompanying adulthood, trouble ontological boundaries between girlhood and womanhood. Those ideas also point to a close relationship between the physical body or the corporeality of adolescence and shifting diasporic locational formulations—the fluid and disquieted national borders owing to an assortment of historical processes giving rise to a trans-cultural Africana women's literary tradition. Christopher Okonkwo locates his interrogation of the dialogic relationship between texts by Black women writers within a diasporic geography involving the ogbanje or spirit-child destined to enact a cycle of birth, death, and rebirth to the same mother.[2] In a similar manner, the woman-child offers a space for not only examining the cross-cultural conversation between women writers, the figure also heralds the promise of a radically transformed society with redefined race, gender, and sexual identities, a New World Order arising out of the old, offering fresh and, at times, destabilizing paradigms for gender and sexuality.

Octavia E. Butler, Nalo Hopkinson, and Edwidge Danticat construct young female characters whose passage into womanhood occurs in terms of transgressive behavior that disrupts conventional identity constructions. Fictional characters come of age by embracing an alternative reality that privileges a radical Black femaleness—one demanding its own critical space. And they often do so through fantastic encounters with a dark double, a shadowy figure, or a foreboding night-creature hovering on the margins of a prevailing social order. Emanating from a range of folkloric traditions, the vampire, soucouyant, she-devil, night-witch, or sea-goddess serve a didactic function as a means of childhood socialization while gesturing toward the liberating possibilities of Black womanhood. If the crossroads intimate the dangers of strict allegiance to restrictive images of womanhood, they also offer tantalizing prospects for framing oppositional acts and transformed social spaces unencumbered by existing formulae or predictable patterns, thereby mapping the unexplored boundaries of femininity and sexuality in innovative ways.

Children of the Night: Loveable Vampires and Genetically-Engineered Blackness in Octavia E. Butler's *Fledgling*

Roots, Routes, and the Elusive Quest for Home

Octavia E. Butler contributes to the conversation surrounding the Black female bildungsroman as postapocalyptic intervention with *Fledgling*, a contemporary fable conflating science fiction with vampire lore in an intriguing remix of the story involving the growth of maturity on the part of a baffling orphan girl in search of home and family. Shori is at once both a ten-year-old adolescent and a fifty-three-year-old vampire whose maturation parallels an awakening to the realities of a traumatic past leading to the annihilation of her family. The past continues to haunt Shori in the form of repeated terrorist attacks from an unknown assailant intent on eliminating the raced difference that she embodies. Because of a head injury suffered during a vicious round of violence resulting in the death of her mothers and sisters along with all the human members of her family, the novel's central character is unable to recall the identity of her attackers or the circumstances of her childhood. Chance encounters with strangers allow her to bond with humans in a series of symbiotic relationships, derive vital sustenance by consuming the blood of her associates, and piece together fragments of the life she leaves behind.

The crossroads map Shori's evolution from alien "other"—a stranger, foreigner, interloper, or unwelcome outsider without a country, family, home, or past—to her role as a self-assured woman, still deeply traumatized, but capable of shaping her future in a demonstrable way. Butler interweaves the account of Shori's coming of age with a series of catastrophes figuring as rupturing moments that reveal the tendency toward historical erasure and the struggles on the part of the marginalized subject to remember vestiges of a lost, disjointed heritage. Shori's awakening in a cave after the tragic death of her family, followed by the attack upon her father's compound, emphasizes how a past involving a series of traumatic moments complicates efforts to reconstruct a genealogical heritage. Owing to the fact of her existence as part of a scientific experiment intended to create a super race able to remain awake during the day, exhibit superior strength and agility, and withstand sunlight, Shori's efforts to situate herself within existing social arrangements are frustrated at every turn. Much of the novel involves her attempts to create her own self-defined space of autonomous existence in navigating a cultural landscape where racial and sexual codes are in a state of flux.

A contemporary California setting implies our current moment with the ruin, a postapocalyptic wasteland emerging in the aftermath of disaster and cataclysm. Shori's faint recollections of the fire that destroys her childhood home prompt an association between *Fledgling* and biblical and media images signaling a calamitous end of the world. With its propensity for wildfires, earthquakes, and mudslides, California lends itself to Butler's allegory of a young girl's move toward a radically transformed future in the wake of repeated catastrophe and devastation. Multiple attacks upon Shori's family extends the novel's critique of present-day America beyond a focus on environmental concerns that portend imminent ecological disaster to include acts of terrorism directed toward religious and ethnic communities worldwide. Shori shares with countless immigrant groups a subjection to xenophobic hatred evolving from a fear of the outsider. That the identity of Shori's attackers remains a mystery for much of the novel emphasizes the sinister role that invisible forces of bureaucratic control play in thwarting the individual and collective aspirations on the part of communities of color and the struggle to name the source of the oppressive influences seeking to erase the raced difference Shori personifies.

Butler frames Shori's coming of age in terms of the journey with literal and symbolic overtones and the knowledge essential to an adult constitution. That Shori's evolutionary development occurs both within and outside of the novel's temporal structure speaks to issues surrounding identity construction and the implications of trans-Atlantic travel for the futuristic imaginary Butler limns. Shori's flight to and from the ruin in search of relics from her family past takes on ritual dimensions in her efforts to salvage vestiges of a fragmented heritage and build from it a better world. Saidiya Hartman retraces her ancestor's footsteps along the Ghana coast, only to be confronted by the challenges of reconstructing a family lineage in the face of historical erasure.[3] Issues of memory and forgetting point to the dislocating effects of the Middle Passage and the struggle to remember and therefore reclaim a vanished maternal ancestry. Butler's protagonist experiences the disrupting consequences of cultural displacement in a similar fashion, but in ways that extend the rupturing effects of colonial and neocolonial influences to a present-day California setting with its technological innovations, complex communal and family arrangements, and environmental concerns. The unearthing of a cross and necklace featuring a bird complicates Shori's attempts to rediscover her family past as the necklace offers evidence of genealogical origins based in Christian and pagan belief. Emblems such as this destabilize simplistic notions of family and lineage by pointing the narrative in multiple directions simultaneously. Iosif's revelation of Shori's birth name is no less unsettling in its disclosure of her multifaceted identity. Shori's name associates the protagonist with "a kind of bird—an East African crested nightingale," thereby placing her outside of corporeal designations and setting the stage for her fluid subjectivity as a border figure.[4] The revelation that one of Shori's human mothers assigns that name underscores the role of names as unreliable signifiers in a cultural space where linguistic markers are variable, even as the protagonist's names underscore her distance from a maternal past and its associated semiotic structures.

Toni Morrison's meditation on the quest for home offers useful insights in an interrogation of Shori's role as a bildungsroman protagonist. For Morrison, the contemporary world's work involves "policing, halting, forming policy regarding, and trying to administer the movement of people."[5] Locating the elusive quest for home within a discursive space surrounding the search for authorial sovereignty identifies issues of race and nationhood as central to contemporary political and literary discourses. Readers familiar with Butler's work realize her engagement with contemporary debates about immigration, border-crossing, and home with Shori serving as sign, cypher, and symbol of the alien in our midst. Neither exclusively human nor solely extra-human, not fully a woman but too mature to be a child, Shori defies the essentialist enterprises with which she is confronted. Black feminist criticism traces the objectification of Black women as the "other" to the process of oppositional difference or either/or dichotomous thinking.[6]

The dominant society defines itself in terms of a dialectical tension posing a separation between the self and the "other." The process of "othering" is based in efforts to relegate individuals or groups to a subordinate position in relation to a predefined social norm. Although stereotypic representations of Black women evolve out of the tendency toward raced and gendered objectification, in her multifaceted bodily constituency, Shori moves freely across a range of identities without being subsumed by any one of them. Embracing a fluid self, one owing no fidelity to singularly constituted notions, Shori not only contests the restrictive boundaries of race and gender designations, but she charts a new direction for feminist critique of Black female subjectivity.

As a symptom and cause of her feelings of estrangement, Shori's amnesia prompts her reliance upon "slivers of recovered memory" in a reconstruction of past events (254). Lamonda Horton Stallings astutely observes that Shori's amnesia invokes trans-Atlantic slavery with its history of an erased cultural memory, suppressed affect, and broken family relations.[7] Shori laments the fact that she is unable to mourn the loss of her family. That the past Shori remembers may or may not still exist in its originary form is not Butler's primary concern; rather, the author is intent on inscribing an altogether new history—one that is as fluid as Shori herself and reflects the central character's dynamic role as a border-crosser. As Kristen Lillvis argues, "Transformative Middle Passage experiences in Butler's science fiction cultivate a posthuman multiple consciousness that allows characters and readers to recognize blackness both within and outside of the ontology and cosmology of white power."[8] Central to her argument are the ways in which language functions creatively and subversively in reenvisioning Blackness and the temporal spaces where such identities emerge. Theorizing the Middle Passage as a locus of infinite subject formation liberates Black Atlantic subjects from preexisting identity constructions and prompts a reconceptualization of the trans-Atlantic voyage and its implications for the speculative and fantasy culture. Free of the constrictions associated with an oppressive history, beyond the limitations of the past or future, Shori can fashion an original self and inscribe a new narrative of being apart from established constructions of time, space, and identity. Shori's amnesia liberates her from prevailing social and linguistic structures, allowing her unhindered movement across various identities and social spaces.

When she awakens at the cave in the novel's opening, she does not know herself as Ina, human, black, or female. These semiotic structures hold no meaning for her. She is therefore at liberty to define herself outside existing notions of self. Just as Africans were disconnected from their families during the slave trade, so, too, is Shori separated from her mothers as a result of the violent acts of those who cannot comprehend her existence. Shori elides such negative signification, however, by transforming the dislocating experience of maternal separation and loss into narrative freedom. She no longer adheres to external pressures on her identity because she is unaware of them. This subsuming of signification has implications beyond Shori's own narrative for, as Lillvis notes, "the Middle Passage alters not only black communities and bodies in the past but also black identities in the present," and future.[9] In other words, as Shori produces offspring with a similar genetic make-up, they will achieve autonomy apart from established metonymic structures in the creation of an identity defying established semantic or locational bounds. Like other Ina and their human symbionts, Shori has a propensity for self-healing apart from medical or scientific intervention. But her inability to recall the specifics of her childhood or the circumstances of the death of her mothers and sisters points to memory loss as a catalyst for the dynamic self-construction leading to the creation of an original history—reinvented, reformed, and reenvisioned in relation to a distant genealogical past.

Seeing the Self as the "Other": Self-Reflexive Encounters at the Crossroads

The crossroads imply the usefulness of interrogating self-reflexive engagements with the alien "other" in an appraisal of the black female coming of age narrative as speculative invention. Alien encounters occur in a space of indeterminacy involving linkages between dissolved and reconfigured identities, a site outside of established linguistic and temporal bounds. Such interactions reveal efforts to elide negative raced, gendered significations in the creation of a multiple consciousness that defies strict categorization. Shori is bi-lingual, capable of speaking and reading English and Ina, but she is unable to locate herself in textual or digital spaces. When Wright Hamlin gazes at her image in a mirror, relieved to see that she has a reflection, Shori tries to perceive what others see when they look at her. "I touched my face and the short fuzz of black hair on my head, and I tried to see someone I recognized," Shori discloses. "I was a lean, sharp-faced, large-eyed, brown-skinned person—a complete stranger" (18). The scene is a reminder of the Fanonian lexicon of the gaze with its insinuations for racialized subjectivities. Encounters with the "other" are dislocating in their tendency toward a psychic fracturing prompting a disassociation between body and spirit, between one's corporeal constitution and the image of the self that is imposed from without. Frantz Fanon discloses his confrontation with "otherness" in paradigmatic terms emblematic of the urge toward a deconstruction of the subjective experience of blackness as a marker of difference: "On that day, completely dislocated, unable to be abroad with the other, the white man, who unmercifully imprisoned me, I took myself far off from my own presence, far indeed, and made myself an object. What else could it be for me but an amputation, an excision, a hemorrhage that spattered my whole body with black blood?"[10]

Shori represents a complication of the dynamic processes involved in self-construction; she is neither exclusively woman nor child, not fully human or wholly extraterrestrial. The semiotic structures with which she is confronted either fail to represent her or misrepresent the difference she embodies. Her passage from innocence to a place of knowledge or experience entails a rejection of oppressive representations that would label the protagonist as primitive, savage, and barbaric—a living embodiment of all that is dark, evil, and forbidden. In other words, Shori must defy the false depiction that others would ascribe and carve out an autonomous space of self-representation apart from an oppressive social order. The protagonist's efforts to learn about herself through a reading of late-seventeenth- and eighteenth-century East European vampire lore prove as futile as her attempts to situate herself within media images of vampiric creatures. Shori engages in "a bit of vampire theatre" bordering on the performative in her attempt to conform to popular conceptions of the folkloric night-creature when asking permission to enter Theodora Harden's home (88). "She had probably been brushing up on vampires recently. Of course, I didn't need permission to enter her home or anyone else's. I did find it interesting, though, that human beings made up these fantasy safe-guards, little magics, like garlic and crucifixes, that would somehow keep them same from my kind—or from what they imagined my kind to be" (88–9).

Shori's surprised realization that "no one seemed to be writing about [her] kind" locates the parable of a black female vampire within an unscripted realm of indecipherability (33). Theodora Harden is unable to account for the protagonist through the deployment of a "writerly" perspective or the lens of whiteness or maleness. "You're a vampire," Harden remarks, "although according to what I've read, you're supposed to be a tall, handsome, fully grown white man" (91). Shori cannot credit her existence to mass media, popular culture, folklore, or a written literary tradition. Nor is she solely the result of scientific experimentation. Wright Hamlin renames her "Renee," meaning reborn, in an ironic gesture revealing the unreliability of existing semiotic systems and Shori's propensity for eluding the linguistic and institutional structures with which she is confronted. "Renee ... Shori. It's like being told that extraterrestrials have arrived, and I'm sleeping with one of them" (86).

Toni Morrison's insights are relevant in theorizing the self-reflexive encounters marking a postapocalyptic imaginary. Morrison situates discourses surrounding whiteness and Blackness within the narrative spaces of Early American literature and culture in an interrogation of the politics of "othering." An American literary imagination relies heavily upon a mutually dependent, co-constructed relationship between Black and white, self and "other." Black characters inhabit white textual spaces as the subterranean "other" or "a dark and abiding presence, there for the literary imagination as both a visible and invisible mediating force. Even, and especially, when American texts are not 'about' Africanist presences or characters or narrative or idiom," Morrison contends, "the shadow hovers in implication, in sign, in line of demarcation."[11] She argues that the Africanist presence is a result of white writers' inability to create race-free texts. That project is impossible, since Africans and African-Americans exist within the very fabric of American society and white American consciousness. Morrison implicates scientific racism in the tendency toward "othering" at the center of identity constructions underlying figurations of American-ness. Tracing the impulse toward racial categorization to its precolonial origins, she interrogates whiteness and Blackness as co-constructed categories lending themselves to racial hierarchies that result in the objectification of Africans and African-Americans. "Since no one is born a racist and there is no fetal predisposition to sexism," she asserts, "one learns Othering not by lecture or instruction but by example."[12]

Shori's existence reveals the ways that eugenics makes raced individuals objects of relentless scrutiny, bugs under a colonial or neocolonial microscope awaiting extinction or modification according to preconceived formulations. *Fledgling* is invested in the creation of a youthful protagonist whose evolving subjectivity also reveals the process of "othering" through institutional racism as social practice. As a vampire who enjoys a close connection with the human community, someone who is a genetically engineered night-creature and a loveable adolescent, Shori embodies the signifying difference that troubles a range of discursive modes, from the bildungsroman to vampire narratives to the slave narrative genre. But Butler is as critical of Ina attempts at racial exclusivity through the creation of a genetically engineered Blackness as she is of the genocidal tendencies engaging the Silk Family and their repeated attacks on Shori and her family. Both endeavors emanate from a utopian desire for autonomy apart from constructions of race. As a fictional meditation on race as a social construct, Morrison's *Paradise* locates itself in an ironic linguistic and cultural space involving a dystopia based in a search for racial purity. Male residents of an all-black Ruby engage in an attack on a convent peopled by a multiracial group of women in a gesture of resistance against hegemonic whiteness. Rooted in a fear of the "other," such an endeavor is doomed to failure through an unwillingness to acknowledge Blackness and whiteness, maleness and femaleness, self and "other" as mutually dependent, co-constructed categories. Ultimately, attempts at the creation of a race-free, gender-neutral society—an earthly paradise—prove to be as unsuccessful as the readers' efforts to decipher the identity of the white girl who is first to fall victim to male attackers at the convent.

Wright Hamlin carries out a series of maneuvers designed to protect Shori from her assailants by walling her into an enclosed space. His actions imply the contemporary world's work in policing the movement of immigrant communities of color through public policy or political mandate. Iosif's house serves as a temporary shelter for Shori and her symbionts, but the Silks' assault undermines her efforts to reclaim a home of her own. After Wright learns of Iosif's death, he tells Shori, "What we need to do is find some place safe where we can hunker down, pool information, and figure out what to do" (105). Shori, too, wants to ensure the safety of her symbionts. "If we found the people who had murdered both my both my male and female families, I wanted to kill them, had to kill them. How else could I keep my new family safe?" (105). Commensurate with efforts at nation-building apart from racialized and gendered realities, Iosif's plans to give Shori land so that she can build her own self-contained community, along with Wright Hamlin's attempts to shelter Shori from continued attacks, are frustrated. Such efforts emanate from and lead to an exclusivity that fails to acknowledge difference.

Shori's coming of age implies what Morrison describes as a reconstituted blackness, a designation "loaded with slippery science and invention."[13] Morrison's unfinished novel seeks to answer the question of "how ... one move[s] from a non-racial womb to the womb of racism, to belonging to a specific loved or despised yet race-inflected existence?"[14] Shori hovers on the margins of society as a sinister night-creature who manifests the latent fear and loathing on the part of an established social order while moving toward an intersectional subjectivity. Her awakening at the cave is resonant with birth or rebirth, a loss of innocence on the part of the adolescent subject, and midlife reinvention. The knowledge that empowers and imperils her involves a realization of difference and its implications for contemporary social configurations.

Shori is, at first, unaware of race. Butler's protagonist is a universal figure coping with an unnamed trauma, disconnected from a Western or European imaginary that would seek to delimit her, in search of the sustenance that will ensure her survival. It is only through her interactions with others, however, that she becomes cognizant of raced identifiers. Wright Hamlin tells her, "Ordinary sun exposure burns your skin even though you're black?" (31). Shori observes that the helicopter pilot who transports her and Wright Hamlin back to the ruin is "blonde and very pale-skinned—not just light-skinned like Wright, but as white as the pages of Wright's books" (61). Esther and Celia, Shori's brother's symbionts, "had skin as dark as mine" (76). Shori's brother Stefan is light brown, as both he and his sister have the same human Black mother. Joel, the son of Martin Harrison, the man who teaches and befriends Shori at Punta Nublada, is "dark" (154). Hall and Preston Gordon are simply "two more pale blonde men" (208).

Through a series of clashes with the foreigner recast as an effort to banish the stranger in our midst, Shori comes to understand the implications of her unique social positioning. Not only do these self-reflexive encounters occur at the liminal crossroads, but they take place in a realm of linguistic uncertainty. Being subject to species-ism from the light-skinned Silk Family brings to mind the persistent color fetish among humans and efforts to preserve the so-called purity of the white race. The revelation that the Silk Family is responsible for the death of Shori's family represents a naming of the source of that oppression, even as the disclosure undermines the notion that the Ina are incapable of exhibiting human racism. As Rob Gates observes, Shori's body is a sign of degeneracy through Ina-human miscegenation.[15] Ali Brox explains that Shori's hybridity becomes the focus of their hatred because it exposes the falsity of their claims to purity and reminds them of their past abject condition at the hands of humans.[16] Shari Evans attends to the ways in which insults from the Ina invoke human prejudice.[17] At various times, Shori is called a "Dirty little nigger bitch," "Goddamn mongrel cub," "a clever dog," and a "Murdering black mongrel bitch" (173; 238; 300). The Inas' use of dehumanizing terms in reference to the protagonist, along with her inability to identify her attackers early on, offers a commentary on America's persistent color fetish and the challenges attendant upon inscribing cultural conflicts involving the "other."

Missing Your Mother: Mediating Absence through an Identification with the Goddess

That Shori is the only one of her siblings born in the United States to a US mother reveals the particularly American nature of the young woman's experiences. Her mother's decision to change the family name from "Mateescu" to the more Anglicized-sounding "Matthews" situates the protagonist's coming of age within a cultural context involving historical erasure. But Shori's pre-pubescent constitution prompts an association between the physicality of her corporeal development and a utopian social order where she embraces a complex subjectivity existing at once a part of yet separate from national interests in ways that gesture toward a diasporic legacy connected inextricably with the feminine. Postcolonial and African Diaspora literary and cultural criticism attend to the role of Africa as a gendered space associated with mothers and motherhood.[18] The protagonist's growth of maturity, and, equally as important to her adult constitution, her knowledge of what it means to be Ina, necessitates mediating the gulf between her awareness of her compound identity and a knowledge of a shadowy female persona emanating from a diasporic past. As a signifier for an erased history, the mother exists in mnemonic fashion, reembodying a lost heritage that remains a part of Shori's memorial structures long after the protagonist leaves the ruin.

The mother's role is consistent with what deconstructionist theory posits as trace or the absent-present. Absent things leave traces of their presence, erasing, in a Derridian sense, the invisible boundaries between what is seen and unseen.[19] Ina are a timeless, matriarchal species originating from another world, and the heritage giving rise to Shori's intersectional self evolves from mythology surrounding the feminine as a basis for the group's linguistic, governmental, and communal structures. References to the great mother-goddess who is the originator of the Ina and the one to whom the Ina return in the afterlife point the narrative in dual directions—toward a utopian future with its reconstituted family and communal relations and an idealized past linked with Mother Africa. Shori reads *The Book of the Goddess*, "some combination of religion, metaphor, and history," as part of her efforts to learn about her heritage (215). Stories of the goddess constitute a vital part of the recovered history that Shori unearths, and that lore lays the foundation for a reappraisal of the protagonist's compound identity—as human, Ina, and scientific experiment.

By creating a disembodied body that is a part of, yet separate from, traditional constraints of linear time, Butler fashions a protagonist who undergoes a radical transformation that reestablishes our concept of Black female subjectivity. Posthumanist literary theory opens up critical spaces that interrogate what it means to be human in light of existing cultural and historic movements. Kristen Lillvis asserts that one of the most distinct aspects of a posthuman body is its a-temporality, wherein it exists outside of time, or, rather, suspended within it. Shori's body is a-temporal in the way that is both woman and child, a ten-year-old adolescent and a fifty-three-year-old vampire. This sense of "limited temporality," as Lillvis defines it, designates a space of re-historicizing for the body.[20]

Rosi Braidotti argues for rethinking subjectivity in terms of multivalent and compound subjectivities issuing from continuing associations between humans and nonhumans, animals, plants, and the universe as a whole.[21] Her insights shed light on Butler's attempts to blur the boundaries between human and nonhuman, between the female body and the realm of science. Neither predator nor prey, Shori defies a strict allegiance to all such designations. She kills and eats deer in a manner bordering on cannibalism. Despite her diminutive stature and apparent youth, Shori is also capable of murder as the young girl is responsible for the death of Hugh Tang, a human symbiont. She is motivated by the need for survival, not malevolence, however, which sets her apart from her violent attackers and Hollywood's notorious vampires. Shori's affinity with youth makes her seem less threatening than popular culture representations, and her treatment of symbionts is kind and understanding. Instead of considering her symbionts as victims or pawns, Shori's relationship with them reflects mutuality and balance.[22] While one Ina disputes Shori's claims of inclusivity within the Ina clan based upon her human subjectivity, Preston affirms that "Shori Matthews is as Ina as the rest of us" (272).

The superhuman strength Shori personifies through an association with blackness and the feminine is crucial to the continuation of the group as a whole. Pramod Nayar correctly asserts that Shori is "deracinated as a dark-skinned Vampire," but her "deracinated identity is what helps her survive."[23] Ina regenerative abilities result in the group's longevity apart from medical intervention as the Ina are self-healing and capable of living up to two hundred years. Whereas the light-skinned Ina eventually die off, Shori can live until she is five hundred years old. Her dark complexion is a consequence of scientific experimentation designed to create a genetic group akin to a super race. She also has enhanced bodily capabilities that she can pass on to her children. Female Inas' venom is more potent than that of the male, foregrounding the central character's ability to exert an extraordinary influence in the lives of her symbionts. "In that sense, the Ina are kind of a matriarchy. And a little thing like Shori might be a real power" (109). She, alone, survives multiple attacks, including the one at the Gordon compound resulting in the deaths of everyone except Shori, Brooke, and Celia. While Shori's dark complexion makes her susceptible to sunburn, her color also enables her to remain alert during daylight hours, a benefit allowing her to thwart an attack on the Gordon compound where she and her symbionts take refuge. "You not only survived twice, but you came to us with what you knew, and you led the fight to destroy most of the assassins and to question the survivors," Daniel Braithwaite reminds Shori following the Council of Judgment. "They thought mixing human genes with ours would weaken us. You proved them very wrong" (225).

Encounters with Newness in a Home of One's Own

Shori's identification with an absent-present maternal figure, a shadowy female persona who embodies a lost diasporic heritage, lays the foundation for the transformed social arrangement Butler reinscribes in her fantastic representation of a world where gender roles and sexuality are redefined. Life at the Gordon compound prefigures a futuristic world with an extended family network recalling an idyllic agrarian homestead, but with an assortment of human and nonhuman subjects, men as well as women. Shori encounters modern technological inventions such as cellular phones, computers, and flat screen televisions. Being there revives Shori's desire for a home of her own. "I figure I might want to have a kid someday," Shori reflects. "I wanted that—a home in which my symbionts enjoyed being with me and enjoyed one another and raised their children as I raised mine. That felt right, felt good" (127). Butler creates a protagonist whose growth into womanhood places her in an in-between moment reminiscent of the time at which Black girls, often defined in terms of latent hyper-sexuality, find themselves vulnerable to the threat of sexual assault. Shori is dark, forbidden flesh, subject to unbridled masculine desire. That Wright Hamlin is unable to resist her appeal is a reminder of the hyper-sexuality society often attributes to Black girls. In discussing issues of cultural appropriation, bell hooks describes the white male passage into manhood in ritualistic terms that involve romantic fantasies of the primitive. White males imagine sexual encounters with Black women in ways that point toward efforts to uphold structures of domination in a fetishizing of racial and sexual difference.[24]

Ina sexual liaisons are polyamorous, however, involving intimate relations with both men and women in challenging conventional sexual designations as Butler endeavors to disengage sex and sexuality from structures of masculine control. Melissa Strong mentions how the relationship between Ina and their symbionts blurs boundaries between familial and erotic love.[25] Susanna Morris situates her reading of *Fledgling* within an Afro-futurist feminist epistemology that takes into account issues of race, gender, and sexualities in the futurist visions Butler presents. Morris makes a persuasive case for how Butler "uncouple[s] dominance from power in queer sexualities."[26] Her reading of the novel prompts a consideration of how *Fledgling*'s symbiotic relationships are linked to the Afro-futurist feminist desire to portray liberation from current forms of hegemonic dominance. Such a portrayal of Black girlhood unfetters the youthful female subject from existing gender and sexual conventions, paving the way for a redefined gender construction that acknowledges sexual agency and autonomy.

The idealized home Shori envisions bears little resemblance to the home under patriarchal domination. Whereas the human community features primarily heterosexual, monogamous associations, the Ina are polyamorous and pan-sexual, engaging in multiple sexual liaisons that include same-sex interactions. Pramod Nayar asserts that Butler creates an alternate history in which humans and Ina exist in "non-hierarchic, interdependent and unified ecosystems."[27] Shori's growth of maturity occurs in terms of her awareness of the differences between Ina culture and practices and prevailing social customs. Ina interrelations depend upon "mutualistic symbiosis," which undermines hierarchal designations and the power dynamics of sexual and gender roles (63). Ina exist alongside, yet distinct from, the human community, with the exception of those individuals serving as the Inas' symbionts.

Apart from her role as a vampire, Shori has much in common with ordinary youths. She is, after all, a loveable miscreant bearing a close affinity with countless other pre-teens. Wright Hamlin notices early on that she is a girl, despite her pre-pubescent anatomy. The Inas' venom enables humans to experience longevity and heal quickly while human blood offers the sustenance necessary for the Inas' survival. Both groups rely upon each other for a continued existence, a condition setting them apart from ordinary humans.

Shori reassures Wright Hamlin that they will not retaliate against each other even after moments of disagreement. The protagonist also resists the possessiveness on the part of William, one of her later symbionts whose desire for a monogamous relationship is a manifestation of masculine dominance and control. "The whole thing was too weird for me," Shori explains. "Worse, I thought is sounded more like slavery than symbiosis. It scared the hell out of me" (204). Wright's aunt finds sexual activity between her nephew and Shori disturbing. However, Shori's father reassures Wright Hamlin that sex with Shori is within the bounds of acceptability. "Once you're living with us," Iosif remarks, "there will be no need to hide. And to us, there is nothing improper about your relationship" (68). But Wright Hamlin is unprepared for an arrangement that would undermine his sexual authority. At one point, he tells Shori, "But I didn't know then that I was agreeing to be part of a harem. You left that little bit out" (83).

As a bildungsroman protagonist, Shori enacts the journey from girlhood to womanhood, but she does so in ways that prompt a move outside the prevailing locational and metonymic structures that seek to circumscribe her multifaceted subjectivity. The Council of Judgment therefore evolves from the novel's semiotic structures as both sides—hers and the Silks'—attempt to label Shori in drastically different ways. Competing narratives surrounding the light-skinned Silks' role in the attacks upon Shori's family reveal efforts to confine the protagonist within Ina laws while passing judgement on the legitimacy of her existence. Shori reconstructs the story of her survival through multiple attacks by relying upon prisoner interviews and memory as Butler discloses the invisible influences of governmental and institutional control responsible for multiple genocidal attacks on Shori and her family. With its biblical significations alluding to Revelation's account of an imminent New World Order, the three-day judicial proceeding figures as an unmasking of the psychologically destructive color fetish at the center of America's social and institutional culture. Seven is a biblical trope that symbolizes completion, and seven joint ancestors serve as arbiters in the dispute between Shori and the Silk Family. Subject to a humiliating line of questioning from a doctor that the Silk Family enlists, Shori, still suffering from memory loss, is unable to recall the specific details of her traumatic past. The doctor—a symbiont of the Silks—tries to place not only Shori, but her body within the confines of traditional Western medicine, which "historically ... has instantiated and facilitated violence towards others defined as inferior."[28] The undertones of their exchange work to perpetuate the semiotic structures that strive to contain Shori's body, even as she continues to escape the limits of a Western imaginary.

The concept of semiotic constructions pursues Shori, and it is these structures that she is able to evade. As if to signify the enabling role of the feminine in Shori's passage through a space of linguistic uncertainty, the male-dominated Council of Judgment becomes the Council of the Goddess. Joan Braithwaite replaces Vladimir as Shori's advocate. The closing reference to the female goddess not only brings to mind a past that predates colonial inscriptions of a raced, gendered identity, it also points to a restoration of the ruptured mother–daughter dyad as site for constructing multiple lines of possible futures. The Ina enfold Shori into their clan in spite of the raced difference she embodies. Their acknowledgment of her association with their species is an affirmation of her constitutive relation with the group as a whole and an unsettling of strict binaries designating self and "other." Preston's declaration that "Shori is as Ina as the rest of us" becomes an avowal of the central character's role as a signifier for restored communal configurations (272). Shori, in terms of her futuristic potentiality, is a reembodied representation of all of us: unbroken, healed, made whole.

The journey that Shori and her symbionts undergo is one "where the self only emerges through its indebtedness to and responsibility for others."[29] Shori's amnesia may dislocate her from her ancestral history, but the family she forms with her symbionts marks the beginning of a new history and family that will turn out to be her future. Although Shori has no breasts, the mention of Zoe, who reminds Shori of a Greek goddess with voluptuous breasts, points to a fluid identity linked with both childhood and adulthood, one that is simultaneously past and futuristic without being confined to either designation. Butler uncouples maternity or sexuality from constructions of race in the creation of a model of femininity existing without respect to identity or locational boundaries.

Shori attracts praise for using her intellect in challenging the Silk Family and Katharine Dahlmer, the sinister mastermind behind the Silk Family's attacks. Vowing to learn about her heritage by reading Hayden, Shori decides not to mate or accept adoption into a family. Instead, in affirming her role as mother, she will live with several families and adopt a daughter in passing on a matriarchal history that represents a reinvention of the past. This continual evasion prompts the realization that existing linguistic structures fail to account for Shori's existence or offer a space of belonging. She cannot be adopted into a prevailing space. Rather, she must move outside the structures that attempt to contain her and create a completely new space of dynamic subjectivity. Her refusal to be absorbed into another Ina family is a testament to the urgency of her project of self-definition, a marker of her ability to define herself on her own terms. She must work to find a liminal space that shares aspects of herself while operating outside of those social arrangements.

In spite of Shori's compound subjectivity, her Blackness remains constant throughout her journey into womanhood. Gregory Hampton observes that while "the narratives written upon her body in the form of scars and other memorable injuries are temporary, her Blackness will always continue as an irrevocable permanence."[30] Thus, the cornerstone of her sense of self lingers even in the face of an end to the semiotic structures that have delimited her existence and her loss of memory. This means that she can construct the Black identity for herself, as both separate from and in connection with whiteness, but outside dominant textual spaces. Shori is thus "driven instead by the double impossibility and pre-requisite to become other and become [self]," and part of this is captured through her relationship with other symbionts.[31]

The nature of symbionts crosses the boundary between self and other and poses a new possibility for Black female intersectionality, a reality that is not peculiar to Ina, but mandatory for their—and ultimately their symbionts'—survival. What the symbionts represent is a dissolution between separate and discrete identities that "advocate the embrace of ambiguity and difference as devices for survival."[32] Such intersectionality acknowledges the isolation required for the formation of the self, while also admitting to the necessity of others in that process. The relationship symbionts and Ina share reveals an alternative reality where "humans are intimately connected with others, including those whose existence may exceed the western philosophical definition of human."[33] Although Shori may have found a space for self-construction, she cannot form such an identity without an "other" with whom she can associate.

Butler deploys the trope of the woman-child as a signifier for unsettled national boundaries owing to the tension between diasporic and nationalist formulations. As a youthful protagonist with "at least one more important growth stage to go through before she's old enough to mate or bear children," the novel's central character summons a poetics of futurity that troubles established corporeal, temporal, and locational limits (64). But Butler's mysterious protagonist is not just a manifestation of the historical progression of slavery and colonization; she is a totally different species whose existence points to the dynamic interplay between methods involving scientific experimentation and the biological processes associating her with a broad assembly of dispossessed subjects. In other words, not only is it possible to situate Shori within the space of Black Atlantic literary and cultural criticism, her association with the realm of science or scientific intervention gestures toward an otherworldly constitution owing no fidelity to fixed temporality. The absence of her breasts signals a childlike physicality connecting her with youth while pointing to her latent biological possibilities as a mother. Adolescence is thus a locus for envisioning utopian worlds of female agency, autonomy, and empowerment undeterred by existing social or cultural limits.

Resisting an overly optimistic reading of the novel, Susanna Morris argues that "the Afro-futurist feminism of the text illuminates epistemologies that do not suggest utopian panaceas but instead underscore the importance of transgressive manifestations of family and intimacy."[34] The futuristic society arising at the novel's close at the novel's close issues from reflections on the goddess, a semi-divine mother whose enabling presence is both maternal and sexualized, pointing the novel in dual directions in relation to reconstituted social arrangements. While the existence of such a figure does not offer a solution to the issues of racial animosity, fear, and exclusivity leading to the Silks' attacks, her existence in mnemonic form bodes well for Shori's ability to mediate the emotional and psychic trauma of maternal loss by translating the dislocating effects of liminality into freedom both within and outside existing semiotic structures.

Shori functions as a figure for the emergent Black female, a stranger in a strange country, a foreigner without a home, remade through her interaction with humans, human symbionts, and other Ina. The project of self-definition in which she participates necessitates the cessation of an old semiotic order and its linguistic limitations. *Fledgling* therefore seeks to reinscribe a space of semantic uncertainty tied to Shori's fluid subjectivity in anticipation of a futuristic world where fixed or established meaning no longer exists. The protagonist's reliance upon others, including Hayden, for knowledge about Ina customs and practices is a veiled acknowledgment of her existence as part of a larger constituent social group. She is, simply put, the Ina "in us."[35] Hayden, who offers insight into Ina customs, along with Shori's role as a medium for the transmission of a new historical record, underscores the urgency of Butler's inscription of a history about a recovered history framed as fiction.[36] In her fictionalization of a world marked by an assortment of social arrangements, a space characterized by reciprocity and mutuality, Butler constructs a meta-history of fundamentally altered communal arrangements that challenges the parameters of existing racial and gendered interactions. For her, this task is not just a flight of fancy on the part of the fiction writer; it is a mission interconnected with efforts to reclaim the future, to reembody it with a hopeful, emancipatory intent in ways that underscore the role children can play in ushering in new worlds of possibility.

Fledgling proposes the utility of locating the Black female bildungsroman within speculative genre conventions of time travel, alien encounters, and the creation of fantastic realms at odds with ordinary experience. Figurations of the crossroads demonstrate the fluidity of language in the creation of an alternative reality lending itself to an oppositional world view. In her evolutionary development from girlhood to womanhood, Shori not only grows up, she crosses over into a space of linguistic uncertainty where the metonymic structures seeking to define her lose all meaning.

The novel deploys legend and lore involving a dark, foreboding figure—in this instance, a young Black female vampire—as a means of troubling the dominant discourses of race, gender, and sexuality. Shori's confrontation with a range of constituent groups—humans, light-skinned Ina, human symbionts, male, female, children, and adults—implies the crossroads as a locus for constructing a fluid self that exists both within and outside established linguistic or temporal bounds. Efforts to sanitize a literary history of the vampire, as it were, to unhinge the genre from an association with difference prove as futile as the Silk Family's genocidal actions directed toward Shori and her family. Her existence mediates against a systematic erasure of the black, female, sexually ambiguous persona from vampire lore, bringing issues of difference to the forefront of scholarly reappraisals of the coming of age narrative through the deployment of an Afro-futurist feminist critical lens.

Childhood as a Site of Utopian Realization: Nalo Hopkinson's *Brown Girl in the Ring*

"Show Me Your Motion": Diasporic Wanderings in a New World Setting

Like Butler, Nalo Hopkinson opens a critical space for a reappraisal of the bildungsroman through the deployment of postapocalyptic linguistic significations. The Black Atlantic's worried border space discloses a crisscrossing network of associations featuring erased and reconstituted identities in the service of utopian worlds where women are empowered to reach their full potential. Vernacular culture encodes the perilous journey toward womanhood on the part of the youthful female subject, making visible that which was once invisible in the passage to an alternative reality existing within and outside temporal history.

Fledgling's vision of a transmuted social order bears a striking resemblance to the innovative cityscape in *Brown Girl in the Ring*, where Black women are saviors of a fractured urban setting threatening to spiral downward into further chaos and ruin. The task of safeguarding the future rests with newly awakened women who acknowledge their latent powers as mothers, daughters, lovers, healers, and seer-women without respect to a compartmentalization of roles. With each designation, female characters cross the boundaries of conventional gender and sexual designations by challenging the invisible forces of hegemonic dominance and control.

Hopkinson is among a thriving tradition of women writers whose fiction reveals an engagement with what Houston A. Baker, Jr. refers to as "spirit-work" or the wisdom embedded in African-American expressive culture.[37] Artifacts such as conjure, root-working, Voudoun, and Obeah underscore the viability of non-material forms of expressivity in the lives of Caribbean-Canadian women in ways that foreground connections between cultural groups in an African diasporic community. *Brown Girl in the Ring* extends the scholarly conversation surrounding black women's interventions into fantasy culture through a focus on a trans-generational assembly of seer-women possessing a close association with the spirit world or the realm of the unseen. Ti-Jeanne grows into womanhood in an urban-technological setting where healing arts, the presence of orisha and loas, and spirit possession are as real as the sounds of rhythmic drumming from the Palais, a temple where Voudoun worshipers gather, or the smell of curry stew wafting through the air at Roopsingh's roti shop. Elena Clemente Bustamante points out that "many speculative tropes appear often in postcolonial fiction even though they are hardly ever identified as science or utopian fiction. This is because some issues, such as environmental control, cultural clashes and imperialism, are actually relevant to both genres."[38] In her seminal book *Dark Matter: A Century of Speculative Fiction from the African Diaspora*, Sheree Thomas affirms that "like 'dark matter,' the contributions of black writers to the SF genre have not been directly observed or fully explored ... They become dark matter ... yet their influence ... would become undeniable."[39]

Hopkinson's dependence upon the supernatural not only raises questions about what postcolonial scholars refer to as the shiftiness of borders in a geopolitical sense, her narrative project also gestures toward Afro-futurist canon construction and the need to reassess the contributions of Black women to fantasy culture.[40] Scholars have cautioned against the reliance upon magical realism as a catch-all for an array of precolonial cultural traditions.[41] But *Brown Girl in the Ring* makes its own case for a reading of the novel apart from the principles of magical realism through an immersion in an Africanist spiritual platform predating the Latin American roots of fabulist writing. Hopkinson attempts to clarify her ambivalent relationship with science fiction in light-hearted terms by describing herself as "a science fiction writer who failed science, except biology and cooking class."[42] Elsewhere, she is more forthright about her engagement with the genre conventions of speculative writing: "Science fiction is still predominantly a white community ... It's a community that prides itself for being unracist ... I think to them 'unracist' means ignoring race ... I kind of feel that if you don't see race you can't see racism either."[43]

Hopkinson attends to what Thomas refers to as "dark matter" by racing and gendering the speculative, making visible that which was once invisible through a recovery of West Indian vernacular lore. *Brown Girl in the Ring* is her authorial attempt to reinscribe the spiritual artifacts emanating from an African-Caribbean heritage by relying upon a contemporary Canadian geography as a backdrop for the collision between traditions from the past and the cosmopolitan influences of a futuristic Toronto. The Burn, the inner-city locale serving as a locus for narrative action, is a demonic parody of hell; it is a place of poverty, violence, and political corruption owing to the influence of Rudy, Mami's former husband and a notorious gang lord. Walled off by an invisible boundary separating wealthy white residents from the largely agrarian enclaves where Black and brown citizens reside, the urban space is a commentary on decades of social, economic, and political practices that have led to a postapocalyptic wasteland, a city within a city, with unequal access to opportunities, goods, and services. "The ruined city was his kingdom," the omniscient narrator reminds the reader in a dual implication of patriarchy and the structural inequalities leading to the oppression of Black and brown urban communities within the dominant culture. "He wasn't going to let Gros-Jeanne's brood take it away from him."[44]

Tropes of unrestricted travel find expression in the intersecting network of journeys to and from the Burn, a perilous passage across nations, cultures, and worlds summoning the trans-Atlantic voyage. Hopkinson allegorizes efforts to evade Rudy and the Posse in ways that prompt an association between a resistance against the invisible influences responsible for the structural inequities of inner-city residents and colonial and neocolonial influences resulting in the subjugation of the post-slavery subject. Rudy's descent into a life of criminality marks the downward spiral of Black and brown urban communities because of rampant drug use, gang activity, and unjust governmental policies. Hopkinson implicates practices involving red-lining, gerrymandering, and white flight in the persistence of color and caste inequities in the inner city. But it is Rudy's introduction of buff, a derivative of crack-cocaine, that gestures toward the contemporary war on drugs and the neo-conservative policies aimed at mass incarceration of Black and brown citizens. A reliance upon buff as a method of social control underscores the destructive effects of substance abuse and the role that inner-city residents play in perpetuating a dependence upon the enslaving substance.

Tony, "a healer turned dealer," abandons his medical training in the pursuit of fast money and a life of delinquency in a cyclic repetition of a history characterized by family strife, toxic masculinity, and domestic violence (99). Ti-Jeanne's wayward boyfriend soon learns that resistance to the menacing influences at work in the Burn carries its own perils as residents find themselves facing Rudy's wrath and, in Melba's case, a horrific death. As a shadow of her former self, Melba embodies the dangers of a programmatic allegiance to sinister forces of institutional control. Her inability to act independently of Rudy offers evidence of an involuntary subjection to the dictatorial powers governing life in contemporary Toronto. Rudy tells Melba to clean the office ashtray and she obeys mindlessly. Once Rudy is no longer in need of her, he flays her alive in a gruesome scene of ritual sacrifice designed to feed the duppy bowl that enables his longevity and the ability to see into the spirit realm.

The Burn's topography signals an inner city caught in a downward spiral of poverty, criminality, and political corruption. Twelve years after violent race riots have shattered the city's delicate infrastructure, Toronto announces itself as a postapocalyptic dystopia under siege from gangs of criminals and feral street children.[45] Narrative description of Toronto as "a cartwheel half-mired in muddy water" directs attention to an entrapment with the structural inequities preventing inner-city residents from achieving economic parity as well as the limiting gender roles and sexual identities confronting Ti-Jeanne, Mi-Jeanne, and Gros-Jeanne, successive generations of Caribbean-Canadian seer-women (3).

Mami exchanges her nature-based healing mixtures and medical knowledge for items that residents pilfer from closed drugstores in a system of exchange based upon barter. Mami is a trained nurse whose medical practice is a lively blend of science and nature-based healing methods. Gifted with second sight or the ability to look into the spirit realm, she is a medium of the gods and a bridge to a forgotten African-Caribbean past. Mami's conflicted interests involving tension between a domestic role and her responsibilities as a healer and Obeah priestess, between the obligations of marriage and family life and a commitment to the well-being of the larger community, herald the issues confronting countless contemporary Black women. Internal conflicts owing to her efforts to reconcile the competing demands of womanhood, along with Rudy's abuse, result in the breakdown of the marriage when she decides to marry Dunston, one of her protégés. Mi-Jeanne, too, is imprisoned within the dialectical tensions of a shifting cultural landscape where social expectations governing marriage, motherhood, and sexuality shift in response to a changing cultural landscape. The birth of Ti-Jeanne is directly responsible for the deterioration of Mi-Jeanne's marriage when the protagonist's father becomes resentful of his wife's excessive devotion to her infant daughter. In each instance, women are imprisoned within domestic roles and the burdens associated with a gendered identity.

Rudy's stronghold on inner-city residents reveals the novel's concerns with temporal history and the challenges and possibilities of a life lived apart from the cultural traditions of the Jamaican Busch country. Hopkinson attends to the invisible powers at work in the Burn through a focus on Rudy's duppy bowl, a trope for the semiotic structures of domination governing life in the inner city. Entrapment within the ominous calabash bowl mirrors the disjuncture between body and spirit resonant with the Black Atlantic journey and the tendency toward psychic fragmentation on the part of post-slavery subjects. Baby functions as a signifier for the uncertain future Toronto faces as the city attempts to liberate itself from decades of neglect and oppressive social policies. That he is unnamed and unvoiced, except as an interlocutor under the influence of Papa Legba, implies the role of vernacular lore in mapping the journey toward a transformed future. If Rudy's calabash bowl refigures the oppressive institutional influences at work in the Burn, the destruction of the duppy bowl constitutes an emancipatory act with ritual overtones offering freedom from the forces of dominance that have held successive generations of Caribbean-Canadians in bondage. While Melba, Dunston, Mi-Jeanne, Tony, and Ti-Jeanne at some point find themselves imprisoned within Rudy's duppy bowl or under the influence of his zombie-inducing drug, Ti-Jeanne's fracturing of the duppy bowl signals a reversal of the body–spirit schism resulting from the dislocating effects of a traumatic trans-Atlantic history. The breaking of the bowl is an emancipatory gesture that releases her from an imprisonment within the semiotic structures that seek to delimit a dynamic Black female subjectivity.

The contradictory expectations of motherhood pose an immediate threat to Caribbean-Canadian women seeking to negotiate their relationships with one another, their daughters, and the larger community. Contemporary Black feminist criticism attends to the dialectical tensions inherent in Black motherhood as a fluid institution that mirrors the oppressive influences of the interlocking structures of race, gender, and class control while offering an opportunity for self-definition and community empowerment apart from existing systems of white, patriarchal dominance. Patricia Hill Collins asserts that "some women view motherhood as a truly burdensome condition that stifles their creativity, exploits their labor, and makes them partners in their own oppression. Others see motherhood as providing a base for self-actualization, status in the Black community, and a catalyst for social activism."[46]

The demands of breastfeeding remind Ti-Jeanne of a matrilineal history that empowers women while simultaneously limiting their ability to explore the range of opportunities for self-actualization apart from the domestic sphere. Throughout the novel and especially as she prepares to confront Rudy, the burdens of feeding Baby pursue Ti-Jeanne, prompting an awareness of the challenges faced by contemporary Black women seeking to navigate a cultural landscape where gender roles are under constant change. "Her breasts were achingly full," the omniscient narrator reminds us as the protagonist pursues Rudy. "As Baby began to suckle, the familiar draining weariness tugged at Ti-Jeanne, as always when it had been a long time between feedings" (174).

The novel's title recalls the ring or circle game, refigured as a trope for existing communal arrangements. The admonition for the girl at the center of the circle to "show me your motion" serves as an oblique interlocutor for female agency within and apart from established metonymic structures (183).[47] It is these arrangements that consecutive generations of Caribbean-Canadian women acknowledge and, later, transgress in the move toward a radically transformed self and society. Only as Ti-Jeanne embraces her compound identity does she find freedom both within and against the communal structures that have sustained generations of seer-women. As if to signal the role of youth in framing the oppositional aesthetics essential to freedom from imposed gender and sexual roles, the novel repeats lines from the popular game as a group of street children attack Rudy.

Ti-Jeanne's evasion of Rudy and the Posse therefore occurs in terms of childhood or the realm of youth as a site of utopian realization, a mode of envisioning a radically transformed future beyond the tyranny of the present moment. During the fanciful flight back to Riverdale Farm by bicycle, Tony and Ti-Jeanne are rendered partially imperceptible within Guinea fog, trope for Africa as a cultural metaphor and imperceptible metonymic presence, as if to convey both the move outside the realm of dominance and control defining Rudy's tyrannical rule and the invisibility of urban youth culture within Toronto's institutional structures. Not only does the rose Ti-Jeanne carries remind the reader of the contradictory impulses confronting the young mother, it also heralds liberation from the body–spirit schism through a new corporeality featuring unity between one's corporeal existence and nature or the outer world:[48]

> What if Tony hadn't been able to slide into Ti-Jeanne's heart like a thorn from a rose and stick there, aching and aching? She probably wouldn't have got pregnant. There would be no Baby constantly demanding her attention and her energy. *She coulda go wherever she want, nobody to stop she.* Suppose she could have chosen her own way, instead of trying to tear herself in three to satisfy Tony, and Baby, and Mami?
>
> (215)

When Ti-Jeanne accidentally drops the rose, she is once again visible and subject to a violent attack from Rudy's henchmen. Later, as Ti-Jeanne makes her way to the top of the CN Tower, Rudy's headquarters and place of surveillance, she is once again enshrouded in Guinea fog. Elena Bustamante rightly observes that the trip to the suburbs depicts the journey home on the part of the expatriate through a reversal of the Middle Passage.[49] With its multilayered significations, the fantastic voyage by bicycle also reroutes an otherwise linear journey toward an adult reality through the realm of youth or childhood, a journey refigured in terms of a liminal bodily constituency leading to a recovered diasporic past with its insinuations for futuristic worlds of female empowerment and agency.

Playing in the Dark: Alien Encounters at the Crossroads

Hopkinson contemporizes the fabulist tale by recasting narratives of transmigration, superhuman feats, and the contest between good and evil as a gendered resistance against the controlling discourses posing a threat to successive generations of Black women. Doing so destabilizes conventional identity constructs and the temporal history undergirding accounts of the trans-Atlantic journey. The novel's opening epigraph (*Give the devil a child for dinner, One two three little children!*), along with the epigraph for chapter 7, is drawn from Derek Walcott's play *Ti Jean and His Brothers*, based on a West Indian folktale about three brothers who seek to overpower the devil. Hopkinson mentions regarding the inspiring role of Walcott's work that she attended rehearsals for his theater troupe and visited his house when she was a child. She recalls vividly the moment when she realized that *Brown Girl in the Ring* "was a novel about three generations of women battling an evil in their lives, and [she] thought of the parallels with *Ti Jean and His Brothers*." So she chose to name the three women in her novel Gros-Jeanne, Mi-Jeanne, and Ti-Jeanne in order "to acknowledge that connection to Derek's work."[50]

Hopkinson addresses her relationship with Walcott through the creation of a trinity of women possessing semi-divine powers enabling them to see into the spirit realm and carry out extraordinary exploits of bravery and strength. Ti-Jeanne's encounters with the dark forces at work in the Burn involve an un-gendering of the masculine figures who people Walcott's work in the interest of a feminist epistemology that unsettles the hierarchal structures of patriarchal domination. As a mediating trans-Atlantic figure, Papa Legba not only discloses the paternal absence marking the protagonist's girlhood, he presides over connections involving erased and reconfigured identities in facilitating the fantastic journey to a postapocalyptic culture featuring enabled Black women. Edwidge Danticat refers to the folkloric figure as Baron Samedi in terms of his role as guardian of the cemetery.[51] For Zora Neale Hurston, it is Legba Attibon (*aka* Baron Carrefour) who serves as Lord of the Crossroads.[52] Maya Deren offers a reading of Legba in relation to his procreative abilities by associating him with the phallus.[53] Elena Bustamante notes that the three symbols associated with Legba—the womb, the umbilical cord, and the phallus—"can easily be identified in the novel as Ti-Jeanne herself, her baby and her baby's father, Tony."[54] Lamonda Horton Stallings's concept of "trickster-troping" is useful in theorizing Legba's role in unhinging the triple marginalization that has led to Black women's exclusion from the dominant culture.[55] In his association with gender indeterminacy or trans-ness a basis for Black Atlantic identity construction, Legba opens critical spaces lending themselves to strategies of critique involving alternative identities based in mutuality and interdependence rather than fixity and closure.

Ti-Jeanne's growth of maturity occurs in terms of her willingness to embrace the spiritual knowledge Mami imparts as a constitutive aspect of the protagonist's multiple consciousness as a granddaughter of Caribbean-Canadian immigrants. Dual encounters with the soucouyant reveal the temporal stakes involved in Hopkinson's reliance upon the bildungsroman account of the journey from childhood to adulthood and the protagonist's efforts to mediate the competing roles presenting themselves as solutions to the issues of identity confronting contemporary Black women. Whereas Butler frames the meeting with a sinister night-creature, second-self, or dark double in relation to legend and lore surrounding the vampire, Hopkinson's reliance upon aspects of West Indian folklore Caribbean-izes the vernacular culture laying the foundation for Ti-Jeanne's efforts to arrive at an intersectional self. Gendering the soucouyant female in the form of a devil-woman who is "a tall, tall woman in a old-fashioned dress, long all the way down to the floor," with her "head tie-up in a scarf" summons the matrilineal history marking the trans-Atlantic passage along with the domineering maternal influences threatening multiple generations of Canadian-Caribbean women (8). Ti-Jeanne, her mother, and grandmother are entrapped in a cycle of trans-generational conflict revolving around issues of guilt, shame, and filial estrangement. Mami suffers emotionally as a result of her attempts to impose bush religion on her daughter and granddaughter. Mi-Jeanne's resistance against the knowledge Mami seeks to impart prompts the mother to retreat into madness.

For the trio of women, the past is a historical void enshrouded in the silences surrounding undisclosed family secrets. Confrontations with the soucouyant disclose a shadowy past by bringing attention to traditional beliefs and practices while gesturing toward the emancipatory role Ti-Jeanne is to play in ushering in an alternative future. Giselle Liza Anatol deploys a feminist critical lens in her reading of the multilayered signification of the night-creature as both "an image of cultural resistance to colonial ideology" and a figure "shoring up colonial notions of propriety and respectability."[56] The soucouyant's attraction to blood is, as Anatol points out, resonant with the gendered bodily functions accompanying womanhood and childbirth. But the sinister night-creature's pull toward blood also summons a traumatic history characterizing the lives of Black Atlantic subjects. Of paramount importance to Anatol are the ways that female authors endeavor to bring "certain bodily encounters out of the dark, so to speak—out of the realm of the soucouyant's secretive nighttime flights, out of the realm of the demonic, out of the obscurity of metaphorical association—and into more explicit depictions of women's bodily sovereignty."[57]

Rebecca Romdhani makes an association between the soucouyant and other folkloric figures, including the zombie and duppy. Her observations not only imply the residual presence of an African diasporic cultural history; they also speak to authorial attempts to translate aspects of African-Caribbean vernacular lore into contemporary fictional form. As Romdhani points out:

> Hopkinson's novel … does translate the *zombie astral* into both Western and Caribbean imaginations, as she brings this African being to Toronto and then Caribbeanizes it by calling it a duppy (a Caribbean spirit) and by also making it a soucouyant, aiding an understanding of the brutal history that the African-Caribbean diaspora have encountered since they were transported from Africa. A soucouyant is a Caribbean vampire who appears as an old woman in the daytime and at night sheds her skin and flies through the air as a fireball to suck people's blood, usually that of children and babies. She can be killed by rubbing salt into her discarded skin after she transforms because the salt will make her unable to return in the daytime.[58]

Ti-Jeanne is at first mortified by the night-creature's attempt to abduct Baby. Later, she remembers the method for distracting the night-creature by leaving drops of blood behind. Her willingness to draw upon Mami's folk knowledge foreshadows her inclination to embrace her grandmother's wisdom in practical ways and in a manner enabling the well-being of her young son and, by implication, the community as a whole.

Find Your Mother: The Power of a Remembered Past

Brown Girl in the Ring foregrounds the complex interrelationships between succeeding generations of Caribbean-Canadians in ways that direct attention to the trans-Atlantic journey and its implications for the utopian future arising in the aftermath of Toronto's collapse. Hopkinson translates the dislocating experience of maternal absence into narrative freedom with the mother-daughter dyad serving as a locus for the construction of an intersectionality that acknowledges the past without being subsumed by it. Motherhood constitutes a dynamic construct that allows Black women to work toward the betterment of the family and community. The presence of what Patricia Hill Collins refers to as women-centered networks offers evidence of "fluid and changing boundaries [that] often distinguish biological mothers from other women who care for children."[59]

Ti-Jeanne's evolutionary development from girlhood to womanhood occurs in relation to linkages involving dissolved and reconfigured identities with a resistance against the controlling influences that would render her passive in the face of patriarchal authority. Mi-Jeanne's declaration that "she head ain't ready to hold no spirits yet," following Prince of Cemetery's possession of Ti-Jeanne, directs attention to the psychological dimensions of the battle against the dark forces at work in the Burn (94). Mi-Jeanne falls victim to those influences when she turns to Rudy after fleeing Mami's punitive wrath. The mother later retreats into madness following a series of disturbing premonitions of the Toronto race riots.

Rudy's buff powder, a hallucinatory drug that is a derivative of crack-cocaine, places inner-city residents in a robotic state that recalls the induced forgetting associated with trans-Atlantic slavery as well as the automaton in Science Fiction lore.[60] The revelation that the drug is a "nerve and muscle paralysant" originating in Haiti and is derived from "poison and toad and some herbs" prompts an association between the out-of-body experience on the part of Rudy's victims and the besieged zombie entrapped between the realm of the living and the world of the (un)dead (211; 210). Hopkinson recasts the encounter between Rudy and Ti-Jeanne in terms suggestive of the zombie as a trope for current cultural or political situations. Rudy reminds Ti-Jeanne during their confrontation that "a zombie can't do nothing complicated ... but if you tell it to wash the dishes, it go wash every dish in the place" (212). But in her astral state involving a separation between body and spirit, Ti-Jeanne translates the dislocating experience of dispossession into narrative freedom by redefining the terms of a raced, gendered subjectivity. Her liminal constituency as a seer-woman allows her to see through Guinea Land eyes in ways that liberate her from the demands of a corporeal existence.

Ti-Jeanne is invisible while making her way to Rudy's observation deck as she moves outside of the structures of panopticon surveillance that Michael Foucault associates with a hierarchal ordering of existing social arrangements.[61] Homi Bhabha theorizes the journey outside the boundaries of an established social order in terms of the stairwell with its insinuations for a liminality that "entertains difference without an assumed or imposed hierarchy."[62] When Ti-Jeanne hears the voice of the Jab-Jab, Papa Legba's double whose playful taunts prompt her to exercise agency in thwarting Rudy, she remembers her grandmother's words, "the centre pole is the bridge between the worlds" (221). Remembering the spiritual knowledge Mami imparts allows Ti-Jeanne to mediate the disjuncture between a Jamaican-Caribbean past and the futuristic possibilities of a revitalized Toronto. Ti-Jeanne's climb up the CN Tower constitutes a symbolic reenactment of her grandmother's ritual at the center pole in the Palais during a voodoo ritual. Once the tallest building in Toronto, the CN Tower, home to Rudy's control station, symbolizes realms of power and control. In her ascent to the top of the tower, Ti-Jeanne reappropriates the symbols of masculine authority in the service of an Afro-futurist feminist consciousness that redefines the terms of existing communal and social arrangements in opposition to the structures of control that have defined life in the inner city.

Ti-Jeanne announces her liminal constituency by calling upon the lwa and spirits of departed souls. As Rebecca Romdhani aptly observes:

> Thus [Ti-Jeanne] calls on the lwa and the spirits of the dead, including spirits from Yoruba cosmology, such as Shakpana and Oya, and together they defeat Rudy. As Olmos and Para-Visini-Gebert explains, Oya traveled to the Americas to become a Santeria deity in Cuba (24). This is significant because, once again, Hopkinson's novel blends traditions from Africa and the Americas, which emphasizes the importance and continuing presence of African cultures for the emotional and spiritual wellbeing of the African-Caribbean diaspora.[63]

Remembering the names of orisha becomes a recuperative act that reverses the rupturing effects of the Middle Passage in the recovery of a diasporic heritage. "Rain pelted down like boulders. The lightening cracked fissures into the tower's structure, and water began to leak in, buckets of it. The water traced forms along the wall, and two majestic Black women stepped out from its current: graceful Oshun and beautiful Emanjah, water goddess both, anger terrible on their unearthly faces" (223). The novel's mention of the two water-spirits renowned for ordering the human realm in terms of motherhood and children directs attention to the invisible matrilineal history undergirding the novel and a reclamation of that heritage as the basis for a new social order featuring empowered Black women.[64]

Ti-Jeanne's discovery of her mother among Toronto's homeless residents where the elder woman exists as Crazy Betty, the mother's death at her daughter's hands, and the mother's eventual return to Riverdale Farm imply the conflicted mother–daughter relationship as a metaphor for the diasporic wanderings marking Ti-Jeanne's entrapment within a domestic role and the liberating possibilities for framing a radical Black female consciousness within existing social and communal structures. Mi-Jeanne's liminal constituency releases her from the unresolved tensions of the past while allowing her to continue as an enabling influence in the lives of future generations. Emancipated from the limits of corporeality, Mi-Jeanne translates the schism between the body and outer world into a space of infinite possibility in becoming a semi-divine mother-figure, a timeless maternal persona whose inspiring presence prefigures a restored relationship between the domestic role and the institutional structures of contemporary Toronto, between the individual and the communal arrangements in the inner city. As a disembodied body, she escapes the dislocating effects of temporal history in becoming "a mother found, lost, then found again" (234).

At the Intersection of Science and Culture: Healing the Body Politic

Ti-Jeanne confronts her discomfort with her multiple, overlapping identities by embracing her role as a healer in addressing the myriad ills plaguing residents of Toronto's failing inner city. Laura Salvini rightly observes that "Ti-Jeanne has done good, but she did it in her own way, adapting the traditional knowledge of the previous generations to her postapocalyptic condition of urban settler."[65] Elena Bustamante refers to Ti-Jeanne in messianic terms as "a savior of a near-future Canada in disarray."[66] Although the protagonist has yet to embrace the Obeah practices of her grandmother in full, Ti-Jeanne is intent on carrying out the nine-day funerary ritual that will usher Gros-Jeanne into Guinea, thereby facilitating the foremother's final return to an idealized diasporic homeland.

Brown Girl in the Ring attends to the encounter with newness in relation to a restored body politic no longer under the domination of the warring factions threatening to plunge the embattled inner city into more chaos and disarray. Premiere Uttley's heart transplant serves as a parable for the transformed social arrangements necessary to rescue a failing Toronto. Initially, Mami's heart, which assumes an autonomous existence apart from its corporeal structure, rejects placement in Uttley's body, as if to signify the tensions between cultural practices and ritual beliefs from the West Indies and the political and institutional structures governing life in cosmopolitan Toronto. Uttley reaches out to Gros-Jeanne's disembodied heart, labeled as a foreign appendage, imploring it to end its resistance: "Uttley became alarmed, had tried talking to the alien organ as if she is in dialogue with a creature from outer space." "Please," she said. "This is my body. You can't take it away from me" (237).

Uttley's premonition of death occurs in terms of her extinction, a return to "blackness. Nothing" (237). Critics have read the fantastical account of Uttley's successful transplant as a narrative of the human heart as a "physical and metaphysical key" and a parody of life in the Burn.[67] Beyond that, the scene refigures the contradictions and tensions inherent in the colonial and postcolonial situation as the novel seizes upon Blackness as a locus for the construction of a new self and society. Laura Salvini correctly observes:

> Ti-Jeanne has done good, but she did it in her own way, adapting the traditional knowledge of the previous generations to her post-apocalyptic condition of the urban settler. Ti-Jeanne has struggled all her life against her hereditary power to have terrifying visions of other people's death. However, with acceptance and syncretism, she finally comes to terms with her Caribbean origin, addressing her uneasiness toward her multiple, overlapping identities by welcoming her hybridized self.[68]

Through a focus on the symbiotic relationship between Mami's heart and Premiere Uttley's body, the scene refigures the Middle Passage as a fantastic journey outside temporal history. At first, the ailing politician fears the nihilism that Blackness represents. Once the grandmother's heart ceases its resistance and cooperates with Uttley's body, however, the Premiere recovers. "And then she was aware again. Her dream body and brain were hers once more, but with a difference. The heart—her heart—was dancing joyfully between her ribs" (237). One is reminded of the cyborg—part human, part machine—as a construct featuring enhanced superhuman capabilities. The scene gestures toward a synergetic union between seemingly disparate entities in a culturally inflected expression of the transformational potential of a unified, socially conscious contemporary Toronto, a welcoming embrace of New World Blackness as a constituent aspect of contemporary urban life.

Uttley's transplant maps the journey toward an intersectionality in ways that signal mutuality and co-construction, even as the Premier's recovery summons an a-temporal space involving a confluence between science or medicine and a vibrant folk tradition with beliefs surrounding astral manifestations. With her changed heart, Uttley not only promises to work toward a more humane organ patron system where no one will be forced to be a donor, but she also vows to embark on a comprehensive program of urban renewal that holds the promise of a rejuvenated Toronto. Her new social consciousness marks a change from the oppressive policies of the past and a move toward a more socially just future for the deteriorating inner city.

Ti-Jeanne's coming of age necessitates her willingness to acknowledge her fluid identity as a border-crosser in embracing aspects of her Jamaican-Caribbean heritage. That her journey toward adulthood takes place within a postapocalyptic space involving the associations between ruptured and restored Black identities signals Hopkinson's concern with African-Caribbean history and its legacy in the lives of contemporary Black women. Hopkinson translates the dislocating moments involving the trans-Atlantic passage into tangible form through a reliance upon aspects of vernacular culture. Childhood or youth becomes, in the novel's futuristic imaginary, an expression of a liminal subjectivity that disrupts the chronological arrangement of a temporal history with its insistence upon a systematic ordering of society and a means of realizing futuristic potential in the here and now.

Children of the Night: Invisible Mothers and Haunted Daughters in Edwidge Danticat's *Claire of the Sea Light*

Migratory Ghosts: Departure, Return, and Places In-between

Emanating from what Edwidge Danticat refers to as "fakelore" or the created stories based upon the Haitian-Creole storytelling tradition, *Claire of the Sea Light* interweaves tropes of twinning, doubling, and mirror-imaging with the immigrant experience in the construction of a futuristic imaginary arising in the aftermath of a devastating category seven earthquake.[69] While Danticat chronicles the events surrounding the massive tremor and efforts toward rebuilding the nation's social and institutional infrastructure, as an artist, cultural critic, and social commentator, she is equally as concerned with the misrepresentations of Haiti and its people within mainstream media reportage of a succession of misfortunes that have befallen the country and its citizens. She addresses issues touching on the distortion of Haitians by presenting a range of uniquely individual characters that resist the controlling narratives that seek to define Haitians as passive victims of catastrophe and disaster. Robyn Cope argues that Danticat responds to negative portrayals of Haiti by "casting Haitians as neither sub- nor superhuman 'Others' but rather as neighbors. Danticat accomplishes this by deconstructing the very notion of humanization, shifting the novel's focus away from legitimizing her characters' humanity and toward cultivating her readers' humaneness."[70] Danticat is not content just to fictionalize the circumstances of the destructive earthquake, but she offers a new narrative of individual and communal survival through a rehearsal of the forgotten stories of the Haitian-immigrant community. As an account of the triumph of the human spirit in the face of unrelenting social, economic, political, and ecological turmoil, the novel seeks to unsettle the temporal history underlying the country's otherwise tragic cosmology and enfold us into a humanitarian circle essential to transformative change.

Narrative events transpire within the course of an evening as the underprivileged Haitian fisherman, Nozias Lanme Faustin, plans to give his seven-year-old daughter away to Madame Gaelle, a prosperous fabric shop owner, on the girl's birthday so that the youth can have a better life. Claire's mother dies in childbirth, leaving the father to raise the young girl with the assistance of female relatives and community members who attempt to fill the void surrounding the mother's untimely passing. When Claire learns of her father's intentions, the young girl goes missing, vowing to return to her seaside Haitian town in order to assume the role of Gaelle's daughter in a performative reenactment of the fractured mother–daughter bond.

Danticat situates Claire's coming of age within the diasporic wanderings on the part of the Black Atlantic subject and the liminality associated with a life lived between nations, cultures, and worlds. Caleb's drowning at sea summons the Middle Passage with its storied accounts of the myriad crossings marking the trans-Atlantic voyage. Ville Rose residents keep a worried vigil for the beloved fisherman in hopes of his eventual return to the seaside village. Interweaving the story of Caleb's alleged drowning with tropes of border-crossing lifts the fisherman's tale out of ordinary experience, the mundane, and the everyday into a fanciful realm of adventure involving the collective experiences of Haitian-Caribbean immigrant communities, a world touching on the speculative. Each of the stories that comprise the novel and, indeed, Ville Rose itself revolves around the sea which Danticat describes poetically as a character and source of proverbs.[71] The author's remarks elsewhere direct attention to the complex significations of water in the lives of Haitian immigrants. "In Haiti," she points out in "The Other Side of the Water," "the same expression, *lot bo dlo*, the other side of the water, can be used to denote the eternal afterlife as well as an emigre's eventual destination."[72] "People like to say of the sea that *lanme pa kenbe kras*," the omniscient narrator in *Claire of the Sea Light* informs the reader using Haitian-Creole idiom, "the sea does not hide dirt. It does not keep secrets. The sea was both hostile and docile, the ultimate trickster."[73] Anissa Wardi speaks to issues surrounding the role of water and bodies of water in terms of their spiritual, cultural, and political implications for Black literature, film, and expressive culture. She points out that "water is employed as a framework for theorizing survival and trauma, diasporic and regional connections, and physical and psychological dislocations."[74] Rather than serving exclusively as locations of separation, death, and loss, diasporas can also function as sites of healing and recovery, places of transformative potentiality lending themselves to infinite bodily and historical configurations apart from established temporalities.

Aside from a focus on gang activity among urban youths or the ecological issues confronting Ville Rose, a "small and unlucky town" facing a series of natural disasters owing to climate change, soil erosion, and a disregard for the natural environment, the novel foregrounds the close relationship between the commercial enterprises of the tiny seaside enclave and the realm of nature (14). At the moment Caleb goes missing, Nozias sees "a wall of water rise from the depths of the ocean, a giant blue-green tongue, trying, it seemed, to lick a pink sky" (3). Danticat situates the fisherman's disappearance within legend and lore surrounding the water-goddess Lasiren, an ambivalent maternal figure who seeks to reclaim the fisherman, or at least his body, in a gesture of communal affirmation resounding with myths of the longed-for return of the émigré.

"Di Mwen, Tell Me" locates itself within the diasporic dislocations of a Haitian-immigrant community so as to imply the role of unrestricted travel for contemporary identity formulations. Louise George's affair with the elder Max Ardin reveals the tangled interrelationships characterizing Ville Rose, uniting the community in a cosmic circle of oneness that mediates against the isolationist tendencies on the part of the modern world. As a teacher at Ecole Ardin and talk show host at Radio Zorey, Louise writes a collage a clef offering a history of the village and its residents. Stories on the part of Ville Rose residents such as Flore, who experiences rape at the hands of the younger Max Ardin, constitute a vital part of the narrative Louise inscribes as the popular talk show hostess offers a platform for voicing the untold narratives of individuals who exist on the margins, excluded from mainstream media reportage and literary representations. Danticat's rendering of Radio Zorey and the station's political role as a medium for the transmission of hidden truths underscores the importance of independent media and artists in the struggle for social change. For her, the immigrant artist possesses revolutionary potential with a mission to create dangerously in "creating as a revolt against silence, creating when both the creation and the reception, the writing and the reading, are dangerous undertakings, disobedience to a directive."[75] Bernard is a news journalist whose anxieties over his ability to tell "his side of the story" signal a concern with re-voicing the untold stories of marginalized subjects (77). His tragic death, along with that of Laurent Lauvaud, radio station donor, points to the life-threatening violence surrounding Radio Zorey in its mission of truth-telling in an era of repression and censure.

Narrative action occurs both within and outside of temporal history as if to imply a diasporic history marked by missing and recovered bodies, loves lost and found. Much like the novel itself, Louise's collage a clef constitutes a meta-history of life in a Haitian village subject to a string of catastrophic events that unite Ville Rose with a broad, transnational community of raced subjects facing a litany of environmental and political calamities. Gang violence, political corruption, and widespread poverty constitute very real threats to Haiti's stability and efforts to rebound from decades of political corruption and unjust economic policies. Lest the reader forget, Danticat is also attuned to ecological issues involving soil erosion, flooding, and mudslides—effects of global warming that speak of a world in crisis and portend a tragic fate for the embattled Caribbean nation. The plague of frogs troubling Villa Rose is a reminder of a delicate ecosystem where the link between humans and nature or the natural world is in peril. Only women can rescue the future, or, at the very least, keep the contemporary world from spiraling further into total chaos. Danticat implies through her salutary representation of marginalized Black women and the influence they hold in bringing about a more auspicious future that these women possess the knowledge, strength, and resilience essential to the survival of the entire circum-Caribbean world.

And that influence extends beyond Haiti to include a diasporic geography with ancient stories of semi-divine female figures whose reach traverses national boundaries. Louise overcomes the shame associated with a peculiar bleeding condition during her adolescence to later empower Flore, a former housekeeper who rears her son, Paxmine, alone after facing rejection from the Ardin Family. Paxmine's fatherlessness, his distance in geographic and psychological terms from Max Ardin, reveals the rupturing effects of forced and voluntary migration in a trans-Atlantic geography. The picture he draws of Max is one featuring a blank face so as to attribute the violence, poverty, and despair among young Black males to the dislocating effects of slavery and colonization and the psychological consequences of paternal absence.

Jessamine, who relocates to Miami, is in a ménage a trois involving Bernard and Max, who commits suicide in response to the death of his male lover. Although the same-sex relationship between Bernard and Max offers evidence of shifting sexual identities in a New World setting, the two are compelled to keep their bond hidden, choosing to remain in the closet for fear of public ridicule. Bernard's death plunges Max into a suicidal depression that reflects an inability to cope with lost love. Max's recollection of his mother's aphorism, "You are who you love," occurring as the young man commits suicide by drowning, links the novel's concerns with erased and reconfigured identities with a diasporic history involving broken and restored relations (198). Danticat's rendering of same-sex love undermines notions of heterosexual normativity in favor of relations that uncouple love from issues of dominance, a new societal arrangement featuring interdependence and mutuality. The revelation that Flore uses hush-money from the Ardin Family to launch a successful beauty parlor business not only points to the radical potential of storytelling in mapping the passage to alternative worlds, it also reveals the power of female agency apart from the controlling influences governing life in contemporary Haiti and the United States, the ways in which the young woman is able to leverage her sexual trauma in building a better future for other Black women. "This is what had kept *Di Mwen* on the air all these years," Louise reflects. "This is why people loved the show. She always looked for the pot of gold at the end of her guests' rainbows" (178).

Self-Reflexive Encounters in the Realm of the "Beyond"

Like that of Shori and Ti-Jeanne, Claire's evolutionary development summons both a redemptive return to a diasporic homeland and the journey into the future, a journey back in recovery of a gendered past as well as a fantastic passage toward utopian worlds announcing an intersection self. In each instance, water and bodies of water relate the shifting bodily constituency of a post-slavery subjectivity to aspects of vernacular culture so as to imply the transformative possibilities of unrestricted travel. Self-reflexive encounters with the alien "other" occur in association with difference and its implications for a transformed society where gender binaries and social hierarchies lose all validity. Notions of raced, gendered, or sexual difference exist as part of the postcolonial condition, and for the assortment of subjects who people *Claire of the Sea Light*'s fictional landscape, ghosts or ghostliness issue from the in-between-ness of living outside established cultural and geographic limits. Postcolonial literary and cultural theorists relate matters of ghostliness to trauma and the unhealed wounds of slavery and colonization.[76] Kathleen Brogan coins the term "cultural haunting" in attending to contemporary ethnic narratives of ghostly intrusions.[77] Elements such as haunted houses, dark passageways, hidden family secrets, scenes of violence, death, and dying, and elaborate burial rituals conjured within the pages of fiction by American multiethnic writers carry a meaning extending beyond the private function critics ascribe to similar concerns in canonical texts by Nathaniel Hawthorne, Edgar Allen Poe, and others. She goes on to point out regarding Black texts that "the figure of the ghost itself emerges from the cultural history of that group: one of the key elements of African religious thought to survive in syncretic forms of new-world religious practice and in slave folklore is the belief in ancestor spirits."[78]

For Marisa Parham, haunting and ghostliness offer important ways of thinking about the complex relationship between memory, art, and representation in African-American literature. "Haunting is not compelling because it resonates with the supernatural," she astutely points out, "but rather because it is appropriate to a sense of what it means to live in between things—in between cultures, in between times, in between spaces—to live with various kinds of doubled consciousness."[79] Relying upon the scholarly work of Cathy Caruth and other trauma theorists, Laurie Vickroy offers an experiential approach to memory and history in directing attention to the ways that contemporary authors utilize fiction in an effort to "fill in gaps left by official histories, pointing to unhealed wounds that linger in or on the body, in sexuality, intrusive memory, and emotional relations."[80]

Ghostly apparitions evolve out of a diasporic history with the interconnection between sacred and secular, past and present, the world of the living and the realm of the dead. *Claire of the Sea Light* seizes upon notions of in-between-ness in refiguring both historical loss and the persistent longing for recovery, a past involving ancient beliefs about the supernatural and a future where historical temporalities no longer exist. Caruth argues that trauma is a "symptom of history," because "the traumatized person ... carries an impossible history within them, or they become themselves the symptom of a history that they cannot entirely possess."[81] Useful to the present discussion are Caruth's observations regarding the referential nature of traumatic occurrences, the manner in which painful events, by virtue of their incomprehensibility, return to haunt the survivor at a later time.[82]

Claire of the Sea Light features an international community of transient subjects haunted by a history of tragedy and loss. Claire, who reembodies the lingering effects of such a past, disappears early on, remaining invisible for much of the novel in a playfully malevolent way, teasing her father, Ville Rose residents, and the reader-audience with her absence. Much like Claire Narcis, the "invisible mother" who hovers outside of existing semiotic structures, the protagonist inhabits a space of linguistic indeterminacy in anticipation of her eventual return to Ville Rose as a ghostly manifestation or dark-double of her former self, or, possibly, a reincarnation of her mother (225).

"Ghosts, or Chime," the radio talk show that Bernard envisions, takes up issues of gang violence, unemployment, police brutality and host of concerns confronting urban youth culture in a critique of systems of political and social dominance responsible for the invisibility on the part of Black Atlantic subjects. As a platform for males to share their stories, the program is a medium for urban youths to express themselves through rap and hip-hop, the language of the unheard and a medium representing those who inhabit the forgotten margins of society. Bernard thinks of launching his radio program with a focus on lost limbs:

> Not just Tiye's, but other people's as well. He would open Chime with a discussion of how many people in Cite Pendue had lost arms, legs, or hands. He would go from limbs to souls—to the number of people who had lost siblings, parents, children, and friends. These were the real ghosts, he would say, the phantom limbs, phantom minds, phantom loves that haunted them because they were used, then abandoned, because they were out of choices, because they were poor.
>
> (82)

Ghosts function as a cultural metaphor emblematic of the rupturing effects of immigrant life, or, as Danticat puts it, "what it means to live with one's feet in both worlds."[83] One is reminded of Danticat's deployment of the multilayered Creole term *dyaspora* as a metaphor for the dualities associated with the Haitian-immigrant experience. *Dyaspora* becomes a signifier for the ambivalent positioning ascribed to Haitian-immigrants separated from their Caribbean homeland through voluntary or involuntary exile.[84] Encoding the story of Claire's passage into womanhood within aspects of vernacular culture interweaves issues surrounding dissolved and reconfigured identities with the linguistic structures of Haitian-Creole parlance in signaling an alternative future existing apart from the realm of ordinary experience.

As a ghostly reembodiment of her mother, Claire is emblematic of the rupturing effects of maternal separation. Her liminal subjectivity enables a reenactment of a tragic past while allowing her to evade a national history marked by alienation, tragedy, and loss. In other words, Claire possesses a multifaceted identity that permits her to repeat the past in ghost-like fashion without being subsumed by it. Claire finds that her growth of maturity entails her developing awareness of female sexuality and the risks and possibilities associated with defying established gender conventions. Bernard and Max are tragically gay, subject to society's insistent homophobia. But the discovery of Max or, possibly, his corpse at the novel's ambiguous end signals the celebrated homecoming of the émigré, a reappearance marking a reconnection with the community in an unsettling of societal structures resistant to same-sex love.

Danticat's deployment of the revenant as bildungsroman protagonist disrupts the chronological progression underlying the passage to adulthood on the part of the novel's titular heroine who embodies both girlhood and womanhood simultaneously. Nozais's anguished decision to give his daughter away stems from the fisherman's insecurities about rearing a daughter alone as much as his concerns about not being able to provide for her adequately. "What did he know about raising a little girl? Maybe if she were a boy, he could try to do it. But with a girl, there were so many things that could go wrong, so many hopeless mistakes you could make" (15). Female sexuality carries its own particular vulnerabilities, as the experiences of Jessamine, Flore, Louise George, Madame Gaelle, and Claire Narcis disclose. Nozais warns Claire of the dangers of walking near establishments where "the women were said to spend days and nights in their bras and panties and the men walked in the doors quickly as they were frightened of being seen" (213). Ville Rose residents find themselves confronting a cultural landscape where sexual codes and gender identities are in a state of flux, with Claire serving as an embodiment of shifting gender roles and sexualities confronting an assortment of fictional characters.

"Anniversary," Madame Gaelle's story of trauma and healing, of love lost and regained, is located within an a-temporal narrative space involving the wealthy fabric shop owner's reconnection with a broad diasporic heritage featuring a range of sexualities. The grieving widow and mother turns to a succession of lovers in order to assuage the grief from her multiple losses, including the deaths of her husband and daughter. On the evening of Claire's disappearance, Madame Gaelle goes to Pauline's, a seedy nightclub and bar located on the outskirts of the village in Cite Pendue, a ghetto section of town peopled by violent gangs and the city's most impoverished residents. There, Gaelle meets Yves, the man responsible for the death of her only child. Wearing "a fancy body-hugging evening gown and rollers," Gaelle abandons her daytime persona involving middle-class respectability as she presents herself to the man whose carelessness results in her daughter's untimely death (155). No longer is she a caring mother-figure; instead, she becomes a beguiling lady of the night. The enchantress engages in a bizarre sexual encounter that is as sensual as it is mystical. Abandoning her maternal characteristics, Gaelle assumes the role of a sexually transgressive night-creature in search of an unwitting male victim.

While both Hopkinson and Danticat reinscribe the soucouyant as a figure for the unhealed trauma associated with a diasporic history, the menacing night-creature in *Claire of the Sea Light* is more closely associated with issues surrounding transgressive sexuality through a complex play of linguistic doubling that unsettles established sexual and gender conventions. The grief-stricken Gaelle exacts vengeance upon Yves who is also traumatized because of Rose's death as she engages in sex with a man who is either unable or unwilling to resist her feminine charms. United by a shared pain, bound by a past featuring trauma and loss, Yves and Gaelle enact a sexual union that heralds the creation of a new corporeality undeterred by existing bodily configurations. In a manner that mimes Voudoun beliefs involving spirit possession, the two wounded souls become one conjoined body.[85]

Mirrored Subjects: Un-twinning the Mother–Daughter Dyad

Claire of the Sea Light attends to the mother–daughter relationship as a cultural metaphor for diasporic wanderings and an ambivalent connection with a gendered past on the part of the post-slavery subject. As a woman-child fated to repeat a cycle of birth, death, and rebirth to the same mother, Claire embodies the liminal constituency of the Black Atlantic subject who exists within and outside temporal history. Distance from the mother induces a disremembering resonant with the trauma of forced migration and the cultural condition involving one's distance from an ancestral heritage featuring transcendent female figures. Claire relies upon the stories from her father, the mother's relatives, and Ville Rose residents in reinventing the events surrounding Clare Narcis whose maternal absence refigures the dislocating nature of the trans-Atlantic journey. Danticat is attuned to the role of memory and storytelling as sites of resistance against historical erasure. "There are many ways our mind protects us from present and past horrors," Danticat asserts regarding "writerly" efforts to mediate the trauma of maternal separation. As she points out:

> One way is by allowing us to forget. Forgetting is a constant fear in any writer's life. For the immigrant writer, far from home, memory becomes an even deeper

abyss. It is as if we had been forced to step under the notorious forgetting trees, the *sabliyes*, that our slave ancestors were told would remove their past from their heads and dull their desire to return home. We know we must pass under the tree, but we hold our breath and cross our fingers and toes and hope that the forgetting will not penetrate too deeply into our brains.[86]

Claire's mother, Claire Narcis, is what Tuire Valkeakare would label as a partially symbolic subject commensurate with Mother Africa, a diasporic home that is neither immediately accessible to nor completely removed from the post-slavery subject.[87] The mother is embedded in the protagonist's memorial structures as a fluid semiotic construct linked with an indistinct past. Claire's longing to hear stories about her mother evolves from a desire to remember a broken maternal heritage as a means of healing the psychological trauma of the trans-Atlantic journey. As a substitute maternal figure who is to fill the void associated with Clare Narcis's passing, Gaelle is a likely source for the retelling of the stories surrounding Claire Narcis. Gaelle's account of her sighting of the mother at the cemetery gate summons the crossroads as a space of transformative potentiality owing to the power of a remembered past. Claire Narcis, in Gaelle's reenvisioning, stands alone under a flame-colored weeping willow in ways that insinuate both the possibilities for a new bodily constituency involving a oneness with the natural environment and the induced forgetting that Danticat attributes to the trans-Atlantic passage.[88] In this regard, the mother's liminal positioning offers a basis for interrogating Claire Limye Lanme's evolutionary growth. The daughter's anticipated return to Ville Rose following her period of wandering constitutes a radical act of disarticulation in the move toward a multiple-consciousness as she breaks the spell of colonial and neocolonial influence, thereby signaling the radical possibilities for empowered womanhood in a diasporic setting.

Gaelle's daughter bears the name, Rose, in memory of So Rose, a "free colored woman, the wealthy affranchie, who'd founded the town after Pauline Bonaparte had left. So Rose herself had been named by her slave mother and French father after Sainte Rose de Lima, the patroness of the southern region" (55). Rose therefore functions as an unstable signifier with a range of possible meanings, including its association with Ville Rose, a history of slavery and French colonial rule, and the birthplace of Danticat's mother.[89] Claire, which means daffodil or self-love, is a name uniting the title character and her mother in a semiotic as well as a familial sense, just as the name implies a shared identity that threatens to undermine the young girl's realization of futuristic potentiality apart from past inscriptions. Nozais is intent on making sure Gaelle does not change the daughter's name. Claire appears as "a smaller version of her mother" (25). Ville Rose residents say that the mother–daughter pair are "like two drops of water" (218). Young Claire and Rose are "milk sisters" as Gaelle nurses Claire after the death of Claire Narcis (23). Claire wonders whether her adult voice will sound like that of her mother. "She must walk like her mother, too," she tells the reader, "and when she was a woman, a true Madame, when her adult voice came in, would she sound like her mother too?" (218).

Remembering the mother serves as a decolonizing gesture of resistance against the psychic rupture of the trans-Atlantic journey. Claire Narcis's work at Albert Vincent's funeral home prompts an association between the mother and all things (un)dead. She and Nozias begin living together before they are married, an act that raises issues about matters of sexual purity. While she is pregnant, Claire Narcis and Nozias go out to sea together for a night of fishing. Nozias describes his wife as a reembodiment of Lasiren, a water-spirit or mermaid-like creature responsible for entrapping sailors: "And in that moment she was his Lasiren, his long-haired long-bodied brown goddess of the sea. With an angelic face like a bronzed Lady of Charity, Lasiren was, it was believed, the last thing most fishermen saw before they died at sea, her arms the first things they slipped into, even before their bodies hit the water" (34). Lasiren is feminine, sensual, and charming, and she draws individuals into the sea so that they can achieve a higher consciousness. Nozias keeps a burlap sack with a mirror, comb, and conch shell—amulets to attract the ethereal water-spirit's protection.

Alien Frontiers and the Maroon Life

Emanating from Haitian-Creole linguistic structures involving mimesis, doubling, and repetition, the fantastic realm emerging at the novel's unresolved end mirrors the freedoms of an idealized diasporic past, but in terms of maroon life as a locus for futuristic potentiality apart from colonial inscriptions. Claire's ambivalent positioning as a border subject allows her unrestricted movement across Mon Initil where the ghosts of former slaves reside, a site associated with Ginen, a metonym for "all of Africa, renaming with the moniker of one country an ideological continent which, if it cannot welcome the returning bodies of its lost children, is more than happy to welcome back their spirits."[90] By envisioning herself as the lighthouse, Claire constructs a model of self-identity that heralds not only a disruption of established social hierarchies and divisions associated with the immigrant life, it also signals a reconfigured bodily constituency where the boundaries between the physicality of youth and the natural world cease. Once connected with a history of slavery involving French colonial rule, the non-functioning lighthouse speaks of the safe arrival of the emigrant. Claire's imagining of her return to Ville Rose therefore occurs in relation to a reembodied body—one that is free of the shattering effects of a fragmenting trans-Atlantic history. Silvia Martinez-Falquina argues that "the novel offers a form of healing by rejecting the position of opposition in favor of 'relation' through Claire's decision to return from the mountain—a symbolic site of resistance—in favor of returning to her town and its people."[91] Similarly, Robyn Cope points out that "as *Claire* moves from the local to the individual to the downright strange, its marvelous realist elements demonstrate that our sameness resides, remarkably, in our difference."[92] Claire refuses to sing the familiar fisherman's song with its inference for separation and loss—the tragic contours of the Middle Passage and its insistence upon a temporal history. The wonn song that Claire intones is an original one that marks her new identity as a border-crosser. She therefore summons the presence of LaSiren, mystical sea-goddess whose appearance signals a reversal of the trauma owing to the perilous trans-Atlantic journey and a restored mother–daughter dyad.

LaSiren mediates against the dislocating experience on the part of the Black Atlantic subject as Claire resolves the double impossibility of either rejoining her mother through death or charting an altogether different course leading to an infinite future. That her passage through the phases of girlhood occurs in terms of the journey from silence to speech underscores the role of language in outlining the fanciful world emerging at the novel's close. Claire is, at first, unable to offer a uniquely individual voice in passing on aspects of the oral tradition that occupies a central place in Ville Rose life. As a revenant, she threatens to repeat the legacy of tragedy, separation, and loss that her mother leaves behind. But "Claire de Lune," the novel's closing section, returns the reader full-circle by echoing the novel's title and the first story with a play of difference involving a French inflection. Centering the title character's evolutionary journey toward womanhood within the contours of Haitian-Creole parlance liberates Claire from linguistic fixedness in ways that gesture toward a speculative world that disrupts established temporal and semantic bounds.

Danticat's reliance upon the wonn game as a structural device underscores a narrative investment in childhood as a locus for envisioning alternative futures.[93] Like the ring game in Hopkinson's novel, the wonn implies issues of fantastic world-building within and against existing communal arrangements. Although she fails to include a discussion of *Claire of the Sea Light* in her interrogation of the

Haitian diasporic imaginary in Danticat's evolving canon, Nadège T. Clitandre points out that Danticat's writing is

> fueled by a desire to engender new imaginaries of identity, belonging, and home spaces that transgress binaries, stable signifiers, and monolithic truths ... But whether these new imaginaries produce revisionary tales, counter-narratives, or completely new frames of reference and mythic fantasies for alternative futures and places of belonging that take flight in new terrains of the imagination, they all emerge, for Danticat, out of both individually embodied and disembodied experiences in historically specific and localized contexts that echo and recall the nation—Haiti as homeland.[94]

Claire's destiny is therefore more hopeful than that of the orphaned Amabelle Desir in *The Farming of Bones* or the unnamed narrator in "Children of the Sea," indicating the author's growing concerns over the course of her decades-long career with fantastic world-building and the possibilities for beginning anew in the aftermath of catastrophe and disaster. The novel's unresolved ending is encoded in Haitian-Creole lore surrounding the Year-and-a-day celebration involving the collective return of lost souls rising from the sea, an event resonant with a Judeo-Christian belief in resurrection, the millennial reign, or the Second Coming of Christ.[95] Listening to the stories of survivors following the catastrophic 2010 Haitian earthquake buoyed Danticat's hopeful anticipation of a revitalized Haiti. "Then I heard one of the survivors say, either on radio or on television, that during the earthquake it was as if the earth had become liquid, like water," the author remarks. "That's when I began to imagine them, all these thousands and thousands of souls, slipping into the country's rivers and streams, then waiting out their year and a day before reemerging and reclaiming their places among us. And, briefly, I was hopeful."[96] A belief in a collective, eternal return destabilizes the otherwise linear chronology marking the Haitian-immigrant experience and reaffirms the prospects for newness in the face of calamity and loss. In its insistence upon the possibilities for recovery and return, the novel's unresolved ending points to the viability of a postapocalyptic culture that looks forward and back simultaneously, thereby reestablishing our sense of reality and our understanding of what it means to be human.

The novel's ambiguous ending with its insinuations for a collective return on the part of a nation of dispossessed subjects also recalls stories surrounding the zombie who is awakened by eating salt. "When zombies ate salt, it brought them back to life. Or so she'd always heard," Claire reflects in a creative engagement with communal lore. "Maybe if she ate enough salt, she would finally understand why her father wouldn't let her wander, flannen" (212–13). A half-dead body whose identity is a matter of the reader's conjecture washes up onto the shore, prompting a temporary pause in Ville Rose's worried vigil for Caleb. But whose body is this? Or does the identity of the ghostly corpse matter? Although the villagers agree that the body is likely that of suicide victim Max Ardin, Madame Gaelle greets him, "as though to kiss him," a gesture implying at once both a celebrated homecoming of the émigré and the healing, redemptive power of love in reawakening the (un)dead (237).

Claire of the Sea Light implies the crossroads as a space of untwining, a decolonizing site lending itself to a radically reconstituted self that is characterized by a multiple consciousness. Whereas, at firstyoung Claire continually identifies with the cultural and ethnic labels others apply to her heritage, she later rejects that identity, using her dynamic self-understanding as a border-crosser as a locus for a dynamic subjectivity. She resolves the dialectical tension represented by the decision of whether to join her mother in death or return to Ville Rose. The novel therefore gestures toward an emergent Black female consciousness as the basis for renewal and recovery on the part of an African-Caribbean community facing a series of unrelenting social, economic, and natural calamities. Claire's growth toward womanhood sheds light on the author's "writerly" efforts to reembody a broken, traumatic historiography in ways that underscore the resilience of those in an African-Caribbean setting, the ability on the part of the Haitian people to transcend a succession of social, economic, political, and ecological calamities with a measure of dignity and grace.

The titular heroine in *Claire of the Sea Light* embodies both childhood and womanhood in her ambivalent relationship with the linguistic structures of Haitian-Creole parlance. Claire Limye Lanme's multiple, overlapping subjectivities situate her within the realm of girlhood and womanhood simultaneously without restricting her to either designation, much like the female protagonists in *Fledgling* and *Brown Girl in the Ring*. The daughter's liminal constituency as a disembodied body—her clairvoyance as a seer—allows her to move freely between worlds, across established boundaries, in and out of time and space, as she seeks to redefine her place in contemporary Haiti.

The journey from girlhood to womanhood is fraught with peril for bildungsroman protagonists navigating a changing cultural scene where gender roles and sexual identities are in a state of constant flux. Unlike their counterparts in canonical texts, these figures journey into adulthood in ways that prompt a movement into an original social space privileging a complex intersectionality, one that challenges conventional notions of a raced, gendered, sexualized self. Moments of catastrophe liberate the Black female subject from the structures of white, male domination, and aspects of vernacular culture map the circuitous passage toward futurist worlds where Black females redefine the terms of Blackness and femininity. Black women writers are united by a narrative project dependent upon efforts to recover a largely unscripted heritage with its investment in transgressive models of female sexuality that call for innovative models of cultural critique.

3

"Queering" the New World Order in Michelle Cliff's *Abeng* and *No Telephone to Heaven*

The image of the ship—a living, micro-cultural, micro-political system in motion—is especially important for historical and theoretical reasons that I hope will become clearer below. Ships immediately focus attention on the middle passage, on the various projects for redemptive return to an African homeland, on the circulation of ideas and activists as well as the movement of key cultural and political artifacts: tracts, books, gramophone records, and choirs.

Paul Gilroy, The Black Atlantic: Modernity and Double-Consciousness

You see, the black Atlantic has always been the queer Atlantic. What Paul Gilroy never told us is how queer relationships were forged on merchant and pirate ships, where Europeans and Africans slept with fellow—and I mean same-sex—sailors. And, more powerfully and silently, how queer relationships emerged in the holds of slave ships that crossed between West Africa and the Caribbean archipelago.

Omise'eke Natasha Tinsley, "Black Atlantic, Queer Atlantic: Queer Imaginings of the Middle Passage"

Black women's literary and expressive culture is as invested in recovering a diasporic past as it is with creating alternative diasporic futures as a new avenue for exploring core themes in contemporary feminist thought, such as motherhood, women's activism, women's relationships, gender roles, and female sexualities.[1] But the task of reclaiming a lost past is fraught, as Mark Dery implies in his landmark essay marking the beginnings of a formal study of Afro-futurist writing, bound with issues of historical erasure and cultural appropriation in ways that complicate efforts to reinscribe a fragmented history traceable to Africa.[2] Michelle Cliff is at the forefront of a flourishing group of contemporary women writers whose literary works offer enriching possibilities for an imaginative reconstruction of past events in the service of utopian worlds existing apart from the interlocking influences of race, class, gender, and sexual domination. Her narrative project frames a radical subjectivity that is linked with a gendered heritage—one that acknowledges her multifaceted identity as a queer woman of color. Writing serves as a means of reclaiming a heritage of difference, of reaching back into a forgotten history featuring transgressive sexualities. In exploring issues of gender and sexual variability, Cliff reveals that she was "claiming—in a way, demanding—to be a whole person."[3] Cliff outlines her authorial intention in terms of efforts to recover a buried narrative of queerness. "As a writer, as a human being," Cliff remarks, "I have had to search for what was lost to me from the darker side, and for what has been hidden to be dredged from memory and dream."[4]

For Cliff as well as countless other Black women writers, the poetics of futurity evolve seamlessly out of a rich heritage involving individuals whose histories are lost, sublimated, or erased within a master narrative of whiteness, maleness, and heterosexual normativity. *Abeng* and *No Telephone to Heaven* serve as companion texts that attend to efforts at recovering a subterranean record of transgressive sexuality through the lens of Clare Savage, a mixed-race girl whose evolving political consciousness reflects the struggle for nationhood on the part of Jamaica within an Anglophone West Indies. Clare's globe-trekking mirrors a growing cosmopolitanism in the mid to late twentieth century involving her travels from Jamaica to the United States to Paris and, ultimately, a return to her homeland where she joins an armed militia group in the Cockpit country. Clare's wandering and subsequent awakening to the political concerns of the postmodern era occur alongside a Pan-Africanist movement insistent upon a cultural arousal among Blacks worldwide in an effort to throw off the shackles of colonial and neocolonial domination. The goal is not only to foster a sense of unity among an otherwise fragmented global assembly of Black nations, but also reclaim a free, independent Africa through a redemptive return to the Mother Country. The protagonist's international travels also exist in tandem with the first- and second-wave feminist moments and women's struggle for equal rights as a means of redressing the lingering consequences of patriarchal oppression. The personal is the political, in accordance with the rallying cry of the 1960s' second-wave feminist movement, as Cliff interweaves the protagonist's subjective experiences with an assortment of events signaling a rapidly changing international scene and the myriad concerns confronting queer women of color.[5]

Reembodied Histories and the Search for a Usable Past: *Abeng*

Bridges to Nowhere: African-Caribbean Dislocations

Post-Emancipation Jamaica's multicultural population reflects the dynamic processes of slavery and colonization with interrelations between Africans and African-descended people, the island's indigenous Indian or Arawak population, and white descendants of the British planter class. As a creolized subject whose identity reflects both the British aristocracy and an African cultural heritage, Clare embodies the edging between whiteness and Blackness; she exists on the border space outside fixed or established cultural limits while representing the permeability of national boundaries. Although Boy Savage is critical of intermarriage between the island's aristocratic, light-skinned inhabitants and Jamaica's brown-skinned peasant class, Clare is a reminder of the challenges associated with policing sexuality between the island's multicultural groups and the impossibility of framing strict raced, gendered, or sexual constructions apart from difference. Boy is a direct descendant of Judge Savage, a despotic British planter and slaveholder who carries out a reign of terror by burning his slaves on the eve of Emancipation, and Clare's elitist father engages in drinking, womanizing, and domestic abuse as if to convey the degeneracy of the British aristocracy. Marriage to Kitty, Clare's dark-skinned mother, introduces Boy to the folk culture that permeates island life, but does little to assuage his disdain for Jamaica's darker-skinned residents. Tensions within the couple's tumultuous marriage climax with Clare's shooting of her grandmother's wild hog, an act signaling the protagonist's transgression of inscribed behavioral codes for upper-middle-class girls. While Boy attributes his daughter's lapse to an inherent degeneracy associated with Blackness, Mattie ascribes her granddaughter's rebellion to whiteness and Clare's genealogical connections with the aristocratic Savage Family.

Abeng situates itself in a space involving transnational travel and its implications for social and cultural formations in the Anglophone West Indies. The novel mediates against a homogeneous inscription of Jamaica's diverse island population through the inclusion of a range of subjects whose identities traverse established limits. Annual visits between a developed Kingston and Mattie's expansive country estate at St. Elizabeth, between urban and rural settings, refigure the mass migration of a raced population during the contemporary era, but on a micro-cosmic level and in ways prompting an association between Clare's evolving subjectivity as creolized Jamaican girl and the global mappings marking Jamaica's move toward independence from colonial rule. Cliff attends to matters of displacement through a focus on the dislocating effects of transnational and local travel, but she is equally attuned to the manner in which identities collide and reconfigure within geographic spaces. A transformed social reality is the inevitable consequence of the interface between migratory subjects and the social spaces seeking to delimit an emergent raced, gendered, and sexualized self.

The Crossroads, a town located outside the movie theater where Clare views a film based on the life of Anne Frank, signals a refiguration of Clare's subjectivity in spatial or locational terms and in relation to the central character's evolving identity touching on matters of queerness or a trans identity. Clare exists outside the boundaries of an essentialist self, in a metaphoric site removed from existing cultural and geographic limits. Her creolized identity serves as a space rife with ontological and epistemic meaning, one lending itself to the ritual of coming *out,* invoking the language of one's open identification with a queer community, as well as coming out *from,* in the sense of travel or migration. M. Jacquie Alexander holds a concern with recovering untold stories in the service of a Black feminist epistemology invested in a resistance against twentieth- and twenty-first-century figurations of empire. By locating her project's central metaphor in the Middle Passage, she relies upon a lesbian feminist consciousness in arguing for a theoretical and methodological framework informed by multiple discourses of feminisms in looking outside narrow, prescriptive scholarly boundaries while searching for submerged truth. The truth that most concerns Alexander involves an engagement with the crosscurrents of feminisms against a global backdrop. Especially relevant to the conversation surrounding the intersection of queer identities, Black feminism, and a futuristic imaginary is Alexander's conceptualization of the crossroads as an intermediary site where "one puts down knowledge and acquires knowledge."[6]

Omise'eke Natasha Tinsley makes a compelling case for a rereading of the Black Atlantic as a locus for the construction of queerness by troubling the identity politics underlying Gilroy's theorizing of ships in motion. In much the same way that forced and voluntary migration holds the potential for transcultural influence, it also facilitates same-sex liaisons in a manner that destabilizes gender binaries. Tinsley attends to matters of a subterranean history of alternative sexual arrangements while offering a discussion of queerness in relation to issues of race, nationality, and gender, with water and bodies of water as emblems of a fluid identity that resists conformity to an established social norm. A central aspect of Tinsley's indispensable project involves an appraisal of queerness as a sign of erotic expressivity as well as a means of resistance against prescribed social hierarchies. I employ the term "queer" broadly in reference to a range of sexualized gestures and performative acts linked with the female body, even acts not overtly sexual or sexualized, including but not limited to close, same-sex interpersonal relations. The term is thus a signifier encompassing gestures, expressivity, and codes that mark what Tinsley aptly describes as "a disruption to the violence of normative, imposed colonial order inscribed in established social hierarchies and binaries."[7]

Lamonda Horton Stallings offers a reading of Black literary and cultural production in relation to the erotic as an expressive medium encompassing a range of gendered transgressive sexualities.[8] Queer relations, whether they entail physical intimacy or an affirmation of the regenerative power of same-sex bonds, involve self-love as a means of undermining the physical and psychic violence of our present moment. Baby Suggs's sermon in Toni Morrison's *Beloved* constitutes a radical call for self-possession, an admonition for a traumatized ex-slave community to carry out a redemptive project of self-love as a means of resisting the imposition of hegemonic control in a post-slavery context where a literal return to Africa is not entirely possible. That this space of self-love is yet uncharted and unmapped, much like the Clearing itself, speaks to the challenges posed by attempts to theorize issues of queerness in relation to race and gender, and while Cliff endeavors to chart the unexplored border space between multiple and, at times, competing subjectivities, her narrative project is as much invested in the process of reclaiming a lost heritage as it is in framing a world after the apocalypse, an invitation to envision the future now.

Cliff's reliance upon Clare Savage as a figure for the dynamic processes featuring trans-ness or a queer identity as a constituent aspect of a multiple-consciousness signals a concern with Black Atlantic subjectivity in a New World setting. As a sexually ambiguous protagonist, Clare embodies the liminality associated with identity construction in a world governed by rapid change and flux owing to transnational travel. The creation of such a figure gestures toward the past and future simultaneously as Cliff asks how one might imagine a utopian world that re-centers the marginalized, sexualized or sexually ambiguous subject, questions the extent to which a reappraisal of the Black Atlantic might lend itself to a reclamation of subterranean accounts of same-sex relations, and opens a critical space for analyzing a future that is not only cultured and gendered, but also queer.

Consistent with a focus on an a-temporal history and its insinuations for the dislocating experiences on the part of nations representing an Anglo-Caribbean geopolitical space, this project considers queer identities, not as fleeting interruptions of a heterosexual, cisgendered imperative, but as radical moments of expressivity along an unbroken historical continuum, the always-already of Black identity formation in a reversal of the rupturing effects of a colonizing history. Women writers attempt to reclaim the terms of eroticism and desire, rescuing sexuality and the sexualized female (and male) body from the strictures of established social practice. The process of repossessing the performative bodily gestures surrounding sexuality, of seizing control over the erotic appeal often associated with a gendered self, signals a turning point in the journey toward wholeness, freedom, and self-identity as same-sex-loving figures subvert the codes marking hetero-normativity. Effort to plot the journey toward self on the part of the queer subject is a project laden with potential complications owing largely to the absence of a historical record documenting the existence of such figures and their associations. Like the unpredictable waters of the Atlantic, the enterprise is subject to change and flux, open to sudden reversals, frequently without warning, altering the scholarly terrain of established critical practice.

Sexing the Margins: Encounters with "Otherness" and the Eroticization of Difference

Abeng and *No Telephone to Heaven* offer a starting point for mapping the unexplored boundaries between queerness or trans-ness in its myriad and, at times, disjunctive figurations and Black Atlantic subject formation. As the first work in the two-part series, *Abeng* gestures toward the island nation's beginnings as part of a natural process involving geological shifts over time, establishing the foundation for critical interventions into a futuristic imaginary unencumbered by existing genealogical or locational formulae. Cliff's narrative project demands its own space of scholarly inquiry, one that takes into account the seismic shifts involved constructions of queerness over time. A visit to Paradise Plantation, site of Judge Savage's genocidal attack upon newly freed slaves, signals the a-temporal history governing the overlapping identities marking Clare's emergent self-hood and the need for a critical perspective that accounts for difference. Boy takes pride in pointing out the lavish furnishings imported from abroad: "Settees and tables. Bric-a-brac. Crystal. China. From Royal Doulton."[9] A relic from Jamaica's colonial past, the plantation is a site for the hierarchal inscriptions of race, color, and caste underlying contemporary island life as well as a signifier for the exploitation of the nation's environmental and human resources. Boy is intent on presenting a revisionist version of the Savage family past, however, in his concealment of the brutalities of life on the sugar plantation. Visitors see Blacks dressed in period costumes in a performative reenactment of a slavery past that is sanitized and repackaged for mass market consumption. As a tourist attraction and a site for the construction of summer vacation homes, the plantation masks a record of cultural appropriation and genocide in the British West Indies.

Cliff counters the tendency toward historical erasure by excavating a subterranean narrative of resistance against colonial and neocolonial domination. Acts of insurrection on the part of the island's darker population—the offspring of African slaves, maroons, and other indigenous people—offer evidence of residual color and caste divisions stemming from slavery and the insurgent potential on the part of repressed subjects. Clare is attuned to the genocidal acts directed toward the Jews in Nazi Germany through the story of Anne Frank. Such accounts link the oppression of Blacks and Jews with that of same-sex-loving individuals, including Clifton and Clare's cousin Robert. An investment in the untold stories of insurgent subjects whose identities challenge established limits prompts a rethinking of the terms involved in Black Atlantic and queer critical interventions by positing a poetics of futurity that encompasses both epistemologies while resisting exclusive containment within either.[10]

Stemming from the dynamic processes of slavery and colonization, self-reflexive encounters with the alien "other" evolve out of the intersection between a diverse group of island residents whose compound identities reflect the growing cosmopolitanism of Jamaica's social landscape. Inscriptions of the island's darker inhabitants as primitive, savage, and subhuman—an embodiment of all that is dark, sinister, and forbidden—encode difference in ways that uphold hierarchal social designations based in the oppressive sugar plantation system. Clare labels her elitist classmates inhuman after observing their rude treatment of an elderly Black woman at a bus stop. The sharply intuitive youth locates her classmates' disdain for the dark-skinned, poor, elderly woman within a cultural context linking imperialism and a colonial history of the subjugation of native people with stories of fantastic clashes with an alien presence in science fiction lore. The invocation of Christopher Columbus summons the role of imperialism in the grand metanarrative of the region's history while challenging notions of racial inferiority and degeneracy central to a white Christian European imaginary:

> Dog-headed beings with human torsos. Winged people who could not fly. Being with one foot growing out of the tops of their heads, their only living function to

create shade for themselves in the hot tropical sun. People who at human flesh. All monsters. All inhuman. The people the explorers and the philosophers of exploration envisioned would inhabit the ends of the earth.

(78)

Mrs. Winifred Stevens voices the racist sentiments of her times in admonishing Clare against interracial sexual relations. Cautioning the young girl not to "let them cross you up" is the elder woman's way of upholding tenets of white supremacy based in notions of the so-called purity of the white race (162). Mrs. Stevens, who fails to follow her own advice, suffers the penalties of a transgressive sexuality through her liaisons with a Black man who works for the wealthy white family. The elder woman's remarks are noteworthy in their insistence upon the subhuman qualities she ascribes to the anonymous Black man and the mixed-race daughter who Mrs. Stevens births:

> Her father was a coon, you see, but he was a nice man. I didn't even touch the little girl after she was born. I just saw her dark little head under the blanket the nuns wrapped her in. Her eyes were still shut tight, so I don't know what color they were—blue like mine, or black like her papa. They crossed me up good, as you can easily see.
>
> (162–3)

Like Clare, Mrs. Stevens is relegated to the margins of society, placed in a convent as a result of a defiance of social mores.

Cliff attends to sexuality in relation to a history of oppression in the circum-Caribbean and efforts to evade the social restrictions that would proscribe intimate physical relations between same-sex-loving individuals. Excavating the stories of gay, lesbian, or sexually ambiguous figures becomes a means of reinscribing the history of the Black Atlantic as a resistant gesture against prevailing discourses tending toward an erasure of sexual difference. Inez's plight complicates the dominant discourses of slavery in the Anglo-Caribbean through a focus on the lives of enslaved and free women of color. Inez finds herself on the wrong side of law, brought up on charges of theft and summoned before Judge Savage. The Judge's rape and impregnation of the mixed-race eighteen-year-old underscores the routine vulnerabilities of womanhood during and after slavery.

But Mma Alli's role among a community of enslaved and free subjects offers a counternarrative to notions of raced, gendered acquiescence in the face of slave-holding authority. As a descendent of a tribe of one-breasted African warrior women, Mma Alli is aligned with a history of female insurgence. Yet is it as much Mma Alli's queerness as her powers as an obeah-practitioner that results in her influence on the plantation. She is what Lamonda Horton Stallings would refer to as a wild woman, someone whose sexual expressivity defies heterosexual normativity.[11] Mma Alli "had never lain with a man," the narrator discloses:

> The other slaves said she loved only women in that way, but that she was a true sister to the men—the Black men: her brothers. They said that by being with her in bed, women learned all manner of the magic of passion. How to become wet again and again all through the night. How to soothe and excite at the same time. How to touch a woman in her deep-inside and make her womb move within her. She taught many of the women on the plantation about this passion and how to take strength from it. To keep their bodies as their own, even while they were made subject to the whimsical violence of the justice and his slave drivers, who were for the most part creole or *quashee*.
>
> (35)

Not only is Mma Alli a guardian of spiritual knowledge from an African past, she also empowers her devotees through a sexual autonomy that uncouples sexuality from a hegemonic slave-holding practice.

Hortense Spillers points out that visual and historical accounts of slavery convey a troubling silence surrounding sexual trauma and Black women's responses to such oppression. The sexual violation of Black female bodies and their resistance, Spillers wryly observes, "did not constitute events that captains and their crews rushed to record in letters to their sponsoring companies, or sons on board in letters home to their New England mamas."[12] But the story of Inez and Mma Alli unveils a buried historiography of gendered trauma and Black women's resistance to sexualized and psychic violence. Although Judge Savage's rape and impregnation of mixed-race Inez highlights the liabilities of womanhood during and after slavery, the account of Mma Alli troubles the dominant discourses of Black female subjectivity to masculine power and authority. Mma Alli embodies queer resistance through her intervention into realms of sexuality and the biological processes associated with womanhood. Her role in the abortion of Inez's child is an act of defiance that liberates the eighteen-year-old woman from the role of breeder often ascribed to women on the plantation, even as it frees Inez from the imposition of motherhood in ways that enable a continued involvement with the maroons in their ongoing struggle for liberation. Through Mma Alli, women wrest control over the terms of femininity, motherhood, and erotic appeal so as to destabilize an exploitative patriarchal system deeply rooted in a capitalistic exploitation of the "other." The newly acquired agency Inez wields involves a level of eroticism that allows her to redefine the terms of her sexuality in undermining Judge Savage's dictatorial rule. The implications of Alli's intervention are measurable by the sexual agency Inez assumes. Inez is compelled to go back to Savage Plantation, "But she went there with a newfound power" (36).

The story of Queen Nanny, legendary leader of the windward maroons, is similarly invested in a reimagined account of female resistance emerging out of the interstices of race, class, gender, and sexual difference. A sorcerer and obeah-practitioner, Nanny exists in an unmapped space of linguistic indecipherability outside fixed locational and identity constructs, in between history and myth, embedded in cultural memory. Accounts of the island foremother's hunting and military exploits offer evidence of a subterranean narrative at odds with the dominant discourses surrounding Jamaica's colonial beginnings as part of Britain's imperialist expansion. Although Nanny's tragic death is attributed to betrayal from an unnamed informant who is likely Cudjoe, leader of the leeward maroons, she emerges as a figure for a resistant subjectivity—one that is invested in sexual ambiguity as well as the military maneuvers marking the struggle for freedom on the part of African and African-descended people.

Toward a Decolonized Future

Accounts of sexually transgressive figures disclose a diasporic heritage featuring alternative sexualities, not as transient moments across a linear or chronological spectrum, but as central to the larger historiography of the Black Atlantic world. While Africa functions as what Tuire Valkeakari describes as a cultural metaphor emblematic of the diasporic condition, England exists a figure for Jamaica's "Anglocentric and imperialist past."[13] Neither Africa nor England offers an altogether welcoming reception for the West Indian immigrant in search of a place of belonging, however. Clare therefore experiences the moments of womanhood outside the prevailing structures of post-Emancipation Jamaica and while she is in the presence of Zoe, a dark-skinned playmate whose mother lives on the edge of Mattie's estate, not when the protagonist is in the company of her mother, Kitty. Kitty introduces Clare to aspects of African culture through bathing rituals in the Black River, herbal remedies, and knowledge about the natural environment and its processes. But the mother's emotional reserve and reticence about the bodily changes associated with youth prompt Clare to turn to Zoe as a source of affirmation.

Carol Boyce Davies centers her reading of fiction by women writers in the United States and Anglo-Caribbean within a context involving the politics of location in relation to the multidirectional crossings issuing from a colonial history of forced and voluntary passage across the trans-Atlantic. Boyce Davies's scholarly project is insistent in its refusal to isolate "heritage/identity questions from say gender/identity issues."[14] "While the evocation of Caribbean geography is strong," she avers, "there is a re-mapping of the terms of that landscape. In many ways, it is a cultural geography and 'cognitive mapping' of one's experience and location. Historical links to Africa are re-examined and relocated. Significantly, many of these writers are critically engaged in an anti-hegemonic discourse with the United States."[15]

The imaginative archives of the Black Atlantic serve as a locus for what Omise'eke Tinsley theorizes as "linkages [that] speak a cross-current of dissolved and reconfigured selfhoods."[16] Mattie's grandmotherly observation that the protagonist is "developing" has implications for Clare's journey through the phases of womanhood as well as the adolescent's evolving political consciousness, the move from a past bound with established sites genealogical origins to futuristic possibilities of a multiple-consciousness (62). The Bush serves as a gendered space of unbridled expressivity apart from colonialist reinscriptions of a gendered self. Patricia Hill Collins offers a basis for imagining the space that lays claim to Clare and Zoe's friendship through a mention of female bonding, storytelling, and the blues as essential aspects of the safe spaces that have allowed Black women to define themselves in opposition to hegemonic authority.[17]

After reading a news account of a rare disease that turns girls into men, the young women survey their bodies for signs of gender indeterminacy or variability:

> They searched their bodies for signs, and tried to figure out what the signs would be. Would they begin by acting differently—they thought about the mannerisms some men had. Walking in a certain way. Stroking their chins— Mr. Powell did that when he was considering something. Spitting against the wind. Would they act differently at first? Or would they begin to grow one of those things they called a "pepsis"? What would they do with a pepsi? They were only just beginning to develop, were waiting around for their "monthlies" to start—and now this.
>
> (103–4)

The second news article involving a five-year-old girl in Peru who gives birth to a baby boy has an equally disturbing effect on the young girls as they contemplate the physical changes accompanying adolescence. What is noteworthy about the scene are its insinuations for trans-ness and the role that nature or the natural world assumes in a reading of the novel's concerns with "fluid bodies under force of brutality."[18] Conceiving the Black Atlantic as a fluid space of gender or sexual construction in response to the exigencies of slavery and colonization unfetters the raced, gendered, potentially queer subject from the moorings of an essentialist identity and liberates the Black self from the strictures of an oppressive colonial history.

Clare and Zoe enjoy a female bond that is laced with homo-erotic appeal. Through bathing rituals in the Black River and moments of play, Clare and Zoe define themselves apart from the dominant discourses embedded in Victorian inscriptions of womanhood. Their friendship interrupts the hierarchal social arrangements emanating from the island's slavery past and signals a new social configuration reminiscent of Jamaica's precolonial existence. Kitty and Zoe recite "The Maroon Girl," a poem prompting an association between Jamaica's struggle for independence and an insurgent female persona—unbound, unshackled, and unfettered. That this figure exists outside of temporal history and canonical textual spaces speaks to the limitations of "official" history in a representation of the marginalized subject within a Europeanized colonial imaginary.

Lewis Powell requires students to memorize the Wordsworth poem, "Daffodils" so that it is "spoken with as little accent as possible" (85). The daffodil is a hybrid flower appearing throughout Caribbean literature as a symbolic representation of the colonial experience. That one of Kitty's classmates chooses to color the flower red—"like a hibiscus"—underscores the viability of a culture of resistance on the part of indigenous people (129). Not only does Clare place a red hibiscus behind her playmate's ear in a commemoration of the pair's Sapphic attachment, she also dresses Zoe using elements from nature in a gesture signaling an erasure of artificial boundaries demarcating the female body and the natural world and a reclamation of the bodily processes associated with womanhood. In a rehearsal of the scene, but in a context involving the entire school at St. Elizabeth's, the Jamaican Tableau features students dressed as flowers and palm fronds in a performance of a reality featuring a series of reconfigured social arrangements involving an erasure of boundaries between the human community and the realm of nature.

The association between Marcus Garvey's Back-to-Africa Movement and Lewis Powell's revolutionary pedagogical practices foregrounds the novel's investment in the various projects involving a redemptive return to Africa and their implications for a queer postapocalyptic culture. Garvey's vision of a decolonized Africa locates *Abeng*'s futuristic concerns within an a-temporal space featuring a collision between a precolonial past and an idealized future where once dispossessed subjects establish their own autonomous society. "Garvey's dream of the Black return to Africa became Mr. Powell's," the omniscient narrator points out. "But it would not be a bushman's Africa—it would be an aristocratic and civilized Black continent, where, finally, after hundreds of years of misery, Black supremacy would be evident, and Black people would prove once and for all that they were capable of existing in a white-dominated world on their own terms" (88). Powell raises the specter of queerness in an era marked by transcultural artistic, artistic, and political exchanges between Haitians, Dominicans, and West Indians. As a poet who traveled to New York in the 1920s and "pirouetted around the edges of the Black literary movement known as the Harlem Renaissance," Powell enjoys a casual friendship with Mad Hannah's openly gay son, Clinton, that hints at an underground gay/lesbian network among Black and white artists, patrons, intellectuals, and activists during the Renaissance and the need to uncover the submerged narratives of figures whose lives are excluded from or misrepresented within mainstream accounts. Boy's mother, Caroline, moves to New York and joins the cast of Noble Sissle and Eubie Blake's Broadway musical *Shuffle Along* where she passes for white. Clare's queer cousin, Robert, faces ridicule from homophobic family members when he returns to Jamaica with his Black American gay lover. Not only does the family attribute Robert's queerness to an illness resulting from inbreeding between English residents and American tourists or insanity, they also ascribe the so-called malaise affecting Robert and Clinton to the role of "crazy or overprotective mothers" (126).

The account of Clare Savage's move toward a revolutionary consciousness informs on a reembodied history involving erased and restored identities. Situating her search for self within the global mappings of an increasingly transnational world lifts her experiences out of the realm of the ordinary, the commonplace, and the everyday, out of the personal and into a transcendent space connecting her struggle for independence with that of countless other marginalized subjects worldwide, including the novel's assortment of gay-lesbian and sexually ambiguous figures, past and present. In Cliff's second novel, the protagonist's globe-trekking culminates with a return to Jamaica, mirroring the transnational travels marking Cliff's evolutionary journey as a writer and queer woman of color. But the country to which Clare returns is riddled with internal tensions owing to social and political unrest, widespread poverty, and neocolonial interference. It is this country, not an idealized

Mother Africa, that functions as a locus for the struggle for liberation on the part of a diverse group of armed militant subjects in opposition to the utopian future Powell envisions.

Hunting Like a Girl: Reclaiming a Militant Trans Consciousness

Slavery and colonization instantiate a loss of worlds resonant with apocalypse through genocide, displacement, and systematic attempts at historical erasure. Yet Cliff attends to the ways in which postcolonial subjects reestablish cultural linkages to a diasporic heritage as a means of mediating the psychic and physical trauma associated with the trans-Atlantic journey. That the encounter with newness central to a postapocalyptic imaginary is encoded in the novel's discrete linguistic structures points to the role of semiotic structures in framing a radically reconstituted social order where women are free to explore their compound identities. The New World Order arising out of the novel's temporal framework therefore summons the past, but in a performative way and in a manner refiguring the past as a liminal, in-between moment.

Clare's accidental shooting of her grandmother's wild hog prompts a consideration of the novel's imaginative engagement with Black Atlantic history and the role that empowered women are to play in redefining the terms of a gendered self. At first, the hog killing is a rite of passage designed to reinscribe socially sanctioned notions of sexuality, masculine power, and privilege. Only males participate in the killing of the animal; the women at Mattie's estate remain in the house or on the porch, within gendered spaces of female subordination. The adventurous young men take pleasure in watching Clare's revulsion upon seeing the hog hanging from the tree during the post-kill phase of the rite. When the males eat the dismembered hog's privates, internalizing masculine powers of virility and potency, the boys further Clare's sense of alienation, dismissing her attempts to comprehend their behavior with the claim, "Is jus' no fe gal pickney, dat's all" (58).

Within the perimeters of a diasporic imaginary involving shifting corporeal and locational constructs, Clare's shooting of Mattie's hog constitutes a reinscription of a once exclusively masculine rite of passage resonant with the African hunting expedition. The protagonist comes face-to-face with a canecutter when she and Zoe are naked on the countryside. Fearful of having the male interloper see her exposed body, Clare shoots over the head of the intruder, killing Mattie's hog. In the rendering of the shooting of Mattie's animal, Clare, who is intent on concealing her nakedness, code-switches when she speaks in standard English in addressing the intrusive cane-cutter, and, later, in her conversation with her grandmother. Clare abandons, at least temporarily, the Patois that signifies her allegiance to an indigenous island culture. Incensed by her granddaughter's rebellious behavior, Mattie is intent on enforcing conservative notions of womanhood and femininity. "She was a girl," the omniscient narrator remarks regarding the communal response to Clare's ill-fated hunting session. "No one was impressed with her" (150).

Clare's transgressive act recalls the exploits of island foremother, Queen Nanny. Stories of the famed ancestress constitute a unifying myth of origins among island residents. But in Cliff's reinscription of a diasporic history, the past is resonant with the supernatural, grounded in militant resistance, and gendered female. Nanny's superhuman powers as an Obeah woman allow her to carry out armed maneuvers indicating the presence of a timeless lineage of Black girl magic that is at once both political and spiritual. In the events surrounding the killing of Mattie's hog, Cliff reimagines resistance through a resignification of a colonial past involving a sexually ambiguous female warrior. The image of Clare and Zoe naked against a natural backdrop can be read as a romanticizing of the primitive with the notion that Black women are close to nature. Clare challenges fantasies based in constructions of difference by appropriating a position marked as masculine, white, and elitist in her interaction with the cane-cutter. Rooted in the performative, her act constitutes a reversal of hierarchal social designations in a plantation system that would ascribe sexual power to dark female flesh while reaffirming male power and authority. Her actions also figure as a reembodiment of the history surrounding Queen Nanny in ways that signal a utopian vision of oneness between the bi-racial West Indian youth and the heroic island foremother, between past, present, and future Black girls. Gender, as Judith Butler astutely observes, is a co-constructed formulation lending itself to repeated interpretation and reinterpretation through a range of motions, actions, and mannerisms.[19] Clare's killing of the hog is thus resonant with what Butler describes as a performative gesture that unsettles fixed identity constructs.

Critics have read *Abeng* variously as a Black feminist bildungsroman and a lesbian coming of age narrative.[20] Clare's latent rebellion through an identification with a history featuring insurgent female subjects also invites a reading of the novel as a genre-bending, hybridized instance of speculative intervention. Part historical recuperation, part dream-fantasy revenge, the hunting expedition is an initiatory moment anticipating *No Telephone to Heaven* with a society of outcast-revolutionaries whose complex identities challenge essentialist constructions, including Harry/Harriet, Clare's transgendered comrade. Like the richly variegated Anglophone Caribbean history Cliff endeavors to depict, *Abeng* ventures into the realm of fantasy culture by presenting itself as a plot resistant narrative that refuses allegiance to conventional science fiction formulae and realistic experience. As a modern-day superheroine who explodes the boundaries of colonial constructions, Clare summons an alternate history involving Black female rebellion bringing to mind a fantastic realm situated both within and outside the novel's temporal framework. Cliff's naming of Mattie's ill-fated hog, Old Joe, a linguistic variation of Cudjoe, the Black male informant who is responsible for the attack leading to Nanny's tragic death, is a gesture pointing to the hunt scene as a defining moment in the young girl's evolving feminist consciousness. The shooting of Mattie's hog is therefore not only a mimesis of a mimesis—a practice that resignifies the young boys' hunting ritual—it also recenters the raced, gendered, and sexually ambiguous subject. An enraged Mattie accuses her granddaughter of "acting like a boy" (134). In response to the potentially subversive implications of Clare's actions, the young girl's parents send her to Mrs. Phillips, a wealthy white woman, so Clare can learn how to be a lady.

Rather than following the predictable pattern of the newly awakened youthful female subject who goes back to a familiar environment and conforms to the traditional dictates of marriage and motherhood, Clare remains in an interstitial space resonant with the diasporic mappings Cliff seeks to employ. That the novel closes with the young girl's dream-memory of her first menses while submerged in the river, a moment recalling her entrance into womanhood, constitutes the final disjuncture involved in the construction of a futuristic imaginary through an erasure of artificially imposed limits. *Abeng* associates a postapocalyptic culture with a revaluation of the female body, not as a site of shame, violation, or trauma, but as a locus for female empowerment and a site of unbridled erotic appeal.

As a previously unacknowledged contributor to Black fantasy culture, Cliff relies upon a non-hegemonic positioning in creating an alternative reality featuring enabled women. The presence of a creolized female narrator—a covert woman warrior—whose multifaceted identity traverses established boundaries lays the groundwork for a more nuanced and cautiously optimistic reading of the novel, not as an appendage to a male-dominated science fiction canon, or even as a Black feminist retelling of the classical coming of age story, but as an instance of the Black woman's novelistic intervention into fantasy culture through the recuperation of a subterranean history highlighting queerness.

Clare's mediation of identities, her reliance upon dream-memory, and her body-consciousness point to a level of agency at odds with an assessment of her journey as an expression of female passivity and a failure to realize authentic womanhood. Such readings involve a model of identity based in a pathologizing of Black girlhood. By self-identifying with a range of diasporic figures, from those who are openly gay to ones whose sexuality is ambiguous, Clare signals the potential for articulating a fluid identity that redefines the terms of a gendered self.

For Cliff, the poetics of futurity evolve organically out of the imaginative archives of the past. The past that lays claim to Clare's latent insurgency is enshrouded in silence, buried in the postcolonial nation's collective unconscious, awaiting reclamation through the bodily gestures and performative rituals on the part of the protagonist and her best friend, Zoe. Cliff's first novel insists upon an original social space that authorizes unconventional definitions of womanhood and motherhood. "When I started writing *Abeng* I was really trying to construct myself as a Jamaican," Cliff remarks. "I was able then to claim the rest of the people that I happen to be as well, as I write."[21] Clare mentions at the novel's end, "everyone we dream about we are," invoking a fantastic, if not subversive, model of self-identity emanating from an a-temporal history featuring linkages between a range of diasporic subjects (166). The history that she summons entails lively intersectional identities that, together, chart alternative geographies of race, nation, gender, and sexuality.

Transgendering the Future: *No Telephone to Heaven*

You Can't Go Home Again: Diasporic Wanderings in the Era of the "Post"

No Telephone to Heaven extends the conversation surrounding the imaginative archives of the Black Atlantic as a locus for utopian futures featuring queerness, but within a transnational geography that situates Clare's migratory wandering alongside that of the Savage Family. Permeable national boundaries, changing immigration policies, the uncertainties of war, and Jamaica's political instability instigate the mass migration of a raced population across a global setting. Clare's travels follow an ever-widening circle prompting the move to the United States, London, Paris, and an eventual return to Jamaica where she joins an armed militia group that takes up residence on Mattie's abandoned estate. Throughout her journeys, she defines and redefines herself in relation to home in its myriad associations with a national and diasporic past. Carol Boyce Davies asserts that in fiction by Afro-Caribbean and American women, Black female subjectivity is constructed in relation to home in is many disjunctive associations: a parental home, the Caribbean homeland, and an identification with an African past.[22] Boyce Davies astutely observes that while a reconnection with an African home exists for Audre Lorde and Paule Marshall, no such possibility for a direct connection with Africa exists for Cliff. Boyce Davies also asserts that Cliff frames an emergent Black female subjectivity in terms of a sexuality existing "as part of the consciousness of the growing sexuality of the girls. These issues unfold in her subsequent works, in *Abeng*, for example."[23] While a full explication of Cliff's oeuvre is outside the purview of Boyce Davies's essential project, insights regarding Clare's realization of multiple, compound identities shed much-needed critical light on the futuristic imaginary laying claim to Cliff's narrative project.

The Savage Family's migration to the United States during the turbulent 1960s prompts an association between Clare's encounters with insurgent political movements in postcolonial Jamaica and those in contemporary America as communities of color worldwide resist structures of colonial and neocolonial domination. That the novel foregrounds the family's arrival in the continental United States amidst an era of continued racial oppression directs attention to Cliff's concerns with the interlocking influences of race, class, gender, and sexual subjugation in the face of globalism and the need for collective action in countering forces of white supremacist control. America proves to be a hostile place for the family as a whole, and their journey from south to north following the trajectory of the Great Migration links the search for belonging on the part of immigrant communities of color with the quest for a national identity. Boy's interaction with a white innkeeper in Georgia undermines the Jamaican father's efforts to assimilate into the dominant culture by passing for white. Later, Boy tells Clare that she is an American, counseling her to hide her racial identity as a means of gaining access to educational, social, and financial advantages denied to dark-skinned individuals. His appropriation of whiteness underscores the performative nature of race in a cultural context where markers of identity are subjective. Boy relies upon his Jesuit upbringing as a descendant of the British aristocracy in mediating the racialized situation in the rural South, only to be reminded of difference and its implications for a national identity. Boy denies his racialized heritage in the service of an identity predicated upon whiteness as a marker of American-ness. "Boy's manner changed from petitioning immigrant to ill-used scion. Pauper tu'n prince. No matter that at least one of the Jesuit's categories applied to him—no matter. He was streamlining himself for America. A new man."[24]

While Boy's encounters with hegemonic whiteness prompt him to envision himself as new man remade through this interaction with the institutions, structures, and systems of the governing society, the innkeeper associates race with an alien presence threatening to upset the South's hierarchal power dynamic. "Because if you're niggers you can't stay here. You ain't welcome. It ain't legal." He paused to let the message sink into the alien's brain. "It don't matter where you come from. Mars. Venus. Timbuktu." The innkeeper smiled (55). "Sometimes it felt to him like the *Invasion of the Body Snatchers*," the innkeeper reflects about the shiftiness of racial boundaries. "Who was real, who was not? Niggers were slick. Remember the county nurse with the bright skin whose husband was the good old boy who ran the filling station and whose baby gave her away?" (56).

No Telephone to Heaven attends to the role of popular culture as a locus for an embodied subjectivity manifesting itself in a range of interpersonal interactions within and across racial lines. Cliff's exposure to B-grade movies and their influence in shaping a national consciousness sheds light on issues of representation that persist throughout Clare's nomadic wandering, from the United States to Jamaica where her armed associates find themselves in confrontation with a counterterrorist group during the filming of a movie based on the life of Queen Nanny.[25] The white innkeeper references *The Invasion of the Body Snatchers*, a low-budget science fiction/horror film that prompts an association between the cultural disarticulation on the part of the West Indian immigrant community and the zombie of Haitian-Caribbean lore, Boy invokes *Gone with the Wind* with its romanticized portrait of the Civil War South, and Clare is fascinated by Shirley Temple movies. Clare is enlightened about the persecution of the Jews during the Holocaust by viewing a movie based on the life of Anne Frank, but *No Telephone to Heaven* summons filmic productions that reinscribe objectifying or romanticized images of Blackness.

Steven Shaviro locates his interrogation of a range of films within a critical framework involving a critique of the Lacanian model for self-identity currently popular in film theory and film studies as he argues against that model's over reliance upon the phallus as a trope for identity construction.[26] Through Simone de Beauvoir and others, Kate Ince attends to issues of embodied female subjectivity in a reading of the ways in which mainstream cinema distorts representations of women, objectifies the female body, and divests women of agency and voice.[27] bell hooks's insightful discussion of visual culture lends a cultured, gendered perspective to issues of cinematic representation as she covers a wide-ranging assembly of topics, from constructions of Black masculinity to issues of cultural appropriation. hooks makes a persuasive case for the political dimensions of the image and how images play a key role in how a cultural group is represented, and, ultimately, how they view themselves. Blackness, hooks avers, assumes commodity status in a capitalist, materialist system, making it a selling point of popular culture: "White men want to sleep with as many darker skinned women as they can. Movies and stories offer blackness as a primitivism that can appease disgruntled whites in a post-imperialist society. Cultural appropriation makes up for a perceived or real lack in white dominate culture. Fashion magazines and other advertising industries utilize blackness as a backdrop to sell their products."[28] For hooks, the construction of an oppositional gaze serves as a site for the critique of raced, gendered, and sexualized representation in the project of framing empowering, self-defined images.

Killing Whiteness

Cliff attends to the myriad forms of institutional control that frustrate the identities and aspirations on the part of a raced population—from the blatant racism on the part of the southern innkeeper to the subtler forms of racism in an urban landscape. Although encounters with the invisible structures of whiteness reinforce the sense of "otherness" confronting Clare and her family, the mother or motherhood serves as a locus for framing oppositional strategies of resistance in the move toward an intersectional self that refuses to distinguish one's political consciousness from the larger project of identity construction. Inferences of the maternal persist throughout Clare's transnational travels and culminate with her return to Jamaica where she and her comrades take up refuge on Mattie's land. Much like her husband, Boy, Kitty Savage embodies the anxieties of belonging on the part of the West Indian immigrant. Rather than denying her raced identity, however, she embraces a radical philosophy of Black empowerment that threatens to undermine the very foundations of a racialized contemporary America. Kitty's efforts to find acceptance within the immigrant community in New York are thwarted as a result of tensions between the various cultural groups who take up residence in her largely West Indian Bedford Stuyvesant neighborhood. Disillusionment with America's persistent xenophobia and the tension between immigrant groups prompt her return to Jamaica where she hopes to open a school for disadvantaged youths.

Kitty's introduction to America or what it means to be an American occurs in the form of a sign in Miami announcing the lynching of a Black man. The sign serves as a reminder of unseen forces of racial domination and the life-threatening implications of a defiance of America's written and unwritten social codes. Clare's mother is torn between a history of social activism involving Mattie's role in lending parcels of land to underprivileged island residents and the example of Marcus Garvey and a deracialized self that is based upon whiteness. Visits to a culturally vibrant Bedford Stuyvesant with its West Indian grocery stores and beauty supply shops mediate Kitty's anxieties of belonging by reminding her of a Jamaican homeland. But European residents of the largely Italian neighborhood tend to lump all immigrants of color together, however, "with an ignorant familiarity, as though they were indistinct places, sharing history and custom, white sands and blue waters indiscriminately," in a disavowal of cultural differences (64).

Unlike Boy, whose assimilationist tendencies prompt his pursuit of European ideals, Kitty appropriates whiteness as a performative act that liberates her from the hierarchal structures of race while allowing her to convey her radical ideas of social justice. Employment at White's Sanitary Laundry offers a space for Kitty to challenge white supremacist ideology by enclosing incendiary notes with the customer's laundry. Not only does Kitty's use of the pseudonym "Mrs. White" conceal her racialized identity, her reenactment of hegemonic whiteness under a pseudonym points to the novel's concerns with the linkages between dissolved and reconfigured identities in the service of a radically transformed subjectivity.

Kitty's latent activism situates the shifting identity on the part of the West Indian immigrant within the dominant discourses of American culture and the role of names as emancipatory mnemonic devices. Kitty both is and is not "Mrs. White," defying the labels that the larger society would ascribe. She is no more delimited by that designation as is Mrs. B, the laundry's Italian business owner. Sending anonymous messages that unsettle America's racialized assumptions allows her to present her ideas of equality in a subtle way and in a manner that destabilizes the raced politics underlying social relations late-twentieth-century America. So convincing is Kitty's performance that Mr. B attributes the authorship of the notes to Georgia and Virginia, two Black women employed at the laundry. Kitty's bold declaration that she killed Mrs. White constitutes a decolonizing gesture that signals her rejection of imposed identity constructs, even as it links her actions with efforts on the part of armed liberation groups intent on freeing Jamaica from neocolonial rule.

Like *Abeng*'s Lewis Powell, Kitty is a devotee of Marcus Garvey, and her goal of opening a school for underprivileged youths speaks of a history of social activism stemming from a nationalist ideology. Patricia Hill Collins seeks to conceptualize a history of Black women's insurgence through a focus on the various sites serving as a locus of female resistance. Teaching serves as "a form of Afrocentric feminist political activism," and Hill Collins asserts that "by placing family, children, education, and community at the center of our political activism, African-American women draw on Afrocentric conceptualizations of mothering, family, community, and empowerment. Moreover, offering a vision of what is possible in human relationships furthers the recurring humanist vision in Black feminist thought."[29] As part of her articulation of patterns involving Black women's activism, Hill Collins notes that "many women begin their political activism as advocates for African-Americans, the poor, or, less frequently, women. But over time Black women activists come to see the interconnectedness of race, class, and gender oppression and the need for broad-based political action."[30]

Hill Collins calls for a theoretical model in examining strategies of resistance that takes into account the interlocking influences of race, class, and gender domination. Recent scholarship points to efforts to map the terrain of Black women's activism through a focus on the new strategies that Black women employ in dealing with the challenges of contemporary race, class, gender, and sexual oppression.[31] Those strategies entail efforts to marshal gender variability in the service of an activist consciousness that refuses to make a distinction between one's sexualized, gendered self, and the larger political struggle for a radically transformed society. That Kitty dies without realizing her dream of a revitalized West Indian nation points to the challenges of an activism responsive to gendered difference or sexualized variability in the face of colonial and neocolonial rule.

Reclaiming the Feminine as a Space of Radical "Otherness"

Clare's international travels summon the growing cosmopolitanism of the contemporary era along with the political crosscurrents prompting her eventual return to Jamaica. Among all of the individuals who align themselves with a small group of militants, including Paul and Bobby, it is Harry/Harriet who is an embodiment of a trans-identity presenting itself as a possible solution to issues of difference and the oppressive political structures at work in postcolonial Jamaica. Harry/Harriet remains in contact with Clare, reminding her of her social obligations in her besieged homeland, and he plays a key role her involvement with an armed militia group. Clare's queer friend situates the story of his move toward an activist lifestyle alongside the account of his journey toward trans-ness in ways that signal a refusal to distinguish between a revolutionary ethos and the gay-lesbianism laying claim to his emergent identity. His account of childhood rape by an older white soldier relates his sexual trauma to issues of the imperialist conquest of Jamaica at the hands of white European colonizers. Yet it is Harry/Harriet's description of one of his favorite nightclubs that situates the trans-Atlantic voyage in relation to issues of cultural appropriation and historical erasure:

> Of course, if they were really imaginative, girlfriend, they would hang some whips and chains on the wall, dress the waiters in loincloths, have the barmaid bare her breasts, and call the whole mess the Middle Passage ... Sorry, these places bring out the worse in me ... especially since I know I am more welcome here than I would be in a rum shop at Matilda's Corner. He paused. "Our homeland is turned to stage set too much."
>
> (121)

Harry/Harriet's pronouncement that "we have taken the master's past as our own" implicates Black and brown communities in perpetuating a system of hierarchal domination (127). But it is a refusal to define himself in relation to strict gender binaries that signals the transformative potential of a Black identity in terms of Cliff's insistence upon queerness or trans-ness as a constituent aspect of an intersectional self. Harry/Harriet questions Clare Savage about queerness in order to find out what the protagonist knows about same-sex relations. No doubt Clare would have heard stories about gay/lesbian individuals, encountered queer individuals, or even participated in same-sex interactions during her international travels. Their exchange is worth noting:

> "Tell me something, you ever been tempted?" He raised a meticulously shaped eyebrow as if to mock his question.
> "Tempted by what?" she asked, knowing full well what he was asking her.
> Pussy, sweetness ... loving your own kind.
> "Jesus, Harry! Sometimes you are too much." She was annoyed that the question made her uncomfortable and answered her friend too sharply.
> "And here I thought we was girlfriends ... company," Harry/Harriet pushed out his tinted bottom lip as if to make to cry.
>
> (122)

Clare's hesitancy in responding to her friend's explicit query directs attention to the silence surrounding same-sex associations, the ways in which queerness operates outside the realm of social acceptability, just below the surface of a world that privileges heterosexual normativity. Harry/Harriet is compelled to hover on the forbidden margins of society while frequenting nightclubs and bars in search of affirmation in a world that privileges whiteness, maleness, and a cisgendered norm. Yet it is this space that becomes a site for framing the gender indeterminacy that Hortense Spillers associates with the historical currents undergirding Black Atlantic identity construction.[32] As a figure for an embodied trans identity, Harry/Harriet reclaims the long-suppressed feminine or the power of "yes" to the "female" within, not in ways that would pose a separation between masculine and feminine, but in a manner signaling the female as the basis for a new identity free from externally imposed limits.[33] The move toward an trans-identity culminates with the declaration that "Harriet live and Harry be no more," a radical gesture of self-naming signaling liberation from the discourses of heteronormativity and whiteness (168).

The Senseless Ending: Dystopic Visions of a Post-Catastrophe World

The radically transformed future Cliff imagines emerges out of a space of in-between-ness existing outside the perimeters of whiteness, maleness, and heteronormativity. It is this space, one given to the nihilistic tendencies on the part of a liminal subjectivity, that holds the potential for framing an original self and society, a decolonized world of transformed Blackness existing within and outside of temporal history. Clare's international travels disclose the connections involving dissolved and reconfigured identities leading to an embodied trans-identity and its implications for a postapocalyptic world. Her evolving insurgence occurs in terms of an evolving political consciousness and its implications for an awakened, decolonized Jamaica—a nation lifting itself out of the shadows of a past mired in British imperialism.

Although Clare's final return to Kingston constitutes a symbolic reversal of the Middle Passage, the country to which Clare returns is one riddled with social and class divisions. In a dystopic portrait of late-twentieth-century Jamaica that easily rivals George Orwell's postapocalyptic classic *1984*, "Film Noir" explores the challenges of realizing a radically transformed Jamaica through a focus on the ways in which mainstream media perpetuates raced and gendered stereotypes. A group of European directors select random Blacks to assume the roles of Nanny and Cudjoe in a filmic account of the life of island foremother Queen Nanny. As a glaring instance of the appropriation of indigenous people and their cultural traditions for mass market consumption, the film seeks to reinscribe structures of hegemonic whiteness by divesting the story of Nanny from its cultural context and by ascribing subhuman characteristics to local residents featured in the film. Christopher, the yard man responsible for the murder of Paul's family, appears as an ambiguous Christ/Anti-Christ in a multilayered rendering of colonial and imperialist interventions in the British West Indies. Not only is he associated with Christopher Columbus, as a folk embodiment of Revelation's beast, Christopher assumes the role of the grim reaper. "He had no past. He had no future. He was phosphorus. Light-bearing. He was light igniting the air around him. The source of all danger. He was the carrier of fire. He was the black light that rises from bone ash" (47). Among the folk, he is also known as Sasabonsam, a vampire-like being drawn from the Ashanti tribe. In the film, he is named "De Watchman," as if to signify his shifting identity within the communal lore surrounding his murderous attack on Paul H's family. The family's blunt refusal to grant Christopher land in order to bury his deceased grandmother pits the interests of the island's elite against the spiritual values of the indigenous population with their belief in observing traditional funerary customs. Christopher is responsible for the brutal deaths of Paul's family, and he is likely the source of the betrayal leading to the deaths of Clare and her comrades.

Visual culture presents itself as a potential site for historical recovery and authentic representation, but the film directs attention to the persistence of raced stereotypes in an era of unprecedented globalism and expansion. That the novel culminates with an Armageddon-like conflict between anti-terrorist forces and the guerilla group enlisting Clare and her companions reveals the difficulties of mounting a successful overthrow of the forces bent on maintaining control in the island nation. Clare's death, like that of Nanny, occurs as a result of a Black male informant. Cliff imagines a possible future in which marginalized individuals challenge the forces of hegemonic authority, but intra-racial tensions undermine the idealized future the author envisions.

As much as any other woman writer on the contemporary literary scene, Cliff attends to issues surrounding Black Atlantic identity construction and its relation with an embodied trans-identity. A recovered history involving subjects whose complex identities defy established identity constructs attests to the utility of such accounts in a reappraisal of queerness as a constituent aspect of a diasporic heritage. Postapocalypticism pushes the boundaries of an Afro-futurist canon in relation to Black women's literary and expressive culture through an engagement with a subterranean history of sexual difference. *Abeng* and *No Telephone to Heaven* lay the foundation for a critique of cultural criticism in its responsiveness to issues of gender variability and the contribution on the part of queer subjects to Black Atlantic history and culture.

4

Un-zombifying Blackness in Erna Brodber's *Myal* and Gloria Naylor's *Bailey's Café*

We discussed at great length the theories of how Zombies come to be. It was concluded that it is not a case of awakening the dead, but a matter of the semblance of death induced by some drug known to a few. Some secret probably brought from Africa and handed down from generation to generation. These men know the effect of the drug and the antidote. It is evident that it destroys that part of the brain which governs speech and will power. The victims can move and act but cannot formulate thought.
Zora Neale Hurston, Tell My Horse

Everyone told me a different story about how the slaves began to forget their past. Words like "zombie," "sorcerer," "witch," "succubus," and "vampire" were whispered to explain it. In these stories, which circulated throughout West Africa, the particulars were varied, but all of them ended the same—the slave loses the mother. Never did the captive choose to forget; she was always tricked or bewitched or coerced into forgetting. Amnesia, like an accident or a stroke of bad fortune, was never an act of volition.
Saidiya Hartman, Lose Your Mother

Issues surrounding a postapocalyptic sensibility insinuate the body or the physicality of Black femininity as a locus for the revisions of a traumatic history involving slavery, the Middle Passage, and colonization. In fiction and expressive culture by Black women, the journey to fanciful worlds of adventure, conquest, community activism, or romance necessitates a new corporeality evolving from, but not limited to, existing somatic constraints. As a metaphor for current political or cultural situations, zombies or zombie-ism points to the imaginative archives of the Black Atlantic as a rich source in interrogating emergent identities in relation to a postapocalyptic imaginary where hierarchal designations and gender binaries cease. Colonial and neocolonial influences have a fragmenting effect on Black female subjectivity through ideologies of whiteness, maleness, heterosexuality, and a cisgendered norm. While these forces seek to delimit identity and achievement by restricting individuals to conventional gender roles or rendering the Black female subject passive in the face of patriarchal domination, Black women's fiction and cultural production deploy African-Caribbean vernacular structures as a method of critiquing established subjectivities and the temporal spaces where such identities are formed.

Although zombies are popular in Western film and television, their origins in a perversion of Caribbean and African spirituality are routinely ignored. Bound with a colonial history involving incarnation and reincarnation, zombies not only point to fluid and disquieted national boundaries, they also constitute an avatar of "dark matter" stemming from the worried border space between vernacular culture and speculative or Afro-futurist tropes.[1] Zombies exist within the unexplored margins of a colonial history involving genocide, familial separation, dislocation, and forced migration. They relate to issues of history, trauma, and maternal loss while prompting a reevaluation of the intersection between Black women's evolving subjectivities and a diasporic heritage featuring unspeakable emotional and physical suffering. In their literary or folkloric manifestations, they are as responsive to necromancy in relation to an African-Caribbean epistemology as they are to the machinations of science or scientific intervention in the context of the speculative, bending to external influences of manipulation, domination, and control.

Drawn from African-Caribbean (Haitian) lore surrounding the undead, the condition is an ontological one that entails an enslaved individual who exists indistinctly between life and death, passivity and agency, hovering in a semiconscious state of robotic animation—cold, unfeeling, and mechanical, much like an android. Zombies summon figurations of the duppy, a folkloric cousin in ancestral terms, or a malevolent spirit who usually comes out at night. One is reminded of vampires, night-witches, ghosts, or other spectral figures as representative of a life lived in-between nations, cultures, and worlds.[2] Zora Neale Hurston speculates that the zombie exemplifies a drug-induced state issuing from a secret concoction brought from Africa.[3] Saidiya Hartman deploys a cultured, gendered approach while theorizing the zombie in relation to maternal absence or loss. For African abductees and their descendants, the trans-Atlantic journey instantiates a cultural dislocation resulting in what Hartman fittingly describes as an unnatural death owing to a bewitching influence "in which herbs, baths, talismans, and incantations transformed slaves into black and passive automatons."[4] Only by eating salt does the unfortunate creature awaken from a life-in-death state, at which time the zombie can go back to the grave and be put to rest, returning, happily, to Guinea, an idealized African homeland.

As an embodiment of a trans-Atlantic history marked by trauma, dislocation, and loss, the zombie maps the passage to fantastic worlds that exist beyond the realm of ordinary experience or the present moment. Rather than attending to an individual purpose, these figures serve an artistic function in revealing the situation of the larger diasporic community or the cultural group as a whole. Zombies, in Black women's literary and cultural production, are the inevitable consequence of a programmatic adherence to white, patriarchal standards or the invisible forces of domination and control present in Western or European culture. But by taking on a life of their own apart from patriarchy, "official" history, or authorial invention, zombies are also emblems of a resistant female subjectivity. As robotic figures entrapped within the crosscurrents of a spiritual contest involving the invisible forces of good and evil, they are transgressive beings who just decline to stay put. Black women writers mention how fictional characters can assume a life independent of the textual spaces seeking to inscribe those figures.[5] Writers and creative artists capitalize upon this tendency by exhuming the erstwhile zombie from a forgotten cultural gravesite in the service of an Afro-futurist feminist agenda that entails a defiance of recognized race, gender, and sexual limits. In their refusal to remain quiet, invisible, or passive, zombies personify the uncharted margins of an emergent Black female subjectivity, traversing the frontiers of Blackness and femininity in diasporic wanderings that plot the risky journey to previously unexplored worlds.

Erna Brodber's *Myal* and Gloria Naylor's *Bailey's Cafe* shed critical light on "un-zombification": the reliance upon resistant strategies involving a disassociation from objectifying structures of raced, gendered, and sexualized representation in the construction of a radical Black female subjectivity. As a discursive method, un-zombification is a decolonizing gesture that functions as a locus for the transcultural conversation between Black women in a diasporic geography. Through an acknowledgment of alternative spaces of female empowerment, Black women inscribe a poetics of futurity that takes its discursive cue from African-Caribbean folklore in framing a subjectivity existing within and outside existing temporalities. Such an identity relies heavily upon intersectionality or co-constituency as the basis for self-fashioning, a practice that, in the Black woman's narrative, serves as a method of self-construction in opposition to the politics of cultural representation in the dominant society.[6] The transformed social arrangements appearing in Black women's narratives are undeterred by psychic or bodily fracturing owing to historical rupture, not because they are unaware of such breaks, but because of an unwillingness to accept those estrangements as final or an impediment to newness. By naming the space from which Black women define themselves, making visible that which is invisible in the struggle against ideologies of race, class, gender, and sexual oppression, Black women writers and artists seek to undo the witchery of colonial and neocolonial interference through a focus on what bell hooks describes as language as a place of struggle: a fluid discursive site for framing a completely new space of radical Black female subjectivity unencumbered by existing formulae or prevailing critical practice.[7]

Writing a Zombie Apocalypse: Erna Brodber's *Myal*

"Choked on the Foreign": Language and the Ritual of Dispossession

When Ella O'Grady-Langley falls victim to a mysterious illness, Mass Cyrus undertakes an unconventional healing designed to rid the young woman of the toxic substance that threatens her physical and psychological well-being. Brodber's protagonist returns to Jamaica as a shadow of her former self, covered with boils, and carrying a huge mass in her belly. Staring blankly into space with routine utterances is evidence of a psychic disorder that has taken hold of the young woman in ways preventing meaningful social interaction with Grove Town residents. Mass Cyrus offers a vague diagnosis of Ella's malady before carrying out a rather bizarre seven-day ritual allowing Ella to expel the large gray substance. With overtones of a drug overdose, childbirth, or exorcism, Ella's illness and healing are a catalyst for a lightning storm of apocalyptic proportions accompanied by destruction of the natural world and homes along with a widespread loss of life.

Ella's migration from Jamaica to the United States underscores the persistent alienation marking the young woman's experiences as the mixed-race daughter of Mary Riley, a housekeeper of African-Moor descent, and Ralston O'Grady, an Irish policeman. Separated from her dark-skinned classmates by color and caste, Ella has no identity apart from the one others ascribe to her. She is, within a British colonial imaginary, a noble savage in need of civilization and Christianization. Only after her practiced recitation of a Rudyard Kipling poem does she attract the attention of a local Anglican priest and his wife.[8] Reverend Brassington's repetition of the poem's closing stanza in unison with Ella situates her illness and recovery in a historical context involving not only the subjugation of indigenous people in the interest of imperialist conquest, but also the speech acts emanating from the rich vernacular lore of West Indian culture. Brassington and his wife Maydene envision themselves as "Tak[ing] up the whiteman's burden" in adopting the young woman as their daughter.[9] By immersing the young woman in the Christian faith, introducing her to a life of wealth and privilege, and grooming her for a domestic role, the couple prepare Ella for a place among Jamaica's elite.

Frantz Fanon implicates French colonial and neocolonial influences in the neuroses prevalent among an indigenous people. The colonized tend to adopt the customs, manners, and language of the dominant society in an effort to find validation, often with negative psychological consequences owing to the Manichean tensions between the colonizer and the colonized, whiteness and Blackness, self and "other." Basing his assertions regarding colonization on his observations of racial interaction within an African-Francophone geography, Fanon mentions language as a sign of the self-division issuing from colonialist subjugation. "The colonized is elevated above his jungle status in proportion to his adoption of the mother country's cultural standards. He becomes whiter as he renounces his blackness, his jungle."[10] One might add that the colonized becomes whiter as he embraces the mother country's tongue. Fanon prescribes a cure for the urge toward whiteness by advising his patients not to acquiesce in the face of racial oppression, but challenge the social structures responsible for the subjugation of a raced people. He suggests that "the black man should no longer be confronted by the dilemma, turn white or disappear; but he should be able to take cognizance of a possibility of existence. In still other words, if society makes difficulties for him because of his color, if in his dreams I establish the expression of an unconscious desire to change color, my objective will not be that of dissuading him from it by advising him to 'keep his place'; on the contrary, my objective, once his motivations have been brought to into consciousness, will be to put him in a position to choose action (or passivity) with respect to the real source of the conflict—that is, toward the social structures."[11]

Homi Bhabha conceptualizes the colonial condition in terms of mimicry which calls attention to metonymic presence in troubling semiotic structures of dominance and control. Among a colonized population, the tendency to mimic or imitate the colonizer through customs, dress, and language is an adaptive strategy designed to erase difference and ensure a measure of acceptance and mobility within hierarchal social configurations. Issues of cultural appropriation, historical erasure, and representation relate to the tendency to simulate the dominant society and its mannerisms, even if such replication results in a loss of identity on the part of the raced subject. He sees mimicry as a double vision which in disclosing the ambivalence of colonial discourse also disrupts its authority. And it is a double vision that is a result of what [he has] described as the partial representation/recognition of the colonial object ... the figures of a doubling, the part-objects of a metonymy of colonial desire which alienates the modality and normality of those dominate discourses in which they emerge as "inappropriate colonial subjects."[12]

Although mimicry results in an entrapment within colonial discourses, Bhabha implies that, as a culturally inscribed linguistic enterprise, the language practice can also function as a decolonizing method leading to an elision of established meaning.

Ella's unnamed illness stems from a cognitive dissonance associated with an internalized whiteness divorced from the indigenous cultural traditions of the West Indies. Evidenced by a disassociation from the realm of nature and its processes along with an inability to participate in expressive social engagement, including language use, the young woman's malady is a manifestation of the assimilationist tendency on the part of the younger generation rather than an African-derived concoction, as Hurston's ethnographic work implies. Mass Cyrus's declaration that "this little cat choked on the foreign" speaks to the novel's concerns with the cultural shifts accompanying cosmopolitanism at the beginning of the twentieth century and the dislocating effects of forced and voluntary migration in terms of authentic Black expressivity for African-descended people (4). Simply put, Ella's malady is the inevitable consequence, with cognitive, social, and dialectal implications, of a life lived apart from an African-Caribbean past and its vibrant culture, practices, and beliefs. Although Ella exists in relation to the symbolic order of language, she has no self apart from her representation or misrepresentation within the metonymic structures of a white European imaginary.

Maydene notices Ella only after the young woman recites lines from the Kipling poem about the white man's burden. The poem's closing lines in reference to the need to rescue those who are "half devil and half child" underscore the hybridity Ella experiences as a result of her mixed-race identity (6). In her imaginative reconstruction of storybook characters, Ella envisions figures who exhibit a destabilizing vision of disembodied whiteness:

> When they brought out the maps and showed Europe, it rose from the paper in three dimensions, grew big, came right down to her seat and allowed her to walk on it, feel its snow, invited her to look deep down into its fjords and dykes. She met people who looked like her. She met Peter Pan and she met the Dairy Maid who could pass for her sister—same two long plaits and brownish.
>
> (11)

Peter Pan and the Dairy Maid become shadows without substance, summoned at will as they drift on the margins of a dream-fantasy world divorced from the contextual clues and textual meaning lending themselves to a full, comprehensive reading of the characters and the worlds out of which they evolve. Like Ella herself, they are dislocated and dislocating figures, marginalized, uprooted, and displaced within a master narrative of unmediated whiteness. Ella resummons her storybook friends in Baltimore, no doubt in an effort to assuage the loneliness of her migration to the United States where she passes for white. "This was the kind of life—pale-skinned people floating—that Ella had seen for most of the many years of her daydreaming existence" (46; 80).

Pecola Breedlove displays a similar psychosis in Morrison's debut novel of the self-reflexive encounter with the dominant society and its controlling narratives. Pecola's madness, like that of Ella, manifests itself in a double vision involving a split subjectivity owing to the collision between opposing cultural identities. Morrison's protagonist is entrapped within the semiotics of whiteness through her immersion in the Dick-and-Jane primer, with her mirrored reflection revealing her fracturing in the unmapped delineations of a Fanonian lexicon of the gaze.[13] While Pecola's madness symbolizes the psychosis owing to the schism between body and spirit, the rupture between her burgeoning physicality and the discordant realm of nature, her insanity also allows an escape from the limitations of a racialized subjectivity. Pecola's duality becomes a locus for exercising agency, and, as her self-referential conversation discloses, vocality apart from preexisting metonymic structures. bell hooks mentions the lack of affirming images of Black women as being a catalyst for psychological trauma stemming from internalized racism. She calls for the invention of "images and representations that show us the way we want to be and are."[14] hooks points out regarding the invisibility associated with encounters with white-defined representation, "I was dismayed by how many paintings showed us without eyes, or noses, or mouths. And I began to wonder if these body parts are 'forgotten' because they represent the unloved, unliked parts, because they take us into the realm of the senses."[15]

Dominican-born Jean Rhys attends to the effects of colonialism and patriarchy in *Wide Sargasso Sea*, giving voice and agency to Antoinette/Bertha, the infamous mad-woman in the attic, in a prequel to Charlotte Bronte's *Jane Eyre*. Christophine's observation that Antoinette/Bertha's "face like dead woman and your eyes red like *soucriant*" evolves out of an awareness of the ways in which Rochester attempts to erase the embodied difference on the part of his Creolized Jamaican bride in relation to British colonial power structures.[16] Bertha's act of defiance in burning down Rochester's mansion is an emancipatory gesture of self-liberation signaling her awakening to female subjugation and a resistance against the domestic role to which she is consigned. The benighted housewife carries out a symbolic challenge to "the architecture of patriarchy," or, what Audre Lorde describes as the master's house of semiotic construction, in an effort to liberate herself from patriarchal structures with their insinuations for architectural and linguistic containment.[17]

Drawing upon insights from Abena Busia and Gayatri Spivak, Jean Armstrong reads Ella's recovery in relation to a participation in speech acts. "Selwyn aka Rochester aka Breuer/Freud attempts to 'civilize' Ella, however, she metamorphoses into Bertha, the madwoman in Rochester's attic and the hysteric in Freud's office. Thus as subaltern/hysteric, Ella does speak with her body."[18] While Armstrong astutely asserts that "Brodber's characters use the terms 'zombie' or 'zombification' as metaphors for the process of colonization that deprives the colonized of the ability to think for themselves, she fails to acknowledge the strategies of disassociating lending themselves to a resistant self-fashioning."[19] Both Brodber and Rhys rely upon an African-Caribbean spiritual epistemology in charting the imaginative space leading to freedom on the part of the subaltern whose struggle for autonomy is bound with issues of language as a medium for self-expression and self-representation. In much the same way that the descendants of African abductees seek to liberate themselves from the invisible forces of neocolonialism, so, too, does Bertha/Jane carry out a symbolic challenge to hegemonic authority by destroying the master's house of patriarchal and linguistic domination.

Stealing the Soul(s) of Black Folk

As a descendant African Moors, Ella's mother, Mary, embodies an Africanist past with its investment in aspects of vernacular lore. Although Maydene's adoption of Ella separates the young girl from an indigenous culture, the mother hovers in the background as a shadowy presence, ethereal, ghost-like, embedded in the daughter's subconscious. Mary is thus a partially symbolic subject whose absence-presence erases the boundary, in Derridian terms, between what is seen and unseen.[20] The mother's role as a housekeeper for the wealthy O'Grady Family and subsequent impregnation conceals a history sexual exploitation and cross-cultural influence marking life in modern Jamaica. In a similar fashion, Ella's American husband Selwyn fetishizes the protagonist as the sexualized, exoticized "other," a figuration of white male fantasies of Black women.

More than any other tales, the poltergeist stories that Ella tells her husband in broken English "excited Selwyn" (54). What Selwyn fails to realize is that the stories Ella recounts second-hand are just that: rehearsed and divorced from their cultural context. But he is fascinated by her accounts of spirit possession, eager to translate those stories into his dramatic production, a minstrel show based on the lives of Grove Town residents. "That which Ella had given him was for him purest gold," the narrator discloses using terms linking Selwyn's "writerly" project with an imperialist exploitation of indigenous people and their material resources. "He had only to refine it. He was going to put on the biggest coon show ever" (79–80).

In "Eating the Other," bell hooks frames the white male passage into manhood in relation to cultural appropriation and the power dynamic involved in the commodification and violation of Black women's bodies.[21] White male sexual fantasies of Black womanhood evolve out of a desire to participate in the qualities of the "other" while maintaining arrangements of dominance and control. Selwyn uses prophylactics while engaging in sexual relations with Ella, and, naively, she wonders why she does not conceive. The question, "How can a black woman really be Eve when the garden had stacked the cards so that she could not say 'No?,'" conveys Reverend Brassington's awareness of the challenges of sexual purity in the lives of Black women as well as Black women's dual displacement from a white Christian imaginary (87). The novel implicates O'Grady, Selwyn, and Brassington as figures for a colonial presence resulting in the misuse of Jamaica and its people, including the women whose invisible labor contributes to a national history and culture. As an embodiment of European dominance, Selwyn is a writer who dedicates "his whole career to animating that doll" in his efforts to transform Ella into an idealized representation of womanhood (47).[22]

Although Brodber associates the exploitation of the land or natural resources with the subjugation of the female body in a dual critique of imperialism and patriarchal structures, Ella's migratory wandering constitutes an act of cultural disarticulation that liberates her from white, patriarchal domination. The young woman's dissociative tendencies continue after her move to Baltimore where she passes for white as a personal assistant for Mrs. Burns. Under Selwyn's influence, "Ella was hooked," the omniscient narrator reminds the reader in terms associating the woman's willful subordination to hegemonic whiteness with inferences of a zombie-inducing potion, "and she liked the drug" (43). William Brassington's vision of Ella "as if she was flying" summons not only the psychic fragmentation owing to a schism between body and spirit reminiscent of the out-of-body condition on the part of Ti-Jeanne in Hopkinson's *Brown Girl in the Ring*, but also the dislocating effects of forced and voluntary migration (17). Bereft of the cultural moorings that once nurtured her spirit, Ella is fragmented within the contours of an objectifying gaze. "Ella in a range of animal skins went to this social and that, this lecture and that, quietly waiting on Mrs. Burns. A silent Alice waiting on the Duchess. Very quiet. A marvelously sculpted work waiting for the animator" (46). Selwyn's co-opting of West Indian culture in *Caribbean Nights and Days* is a reminder of the commercialization of Black culture for mass market consumption on the part of white American patrons, publishers, and filmmakers (79–80). The minstrel show offers a romanticized portrait of African-Caribbean culture bordering on the primitive. Separated from the authentic experiences of African-descended people, the show constitutes an act of "spirit thievery" resulting in an entrapment within white-defined representation (18; 37).

Brodber is attendant to the myriad ways that white, patriarchal structures attempt to appropriate the vibrant cultural traditions of an indigenous population. Mrs. Brassington's realization that "spirit thievery comes in so many forms" after hearing her adopted daughter's story points to the far-reaching implications of colonial and neocolonial influences (83). Maydene Brassington's visit to the Tabernacle at Morant Bay where she watches the necromancer, Ms. Gatha, under the influence of the spirits reveals a white fetishizing of Blackness or Blackness as spectacle. One is reminded of efforts on the part of wealthy whites to steal the soul(s) of Black folk in Jordan Peele's gothic fantasy, *Get Out*. The performative exchange between Maydene (aka White Hen), the necromancer (aka Willie), and Reverend Simpson (aka Dan) underscores Ella's entrapment within a white spatial imaginary: "Willie: It has a head but does not nod. Mother Hen: Hair but it does not brush it. Dan: Throat but it does not drink. Willie: Arms but it does not lift. Mother Hen: Legs but it does not kick. Dan: It is a doll" (92).

Ella's willingness to challenge Selwyn's romanticized representation of African-Caribbean culture constitutes a voiced resistance signaling her emergence from the structures of dominance that have rendered her passive, silent, and invisible—zombie-like—within the realm of unmediated whiteness and gender conformity. Speaking out or talking back becomes an act of counter-conjure against the witchery resulting in the compulsory amnesia attributed to the postcolonial condition. While watching Selwyn's Black-face minstrel show, Ella critiques his imaging of Jamaica as unnatural:

> The black of their skins shone on stage, relieved only by the white of their eyes and the white of the chalk around their mouths. Everybody's hair was in plaits and stood on end and everybody's clothes were the strips of cloth she had told him Ole African wore. Ella groaned. Where was Mammy Mary's cool tan-tuddy-potato skin? The major character was a white-skinned girl. Ella

was the star. He had given her flowing blonde hair. Our heroine was chased by outstretched black hands grabbing at her and sliding, and being forced into somersaults as they missed their target throughout the *Caribbean Nights and Days*.

(83–4)

Memory, Forgetting, and the Search for Maternal Origins

The notion of semiotic structures pursues Ella, reminding her of racialized narratives that seek to contain her creolized identity, and it is these structures that she evades. Saidiya Hartman's reenactment of the trans-Atlantic journey in search of genealogical origins is instructive in its revelation of the mother as a critical link in the articulation of Black identity.[23] Hartman's compelling story is not just hers; instead, it bespeaks a diasporic history aligned with the individual and collective attempt to recover a lost maternal past. Like the trans-Atlantic journey itself, Hartman's efforts at retracing her ancestors' footsteps declare a-temporally the possibilities for a transformed self in the present as well as possibilities for a radically reconstituted self in the future. Notions of forgetting and the challenges of recalling an erased heritage become hallmarks of the risky journey toward futurist worlds, a reminder, in mnemonic form, of the difficulties attendant upon mapping alternative realities in a context where the very foundations of a utopian experience are under assault. But Ella's remembrance of her mother's reddish-brown complexion not only inserts raced difference into the otherwise deracialized representation of Grove Town, but the young woman's recollections of a gendered heritage also summon the erased feminine as the basis for a reconstituted self.

Here, again, *The Bluest Eye* is useful in an appraisal of the language structures underlying Ella's transformative passage from a life of passive compliance to one of agency and empowerment. Ella's disordered exclamation during a moment of self-reflexive utterance recalls Pecola Breedlove's psychic fracturing: "Mammy Mary's mulatto mule must have maternity wear.—She said it fast:—mammyMary'smulattomulemusthavematernitywear—She said it slow:—Mammy Mary's mulatto mule must have maternity wear:—She sang it. She said it in paragraphs. She said it forever. Ella had tripped out indeed. Selwyn was scared stiff" (84). Ella's practiced, repetitive uttering, conveyed in terms of her "tripping out" in its insinuations for drug use, points to the novel's invisible linguistic structures as a locus for the construction of a new bodily constituency. Her "otherness," which the mule signifies, becomes a site of dynamic self-definition, a space between sign and signifier where words are reclaimed, reworked, and read anew.

In a similar sense, Ole African's voicing of the line, "The half has never been told," in reference to the untold history of the African-Caribbean world, becomes "Now the half has been told—brother" (63; 67). Occurring in call-and-response fashion, the exchange between Willie (aka the necromancer), and Dan (aka Reverend Simpson) situates issues of colonial and neocolonial power within the context of Marcus Garvey's project involving a redemptive return to a decolonized Africa. Brodber reinscribes the vernacular forms—including naming, renaming, misnaming, and un-naming—that comprise the region's dynamic cultural heritage in ways that gesture toward an unvoiced history of raced and gendered difference, a symbolic recovery, in linguistic terms, of a decolonized space of radical self-definition.

Ella's retreat into madness occurs in terms of a-temporal bodily and locational formulations with the Middle Passage serving as a symbolic space lending itself to an unsettling of hierarchal social designations. The linguistic shift accompanying that journey manifests itself in a radical restructuring of the taxonomy in her storybook world where humans and animals once existed in a rank-ordered fashion. Ella's recollection of her mother's complexion points to the racialized difference that inserts itself, often without warning, into a white spatial imaginary with its concomitant ordering and authoritarian gender designations. Through a process of identifying Grove Town residents with storybook figures and farm animals drawn from her childhood readings, Ella disassociates residents of her community from colonial inscriptions. Renaming members of the community after imaginary figures locates the novel's central metaphor within the trans-Atlantic voyage, even as it points to vernacular culture as the uncertain linguistic grounds for destabilizing the master narrative of black, female subjugation.

In its insinuations for the novel's title and as an African-based belief system, *Myal* announces itself not only as a form of divination and healing, but also as a semiotic space of linguistic indeterminacy apart from the rupturing effects of temporal history. Ella's double vision therefore gestures toward the existence of what Homi Bhabha would label an alternate, Third, Space existing outside fixed cultural and linguistic bounds.[24] This interstitial space is one where the boundaries between human and nonhuman communities are easily traversed, and it is also one that attends to disambiguation owing to a complex language use. The space between signifier and the signified offers unlimited possibilities for linguistic meaning apart from existing structures of colonial authority with double vision working as a means of deconstructing objective reality and recognized truth. As if to imply the indecipherability of Ella's mysterious illness or the indescribability of her encounters with the unseen realms of whiteness and patriarchy, Grove Town residents struggle to name the source of her ailment: as a consequence of a zombie-inducing drug, sexism, racism, a huge fibroid, or, possibly, a combination of factors. Grove Town residents even joke about the storm ensuing from Ella's healing being a result of gas, a huge burst of air from gastrointestinal upset because of a Western diet. Reverend Brassington labels Ella's release of air during her expulsion of the gray mass as a "mini-Armageddon" likely resulting from the intake of rich food (95).

Brodber's retelling of the circumstances surrounding Massa Cyrus's healing ritual signals the novel's multilayered significations interweaving tropes of postapocalypticism emanating from Judeo-Christian mythology with Myal, an African-Jamaican form of divination dependent upon a close relationship between humans and the spirit world or the realm of nature. Although Ella is subject to the destructive influences of the outside world, un-zombification summons the liberating nature of vernacular language through symbolic acts of speech, religion, and music. One can discern this lore in Reggae, a popular musical form that voices the subterranean history of the oppressed, in the verbal rituals between Maydene Brassington and the indigenous population, and in the fanciful stories Ole African rehearses.

Embedded in the novel's linguistic structures involving direction and indirection, the exchange between Amy and Maydene surrounding the adoption of Ella occurs within a context involving the commodity status of Blackness in a capitalist system. "You should know though that I fell in love with the little girl that day when I saw her reciting," Maydene tells Amy. "You do know that my husband is Jamaican."—Amy knew she meant "not full white" and at another time would have feigned surprise, "But Mrs. Brassington, how extraordinary" (23). Amy, of course, is able to discern the truth underlying Maydene's words: "The matter on the floor was of course the exploitation of people's natural god-given gifts—their selves or those of the beings they made. Amy had accused her of stealing her people and exploiting their bodies" (22).

Resonant with diasporic locations and dislocations, however, the novel announces a new history with Ella as the speaking subject: reborn, reclaimed, and revoiced. Audre Lorde's remarks shed light on Mass Cyrus's diagnosis of Ella's dis-ease as a consequence of a life lived under colonial domination:

> We can sit in our corners mute forever while our sisters and ourselves are wasted, while our children are distorted and destroyed, while our earth is poisoned; we can sit in our safe corners mute as bottles, and we will still be no

less afraid. People are taught to respect their fear of speaking more than silence, but ultimately, the silence will choke us anyway, so we might as well speak the truth.[25]

Ella, Brodber insists, must "beat back the spirit thieves and make [her] way back home." (67)

The Politics of Pedagogy: Teaching as an Oppositional Strategy

Ole African expresses a novelistic concern with healing the communal wounds owing to white dominance. "Curing the body is nothing," he points out. "Touching the peace of those she must touch and those who must touch her is the hard part" (93). For Ella, teaching becomes a decolonizing gesture, a resistive act of community empowerment resonant with bell hooks's description of instruction as a subversive method that is "meant to serve as a catalyst that calls everyone to become more and more engaged, to become active participants in learning."[26] hooks asserts that "the engaged voice must never be fixed and absolute but always changing, always evolving in dialogue with a world beyond itself."[27] Brodber addresses what hooks refers to as "the deep, often unnamed psychic wounding that takes place in the daily lives of black folks in this society."[28] By doing so, the author offers an imaginative road map to healing and recovery, one encoded in the uncharted structures of African-Caribbean legend and lore, a course summoning the powers of awakened Black women.

Through her role as a teacher, Ella frames a counter-hegemonic discourse signaling an erasure of established social arrangements. Her pedagogical method undermines the power dynamic in colonial inscriptions tending toward division, separation, and fragmentation. As if to signal the postapocalyptic insinuations of Ella's new role, Percy, the chick, says that Ella will "short circuit the whole of creation ... That little gal's gonna break it up and build it back again, man" (110).[29] Percy goes on to disclose, "Now, White Hen, now, we have people who can and are willing to correct images from the inside, destroy what should be destroyed, replace it with what it should be replaced and put us back together, give us back ourselves with which to chart our course to go where we want to go" (110). Ella's blank stare and robotic actions continue after her healing, but her voicing of the plight on the part of the subaltern offers possibilities for a reconfigured self and society.

Myal features a futuristic imaginary with nonhierarchal communal engagements where the symbolic order of language is revised, and Brodber engages with contemporary feminist, Black, and postmodern theories of representation in her literary choices. In the New World Order arising in the aftermath of Ella's healing, one can entertain difference without respect for rigid social stratification. Audre Lorde concludes that to bring about real change, we cannot work within the racist, patriarchal framework because change brought about in that system will not remain.[30] Using terms reminiscent of Lorde's assertions about a dismantling of the master's house of racial construction, Toni Morrison situates her deployment of a linguistic method that is at once both raced and race-free in relation to the elusive search for home.[31] For Morrison, authorial sovereignty is bound with a discursive strategy that holds the possibilities of collapsing preexisting dialectical tensions and hierarchal designations. Morrison therefore issues a call for the creation of a "new space [where] one can imagine safety without walls, can iterate difference that is prized but unprivileged, and can conceive of a third, if you will pardon the expression, world "already made for me, both snug and wide open, with a doorway never needing to be closed."[32]

In its reliance upon un-zombification as a decolonizing gesture, *Myal* makes a case for the viability of strategies of critique drawn from an African-Caribbean epistemology with beliefs about the coexistent relationship between good and evil, illness and healing, and the human community and the realm of nature, including nonhuman subjects. Although using the master's tools to dismantle the master's house of racial and gendered construction may not yield permanent results, it is imperative to shake the foundations upon which the house is built from within, using linguistic stratagems arising out of an indigenous past. Such an approach carries emancipatory possibilities for self, autonomy, and voice, and will enable the creation of a new house of narrative freedom unencumbered by predetermined interpretive limits.

"Unhomely" Haunting in the Garden of Eve: Gloria Naylor's *Bailey's Café*

"Between the Edge of the World and Infinite Possibility"

Zombies embody a new social identity—one of their own making—and they do so through a series of dissociative maneuvers prompting an evasion of semiotic structures of containment. The dislocating experience of trans-Atlantic passage gives way to a reconstituted self that serves as the basis for utopian worlds featuring once dispossessed subjects who liberate themselves from prevailing identity constructions. The hapless undead find a comfortable, if not unlikely,

US home in the fiction of Gloria Naylor whose multiple-text canon attends to the interlocking influences of race, class, gender, and sexual domination. *Linden Hills*'s Willa Prescott Nedeed has much in common with the heroines in Jean Rhys's *Wide Sargasso Sea* and Charlotte Bronte's *Jane Eyre* who find themselves entrapped between the demands associated with patriarchy and a life of freedom apart from masculine authority. Willa ascends the stairs leading to the kitchen of the Nedeed mansion as a shadow of her former self—silent, defeated, and bedraggled, but determined to recover her role as wife and mother. Although she fails to leave the house, her ascent from the basement leads to the fire that destroys the Nedeed mansion, site of centuries-old female subjugation. What ensues in a textual sense is *Mama Day*'s postapocalyptic Eden featuring semi-divine women whose interventions into the realms of magic, mysticism, and the supernatural herald a new era of unbridled female power and creativity.

Like Ella O'Grady-Langley, Cocoa falls victim to a mysterious illness brought about, in large part, through an association with the institutional structures of urbanized America.[33] Mama Day's involvement in Cocoa's illness and healing positions the elder wise woman as an embodied Eshu Elegbara as the novel's titular character presides over the linkages between dissolved and reconfigured identities leading to Cocoa's cure. Cocoa emerges from a catatonic state revived, revitalized, and restored through a reconnection with rituals of healing emanating from an Africanist past, a community of dispossessed women, and the storytelling tradition surrounding island foremother Sapphira Wade, ready to assume a place in an increasingly global South.

Last in a tetralogy, *Bailey's Café* broadens the scholarly conversation surrounding zombies or zombification to include a postwar geography as an international assortment of dispossessed subjects arrive at Bailey's Café, a magically real establishment located on the unexplored margins "between the edge of the world and infinite possibility."[34] Diasporic wanderings leading to and away from the café direct attention to the transecting network of journeys defining the trans-Atlantic voyage and its insinuations for utopian futures arising in the aftermath of world war. In its insistence upon the dislocating experience of intermediacy as a locus for the construction of alternative realities, the novel summons Houston A. Baker, Jr.'s troping of the blues as a vernacular method. The café functions as a matrix, much like the railway junction in Baker's theoretical musing on the transformational nature of the blues, rerouting a multinational community of migratory subjects through a space of indeterminacy leading to a totally new reality manifesting itself at the novel's unresolved end. The newness that George Andrews's birth prefigures occurs outside the perimeters of racialized (or gendered) inscriptions or what Baker would refer to as the "economics of slavery" in ways that underscore the transformative potential of forced and voluntary migration in the lives of post-slavery subjects.[35] Baker's interrogation of blues moments in African-American expressive culture speaks to the transformative potential of unrestricted travel as a method of undoing the effects of colonial and neocolonial influence:

> At the junctures, the intersections of experience where roads cross and diverge, the blues singer and his performance serve as codifiers, absorbing and transforming discontinuous experience into formal expressive instances that bear only the trace of origins, refusing to be pinned down to any final, dualistic significance. Even as they speak of paralyzing absence and ineradicable desire, their instrumental rhythms suggest change, movement, action, continuance, unlimited and unending possibility. Like the freight-hopping hobo, they are ever on the move, ceaselessly summing novel experience.[36]

As a shadowy figure whose disembodied voice weaves itself in and out of the narrative, lending unity to an otherwise disjointed collection of mournful tales, "Bailey," the Second World War veteran and fatherly café proprietor, personifies a liminal constituency resonant with what Baker posits as the blues-like ambiguity involving a multiplicity of co-constructed meaning. Not only does the war veteran signal the uncertainties of identity in an era marked by shifting cultural codes and gender roles, but he also heralds the liberating possibilities of a life lived apart from the objectifying images present in the larger society. Naylor's reliance upon "Bailey's" voice and its relation with a range of embodied and disembodied voices announces a concern with the "post" and possibilities for newness after catastrophe and disaster. That he both is and is not "Bailey" discloses a narrative investment in the semiotic structures that would circumscribe Black identity while revealing the propensity for eliding fixity through a complex play of linguistic meaning.

"Bailey" establishes the time, place, and character for each narrative, with the exception of "Mary, Take Two," as he can offer sympathy but not immediacy in a retelling of the story involving an Ethiopian girl's sexual trauma and her perilous voyage to the mysterious café. Chapter titles drawn from the realms of music and drama gesture toward the performative and aspects of vernacular lore in signaling a concern with identity construction and efforts on the part of border subjects to mediate the space between raced, gendered, and sexualized representation. "The Vamp," a telling and retelling of the forgotten stories of marginalized women and one trans man, resists established meaning in its dual insinuations for an introductory musical passage and a woman who uses her charms in order to harm or seduce men.

Naylor endeavors to reclaim the histories of dispossessed trans-Atlantic subjects by framing a new narrative of radical Black subjectivity in a critique of a white Christian imaginary with its static portraits of gender and sexuality.[37] "Eve's Song" announces the terms of that critique through a reinscription of the story of the Fall. Naylor liberates the account of the first woman from the historical baggage ascribed to the biblical figure as a passive victim of a totalitarian masculine presence and the unwitting source of a centuries-old curse. In both the biblical narrative and Naylor's reinscription, Eve's transgression of woman's place unsettles assumptions of a preeminent male figure who bears exclusive responsibility for Eve's existence. The thousand-year journey on the part of the fictional Eve summons tropes of unrestricted travel resonant with the border-crossing on the part of the Black Atlantic subject. Eve's remarkable narrative of interaction with Cajuns in the trip from Pilottown to Arabi, occurring in terms of self-reflexive encounters with the impoverished residents of the region, reinscribes a resistant female subjectivity framed in response to the hard-scrabble setting in which she finds herself.

Kristen Lillvis argues that "the boundary crossings that exist within posthuman cultures enable black subjects to make connections to diasporic history in the present and also image the future as a site of power."[38] Eve's journey to Bailey's Café therefore reenacts the dislocating experiences constituting a vital aspect of her disassociation from the interlocking influences of race, class, gender, and sexual oppression in preparation for the role she later assumes as a central mother-figure amidst a community of outcast women and one trans man. As the birthplace of the Delta blues and a liminal passage to Africa and the circum-Caribbean, New Orleans figures as a locus for the transcultural interventions surrounding transformed identities in a New World setting. The city is a border space between nations, cultures, and worlds, a site of identity construction and reconstruction apart from conventional identity formulations. Oneness between Eve and the rich Delta soil points to an erasure of boundaries between the body and nature or the natural world, between the physicality associated with the young woman's growing sexuality and the spaces in which such subjectivities are formed:

> Up my thighs and deep into my vagina, so much mud that it finally stilled my menstrual blood. Layers and layers of it were forming, forming, doing what it existed to do, growing the only thing it could find in one of the driest winters in living memory. Godfather always said that he made me, but I was born of the delta.
>
> (90)

Dorothea Buehler's reading of Eve's move toward a radical Black female subjectivity suggests how "tropes of corporeality serve to reconfigure links between subjects, moments, and location."[39] Eve's arrival in New Orleans speaks of possibilities for dynamic self-construction apart from gender binaries: "I had no choice but to walk into New Orleans neither male nor female—mud," she proudly announces, "But I could right then and there choose what I was going to be when I walked back out" (91).

A reappraisal of Naylor's critically acclaimed fourth novel in terms of un-zombification encourages a rethinking of metonymic presence and its implications for race, class, gender, and sexual domination. Through a focus on a global community of dispossessed subjects, Naylor attempts to name the space lending itself to a radical Black subjectivity. *Bailey's Café* intervenes in the project of illuminating the unseen forces of dominance responsible for sexual and gender oppression by making visible the invisible forces of control seeking to circumscribe a range of subjects, from Sadie, a homeless woman on Chicago's south side, to Miss Maples, a Stanford-educated cross-dressing housekeeper/bouncer. Godfather's grandiose claim that Eve "never had a real mother or father and wouldn't be alive if it weren't for him" recalls the stratagems on the part of necromancers attempting to induce forgetting among African abductees (82). The dictatorial position that Godfather assumes as Eve's guardian, no less that the roles he occupies in Pilottown's school, cotton exchange, and church, contemporizes the invisible influences of dominance manifesting themselves in the formal and informal institutional structures of the mid-twentieth century. But it is not African captives and their descendants who find themselves in transit across a trans-Atlantic geography; rather, it is the mother who engages in an arduous search for belonging following banishment from her provincial Louisiana home. Eve's journey constitutes a ritual reenactment of the passage to a New World setting in ways that liberate the trans-Atlantic voyage from its temporal constraints and announces the exalted role she later assumes as an inspiriting maternal influence. Following in the tradition of *Mama Day*'s Sapphira Wade, Eve inhabits a space of linguistic indeterminacy resonant with the global mappings of the magical café or Willow Springs itself.[40] Eve's ambiguous boardinghouse/bordello functions as a liminal site of becoming and possibility, a space evolving from and leading to an enriching complication of meaning. Her lush garden not only marks her journey toward a self-defined positioning, it also locates the novel's concerns with gender variability and sexuality outside the discourses of race, gender, and sexuality in the dominant society.

"Mood: Indigo": Finding Freedom in the In-Between

Sadie's encounters within the institutional structures of mid-twentieth-century America underscore the challenges faced by Black women in the city. Sadie struggles for love, acceptance, and belonging throughout her nomadic life, only to find herself alone on the streets of Chicago, searching for an idealized existence where she is able to define the terms of her existence as a Black woman. At once both a lady and a twenty-five cent whore, Sadie mediates between the dialectical tensions responsible for what Naylor aptly describes as the Virgin–Whore dichotomy, even as her struggles for belonging serve as critique of established sexual and gender designations.[41] By forcing her only child into a life of prostitution, Sadie's mother robs the young woman of her innocence, placing Sadie in a position where she is compelled to sell her body in order to help with household expenses. The threat of losing the only home she has ever known prompts Sadie's return to a life of prostitution in an effort to earn a living wage.

Sadie's wandering invites a reading of "Mood: Indigo" against the historic backdrop of the urban migration and the collective search for a better life on the part of displaced southerners. A chance encounter with the white madam for whom Sadie once worked prompts a realization of the racial disparities preventing the young woman from achieving a life of self-sufficiency. While the white madam leaves behind a life of prostitution, marries, and assumes a place among the middle-class, Sadie remains homeless, struggling for survival among the working-class poor.

Like the legendary blues women in American history and culture, Naylor's fictional characters take to the open road in ways that disrupt what Angela Davis describes as the gender disparity underlying tropes of unrestricted travel, remaking themselves during the course of the journey.[42] The prospect of marriage to Iceman Jones offers the promise of a stable domestic arrangement, but Sadie's blunt dismissal of his marriage proposal virtually guarantees that she will remain among Chicago's underprivileged residents, dependent upon prostitution and the Five-Star wine that offers temporary escape from her painful existence. Although the couple enjoy a celebratory moment of togetherness as they dance on the pier outside the cafe, Sadie does not take up residence at Eve's place. But it would be unwise to interpret Sadie's failure to find Eve's boardinghouse as an admission of defeat. The seemingly irreconcilable tensions with which she is confronted find their resolution, or enriching complexity, in the unmapped modalities of the blues. References to "moon" and "stars," repeated in recursive fashion throughout her lyrical narrative, revive the dialectical tensions associated with fixed gender and sexual identities, even as a mention of "stars" recalls the Five-Star wine that Sadie imbibes. While Sadie's role among a community of displaced citizens on Chicago's south side signals her status as a ghost-like, spectral presence—a zombie-like figure, dispossessed, dislocated, and disinherited—she translates the dislocating experiences of homelessness into a new, resistant subjectivity through the transformative possibilities of unhindered flight.

Reclaiming "Ratchet" as a Space of Radical Subjectivity

Contemporary Black feminist theory seeks to unmask the governing images serving as a nexus for bourgeoisie white male images of Black womanhood. Controlling representations of Black femininity issue from efforts to delineate Black womanhood in the service of systems of patriarchal domination that privilege whiteness, maleness, and heteronormativity. In her discussion of the range of images ascribed to Black women, Patricia Hill Collins rightly asserts that the Jezebel stereotype is linked with efforts to circumscribe Black women's sexuality.[43] Through a reliance upon language structures involving naming, renaming, misnaming, and un-naming, however, Naylor signals the utility of an oppositional strategy that counters objectifying images that would imprison Black women within the discourses of race, gender, and sexual representation.

Dorothea Buehler aptly describes the novel's female characters as "pilots for a new vision that allows for redemption and change."[44] "Jesse Bell" brings issues of bi-sexuality into conversation with an intersectional identity involving race, class, and gender in ways that critique bourgeoisie ideologies of marriage and sexuality. The King Family's urge toward whiteness manifests itself in a reification of structures of dominance dependent upon the subjugation of women. Jesse chafes under the rule of Uncle Eli, a snobbish man whose strict conformity to upper-middle-class belief prompts a rethinking of the respectability politics governing life among Harlem's elite. Simone de Beauvoir offers insight into the ways in which respectability politics dictate that women find fulfillment within the perimeters of marriage and motherhood. While being married gives participants access to a variety of benefits like health care and tax benefits, de Beauvoir argues that this also comes with the necessity to abide by bourgeois respectability.[45] Lara Karaian points out,

> This type of respectability is specific to women, and requires that women "perform a service in the marriage." These services include satisfying men's sexual needs and caring for the household. Attention to routine domestic

tasks of cooking, cleaning, and mothering, along with her efforts to please her husband sexually, imply an attempt to navigate a social space where members of marginalized groups attempt to police the behavior of the group as a whole.[46]

Thera Pickens observes that the strategy of reclaiming negative stereotypes has been acknowledged as having potential for Black feminine liberation.[47] Jesse reclaims what it means to be "rachet" through her reliance upon heroin and same-sex relations. Yet it is her symbolic return to youth following the break-up of her troubled marriage that signals the connection between the transformative journey she enacts and a narrative investment in the zombie or zombie-ism as a metaphor for diasporic dislocations. Eve draws upon her supernatural powers in conjuring a scene from an agrarian homestead. She then undertakes a rather unconventional cure by allowing Jesse unlimited access to heroin, a recreational drug known for its euphoric effects. Whereas *Myal* attributes Ella's reanimation to ancient spiritual practices based in forms of divination surrounding the power of the ancestor to heal, *Bailey's Café* situates the heroin-addicted Jesse's resurrection within the context of the mother–daughter dyad as a site of intimate familial transmission. Readers familiar with Naylor's canon will recall similar scenes throughout her multiple-text canon, including Mattie's bathing of the grieving Lucielia Louise Turner in *The Women of Brewster Place* and Mama Day's bathing of a bewitched Cocoa. In these instances, bathing constitutes a remembrance of a lost, maternal heritage with ancient healing practices and a reversal of the physical and psychic effects of the trans-Atlantic passage.[48] Eve's methodical healing of Jesse Bell over a multiple-day period takes place outside formal and informal institutional structures, outside the boundaries of the gaze, and follows the course of Jesse's deterioration into "something only half-living that Eve sponged and powdered at the end of the next four days" (141). At the end of Eve's intervention, the novel's central mother-figure accomplishes what dozens of rehabilitation centers are unable to do: Jesse is cured in less than a month.

"Tell Me Your Real Name": A Tale of Two Mary's

"Mary, Take One" locates the novel's concerns with un-zombification within vernacular structures announcing a liberation from the objectifying discourses surrounding Black womanhood. Naylor accomplishes this rhetorical feat through the use of names as unreliable mnemonic devices. Sweet Esther, whose older brother barters her in exchange for higher sharecropping wages, insists on being called "Little Sister." Eve renames the novel's transgendered bouncer/housekeeper "Miss Maple." Each of the narrators whose story the novel retells both is and is not what his or her name implies in a complex play of linguistic doubling.

"Peaches," the name that Mary's father ascribes, sets the stage for the alluring young woman's sexual trauma by displacing her identity within a symbolic order privileging the father as progenitor and authoritative figure. Much like Godfather, Peaches's father attempts to police her burgeoning sexuality by proscribing the terms of her sexual expressivity and erotic appeal. Peaches (aka Mary) is, at first, compliant in her adherence to a gendered role as Daddy's Little Girl. Bailey and Sugar Man are no less culpable in extending the young woman's invisibility by imposing a sexualized gaze relegating Peaches to an object of desire. "As the door closed behind her, Sugar Man shook his head and had the courage to whisper what every man in here was thinking: Born to be fucked" (102).

Through an association with multiple Mary's of biblical renown, "Mary," the name that Naylor ascribes to Peaches, summons the dialectical tension associated with competing gender and sexual identities surrounding the mother or motherhood. Peaches embodies both the trauma of such designations and their resolution in her efforts to redefine herself on her own terms and in ways that counter the prevailing images of female sexuality. Her name implies a oneness between the beautiful temptress and Mariam, the pregnant Ethiopian girl whose story unfolds in "Mary, Take Two." Naylor situates both stories outside the center of an ascribed meaning accompanying gender binaries and sexualized identities. While Peaches is a sexualized subject who attracts unwanted male attention, Mariam is a curiously virginal unwed mother. Together, the two women personify the complexities of female sexualities in ways that call into question efforts to establish the terms of gender designations.

Naylor's deployment of the mirror as a trope for dynamic self-construction apart from an objectifying gaze signals a concern with raced, gendered representation in the present as well as the possibilities for a transformed self in the future. In her liaisons with an assortment of men, from a choir master to a gambler—each one anonymous, nameless, and bereft of the identity labels that others readily ascribe to Peaches—the young woman performs a sexualized role in becoming what the mirror implies. Her insistence upon wearing white and being called "Mary" reverses the power dynamic inherent in the degrading business of naming subjecting her to erasure within a masculine imaginary dependent the Law of the Father. Jacques Lacan relies upon a psychoanalytic structure involving a reinterpretation of Freud in conceptualizing the mirror-stage as the paradigm of an imaginary order where the subject turns himself or herself into an object as part of the process of self-identity.[49] The split subjectivity featuring self and "other" intervenes as a necessary rupture in the move toward authentic self-hood. Peaches is engaged in this process as she seeks to define herself on her on terms, apart from the symbolic order of a linguistic system bent on subjecting her to hierarchal constructions and strict gender binaries.

Whereas Brodber's Ella destabilizes a white imaginary that would remove figurations of the mother, Peaches carries out a similar project in an interruption of the symbolic order of metonymic presence that Hortense Spiller maps in her landmark essay involving an interrogation of a cultural continuation leading to a removal of Black women from the traditional symbolics of female gender. Spillers instantiates a clarion call for a critical methodology that acknowledges a "different social subject" created in response to the pressures of an African consciousness.[50] Peaches's startling act of self-mutilation is resonant with what Spillers refers to as "a radically different text for a female empowerment," even as the gesture frees the fictional character from imprisonment within the politics of cultural representation.[51] Mary (aka Peaches) names herself, or rather declares her real name, in a radical act of expressivity that destabilizes prevailing semiotic structures associated with the Virgin–Whore dichotomy. As if to signal her entrance into a new symbolic order responsive to the feminine, a radically transformed social space outside of prevailing linguistic systems, Peaches is first to intone the gospel song inscribing the sacred identities of Mariam and George at the novel's end.

Global Mappings of the New World Order

Bailey's Café critiques the ways in which language structures instigate the dispossession of a global community of migratory figures. In the New World Order arising at the novel's unresolved close, Eve emerges as the novel's central mother-figure who reestablishes the kinship ties uniting an otherwise fragmented community of disembodied subjects. That the new social order presenting itself at George's birth consists of an international assembly of outcasts attests to the urgency of Naylor's project in its implications for world harmony in the aftermath of war and the possibilities for forging bonds between cultural groups across time and space. As a symbolic representation of the future, George's birth, like that of the Messiah, heralds a transformed reality existing within yet outside of established social arrangements and strict gender binaries.

Naylor's attention to temporal history and the cultural shifts marking life in a postmodern era prompt the creation of uniquely individual characters who position themselves at the margins, beyond fixed identity or locational formulations, in an effort to construct self-defined images. "Bailey's" failure to offer narrative closure is resonant with what bell hooks discloses regarding her efforts to find a way to include Black women's multiple voices within the various texts that comprise Black female literary and expressive culture. hooks's concern with creating a new text that "enables me to recover all that I am in language" resounds with *The Postapocalyptic Black Female Imagination*'s insistence upon a futuristic imaginary that reflects Black women's multifaceted identities.[52] For her, vernacular speech serves as a medium for the transmission of memory, not just as a means of recalling past events, but in the service of creating new, resistant worlds that mediate against historical erasure. hooks offers insight into the transformational potential of black cultural modes:

> In much new, exciting cultural practice, cultural texts—in film, black literature, critical theory—there is an effort to remember that is expressive of the need to create spaces where one is able to redeem and reclaim the past, legacies of pain, suffering, and triumph in ways that transform present reality. Fragments of memory are not simply represented as flat documentary, but constructed to give a "new take" on the old, constructed to move us into a different mode of articulation. We see this in films like *Dreaming Rivers* and *Illusions*, and in books like *Mama Day* by Gloria Naylor. Thinking again about space and location, I heard the statement "our struggle is also a struggle of memory against forgetting"; a politicization of memory that distinguishes nostalgia, that longing for something to be as it was, kind of useless act, from that remembering that serves to illuminate and transform the present.[53]

Brodber's *Myal* and Naylor's *Bailey's Café* seek to liberate Black Atlantic subjects from an entrapment within the discourses of raced, gendered representation. Ella O'Grady Langley, no less than the misfit women Naylor fictionalizes, mediates the cultural condition surrounding the "unhomeliness" of diasporic wanderings through a connection with a community of dispossessed individuals, folk healing rituals, and speech acts. Moments of catastrophe instigate a rupture signaling a new self and society arising in response to a history of trauma and the myriad strikes marking life in the modern and contemporary world. What these texts reveal is the need for a critical methodology invested in and responsive to the dislocating experiences of transcultural passage and the dynamic cross-currents of shifting ideological positions.

5

Romance after the Ruin: Looking for Love in the Era of the "Post" in Toni Morrison's *Tar Baby*, Jesmyn Ward's *Salvage the Bones*, and Beyonce's *Lemonade*

Among the many realities brought to light by Hurricane Katrina was that never again could we justifiably deny the existence of this country within a country, that other America, which America's immigrants and the rest of the world may know much more intimately than many Americans do, the America that is always on the brink of humanitarian and ecological disaster. No, it is not Haiti or Mozambique or Bangladesh, but it might as well be.
      Edwidge Danticat, *Create Dangerously: The Immigrant Artist at Work*

Most people who survive a devastating disaster want the opposite of a clean slate: they want to salvage whatever they can and begin repairing what was not destroyed; they want to reaffirm their relatedness to the places that formed them.
      Naomi Klein, *The Shock Doctrine: The Rise of Disaster Capitalism*

This chapter brings *The Postapocalyptic Black Female Imagination* full-circle, returning discursively to the symbolism of the ruin, site of the Silk Family's first genocidal attack in Butler's *Fledgling*. The ruin figures as a place of quintessential nothingness giving way to the recreated self that offers a locus for a reconstituted society constructed around Shori, the Ina, and their human symbionts. But this chapter's discussion attends to romantic love or conjugal relations in an interrogation of the poetics of futurity surrounding moments of disaster and catastrophe. While the Silk Family's assault results in Shori's amnesia and the death of her mothers and sisters, memory serves as means of mitigating acts of historical and cultural erasure as the young woman seeks to translate the dislocating experience of maternal loss into narrative freedom in the construction of a completely new family with its own dynamics. The family structure that Shori hopes to create affirms the traditions of Ina culture without being subsumed by them. That this new family arises in response to moments of personal and communal disaster points to the postapocalyptic dimensions of the novel in total and a narrative investment in catastrophe as a means of framing a radically reconstituted self and society. Shori's new family, which has yet to materialize, has implications for the past as well as for the interfamilial and pan-sexual arrangements emerging futuristically.

Rather than being a finale, this chapter therefore lays the groundwork for a continued investigation of Black women's postapocalyptic imaginaries by mapping the terrain of male–female relations, gender constructions, and sexualities in the era of the "post." If the domestic arena is, as Homi Bhabha famously asserts in his interrogation of the various transhistorical spaces marking the displacement on the part of the postcolonial subject, a "site[s] for history's most intricate invasions," then a scholarly investigation of that space and its role as a possible locus for the formation of utopian spaces of familial harmony and stability is warranted.[1] Naomi Klein's theory of disaster capitalism offers a useful framework for interrogating the dominant culture's work at erasing difference and the struggle on the part of Black women to recover a gendered history. Tracing the account of free market ideology, artificially constructed social and economic crises, torture, and privatization from the Second World War until the present, Klein critiques unregulated capitalism as a tool designed to realign a post-catastrophe society in the interests of a bureaucratic system that favors wealth, power, and privilege. Natural disasters and wars serve as opportunities to seize control of institutions and infrastructures in the service of capitalist advancement, to lay claim to geographic and institutional spaces for free market purposes.

One could easily add pandemics and social unrest to the litany of catastrophes prompting efforts to restructure present-day society in the wake of devastation and ruin. Incidents involving police brutality with acts of violence directed toward unarmed Black men and women could well be considered as evidence of the shock-and-awe tactics of a bureaucratic system intent on maintaining power over an oppressed group. Klein's observations about capitalism's tendency to not only advance the interests of a free market economy, but also render an adversary docile and complacent—zombie-like—through torture and mind-control are relevant in an appraisal of Black women's postapocalyptic narratives and the stories that contemporary writers, filmmakers, and performing artists retell. Vernacular culture offers sites of memory useful in reinscribing forgotten historical narratives as a basis for recovering the multiple voices that comprise the Black woman's narrative project.

Klein presents an insightful analysis of the Shock Doctrine in connection with media and biblical tropes signaling the end of the world. She attends to crisis exploitation or the capitalist misuse of disasters designed to replace existing public spheres in terms suggestive of the creation of "a kind of corporate New Jerusalem."[2] Regarding the Bush administration's policies in response to the Iraqi War, for instance, she asserts that those policies are "part of a movement that prays for crisis the way drought-struck farmers pray for rain, and the way Christian-Zionist end-timers pray for the Rapture."[3] As Klein points out,

> These are the closed, fundamentalist doctrines that cannot coexist with other belief systems; their followers deplore diversity and demand an absolute free hand to implement their perfect system. The world as it is must be erased to make way for their purist invention. Rooted in biblical fantasies of great floods and great fires, it is a logic that leads ineluctably toward violence. The ideologies that long for that impossible clean slate, which can be reached only through some kind of cataclysm, are the dangerous ones.[4]

Vernacular culture serves as a mode of resistance against the imperatives of a bureaucratic machine intent on rendering individuals powerless in the face of unregulated capitalist expansion. Black women seek to retain aspects of a fragmented past, to salvage the bones, borrowing Jesmyn Ward's metaphor for reaffirming a disjointed diasporic heritage, despite attempts at historical and cultural obliteration on the part of corporate and institutional structures. Chapter 2 of the present study reveals that Rudy's torturous acts designed to render residents of the Burn passive in the wake of his reign of terror in Hopkinson's *Brown Girl in the Ring* are no more successful than the shock-and-awe psychic violence that the nameless narrator undergoes at the hands of a group of industry-appointed doctors in Ralph Ellison's *Invisible Man*. Ellison's tragi-comic protagonist plays the dozens in response to the doctors' questioning about Brer Rabbit, clapping back when the white doctors try to perform a prefrontal lobotomy designed to divest him of his identity, and although the narrator's dignity has been under constant assault, he leaves the hospital with his cultural memory intact. His deployment of verbal stratagems involving subversion and disruption discloses a folk sensibility that serves as a locus for Black survival in the past, his endurance in the present, as well as possibilities for navigating an increasingly global postmodern technical urban–industrial society in the future.

Toni Morrison's *Tar Baby*, Jesmyn Ward's *Salvage the Bones*, and Beyonce's *Lemonade* are likewise invested in a resistance against notions of a clean slate that would suggest crisis survivors are bereft of a viable culture, or that indigenous people are passive victims of a history involving a series of calamitous strikes—from riots to earthquakes to hurricanes to rapidly spreading pandemics. The domestic arrangements in these and other works included in the present study point to a culture that is resistant to capitalist or imperialist interventions aimed at historical erasure, a world given to adaptation and change over time in yielding something new, something altogether different from existing societal constructions. Evasive tactics surrounding oppositional gestures of resistance prompt a subversion of established meaning embedded in the controlling discourses of raced, gendered, and sexualized representation with catastrophe and disaster figuring as rupturing moments that give way to cautiously optimistic new beginnings.

Works under discussion in this chapter extend the scholarly conversation surrounding the close relationship between romantic love, or, in many instances, the idealized fairy-tale romance engaging the interests of a range of diaspora subjects and a radically transformed future arising out of the wreckage of the present moment. Male–female relations constitute the foundations for either a perpetuation of the psychic, economic, and sexual violence of a history involving slavery and colonization, or the basis for a utopian society free of externally imposed restraint. Whether the future as writers and artists envision it remains intact revolves largely around the stories that are rehearsed and the willingness on the part of both men and women to challenge ideologies of white, male dominance.

Paradise Lost and Found: Toni Morrison's *Tar Baby*

Race, Space, and the Places In-Between

Tar Baby critiques strategies on the part of imperialist and neocolonial structures intent on displacing an indigenous people and realigning the natural world, and the novel accomplishes this by creating a sentient natural setting resistant to a colonizing presence. The world to which Son returns at the end of the novel—one where insects, plants, rivers, and swamps are impervious to a past involving a series of catastrophes designed to rearrange the social and natural environment—is not only resonant with myth and legend; it also mediates against a history featuring moments of rupture owing to a colonizing presence. It is this world, not the one that Valerian Street embraces, that presents itself as a solution to the tensions threatening to disrupt Son's relationship with Jadine. Although Jadine's decision to return to Paris places the couple's jet-setting romance in jeopardy, Morrison inscribes an altogether new narrative of Black subjectivity with Son as an embodiment of the possibilities of a liminal constituency apart from prevailing communal arrangements.

Morrison is attuned to a colonizing history resulting in a loss of worlds as a result of capitalist and imperialist interventions in the Francophone Caribbean. As the only novel in her multiple-text canon situated outside the continental United States, *Tar Baby* discloses a concern with the cultural legacy of slavery and colonization against a backdrop involving a transnational assembly of subjects, each one manifesting the dislocating effects of mass migration within and outside the structures of race. Mirrored accounts of Son's arrival at Isle de Chevaliers locate the novel's central metaphor within the diasporic wanderings of the Middle Passage and the perilous journey from Africa to a New World setting, even as those narratives chart Son's move outside the structures of dominance and control laying claim to Jadine's Europeanized identity. Rather than announcing a reconciliation between the two star-crossed lovers, the journey to and from the island reinscribes the dialectical tensions that doom their romance, placing the two forever at odds with each other.

Paris figures as a site of self-fashioning apart from the exigencies of race; it is, in the terms that Morrison puts forth, the foreigner's home, a deracialized space attracting a transcultural assortment of writers, scholars, intellectuals, and visual and performing artists, including Morrison herself.[5] Even there, though, Jadine is unable to escape the exigencies of a racialized identity, as the specter of the African woman in yellow discloses. The dream-memory of a Parisian woman in yellow underscores the unseen influences governing racial constructions and the challenges and possibilities associated with an evasion of a racialized past. The woman in Paris is, in Morrison's words, "another kind of Pilate," an ancestral figure who embodies a gendered diasporic heritage.[6] Like the intra-feminine communities that haunt Jadine throughout her travels, the woman in yellow, "that mother/sister/she," re-centers Black subjectivity within an Africanist cultural nexus privileging the feminine as a site for authentic self-construction.[7] Michael serves a similar purpose in reminding Jadine of her disavowal of the social obligations attendant upon a New World Blackness. He hovers over the narrative in ghost-like fashion, absent, but present, reminding the reader of the perils of identity constructions divorced from the rich cultural traditions emanating from an African past.

Tropes of unrestricted travel involve a border-crossing prompting a confrontation with the interlocking influences of race, class, gender, and sexualities in a New World setting. Yet Morrison refuses to capitulate toward any positioning that fails to acknowledge difference and its implications for male–female relations. Eloe emerges as a possible solution to not only the tension between Son and Jadine, but also the issues of a racialized subjectivity. The visit to Son's rural Northwest Florida home raises questions about the viability of home for the post-slavery subject. Inferences of Son's home town as his "cradle" convey multiple insinuations of Africa as metonymic presence and the unacknowledged foundation of modern and contemporary civilization (269). While there, Jadine labels Son's rural home "the blackest nothing she had ever seen," as if to signify her rejection of Blackness as a site for framing a new self and society apart from colonial inscriptions (251). Her decision to abandon Son in favor of marriage to her Parisian lover, Ryk, is likewise invested in a disavowal of the cultural traditions that have nurtured Son. "She would go back to Paris and begin at Go. Let loose the dogs, tangle with the woman in yellow—with her and with all the night women who had *looked* at her" (290).

But Morrison is as critical of the provincialism of Son's home town as she is of Jadine's unquestioning pursuit of ideological whiteness. Neither position takes into account the variegated nature of life in a postcolonial world. Outside the cosmopolitanism of Paris and New York, the spaces that have shaped her Europeanized identity, Jadine finds herself subject to the sexist ideologies that prevent her from realizing her potential as a contemporary Black woman. Her encounters with the men in Eloe along with Aunt Rosa, who refuses to bend to more liberal sexual mores that would allow Jadine and Son to sleep in the same house, underscore the inescapability of the gaze in its insinuations for Black female subjectivity. Although Morrison is adamant about her refusal to privilege the white gaze in her writing by insisting upon her sovereignty as a racialized author, Eloe discloses the challenges of such an endeavor in a world predicated upon hierarchal constructions of difference.[8] Morrison's avowed purpose in writing to and for a Black audience prompts an unmasking of tropes of whiteness manifesting themselves in *Tar Baby*'s insistence upon the invisible structures of race as a catalyst for the dynamic constructions and self-constructions among residents of the Street household as well as the indigenous island population.

The relationship between Son and Jadine underscores Morrison's skepticism about projects involving a redemptive return to Africa as a solution to persistent racial and social issues in the era of the "post." And she seems equally as conflicted about the claims of the feminist and post-feminist movements involving promises of solidarity between Black and white women. Simmering tensions between Margaret and Ondine or Nanadine erupt once Ondine discloses Margaret's secret abuse of Michael. Jadine's rejection of the insularity that Eloe embodies is no less telling than her desire to extricate herself from the mud that covers her at Sein de Veilles, or her longing to "get out of my skin and be only the person inside—not American—not black—just me?" (48). In each instance, competing discourses surrounding race, gender, sexualities, and class undermine notions of Isle de Chevaliers as an unblemished Eden featuring harmonious social and interpersonal relations, and it is those narratives that jeopardize possibilities for a harmonious future for Son and Jadine.

Trudier Harris avers that "the mythic world of Isle de Chevaliers shares with other myths the formation of a civilization or race or place because of a wrong that has been done to it, some pain that has been caused."[9] Rather than considering the island as a tainted or "perverse" Eden, she contends, "it could just as easily be considered a pre-lapsarian natural incarnation of folk imagination, where beings are not bound by their later prescribed natural proclivities. Or it could be considered a reclamation of folk mythology, in which it is just as natural for trees, butterflies, and reptiles to communicate and to experience pain as it is for human beings."[10] One could hasten to add that the world Morrison evokes is also characteristically postapocalyptic with its insinuations for a-temporal historical and identity formations that call into question the validity of colonial inscriptions in the service of utopian worlds featuring an erased boundary between the human community and the realm of nature or outer world.

"Othering" the "Other": Desire, Resistance, and Fetishized Blackness

That *Tar Baby* frames romantic relations in terms of the hierarchal social arrangements governing life in a contemporary setting and the persistence of race, class, and gender issues outside the continental United States reveals the expanding artistic and political consciousness underlying Morrison's narrative project. Morrison critiques the politics of cultural representation present in the larger society through a portrayal of Margaret and Jadine as embodiments of European standards of beauty. As a poor white woman with no identity apart from her role as a child bride who will one day bear a son to continue the Street Family's candy business, Margaret is an object of desire much like the candy bearing Valerian's name. Jadine is constructed in similar terms among the males in Eloe who view her "like she was a Cadillac [Son] had won, or stolen, or even bought for all they knew" (254). bell hooks situates her criticism of fantasies of "otherness" within mass media culture as a site of pleasure, eroticism, and consumption leading to a reification of white supremacist ideology. An interrogation of visual productions involving sexual liaisons across racial boundaries reveals the desire to partake of the forbidden qualities of the "other," stranger, or foreigner as a prominent aspect of a consumerist economy dependent upon a racist exoticization of the outsider. hooks concludes that "white racism, imperialism, and sexist domination prevail by courageous consumption. It is by eating the other (in this case death) that one asserts power and privilege."[11]

Tar Baby features an assortment of male–female liaisons predicated upon a disruption of desire and the consumer-capitalist underpinnings of Valerian's imperialist endeavors. Sexualized longings and resistance exist simultaneously, holding forth possibilities for harmonious love relations while undermining efforts to establish romantic bonds. Valerian fires Therese and Gideon for stealing apples in a demonstration of the hierarchal power dynamics associated with the exploitation of the "other" as an embodiment of transgressive behavior. Son steals chocolate while hiding in the Street home, perhaps out of a latent fear that "the other will be eaten, consumed, and forgotten."[12] His impassioned reaction to the firing of Gideon and Therese implicates Valerian in a history based in an exploitation of difference for pleasure and profit:

> Son's mouth went dry as he watched Valerian chewing a piece of ham, his head-of-a-coin profile content, approving even of the flavor in his mouth although he had been able to dismiss with a flutter of the fingers the people whose sugar and cocoa had allowed him to grow old in regal comfort; although he had taken the sugar and cocoa and paid for it as though it had no value, as though the cutting of cane and picking of beans was child's play and had no value; but he turned it into candy, the invention of which really was child's play, and sold it other children and made a fortune in order to move near, but not in the midst of, the jungle where the sugar came from and build a palace with more of their labor and then hire them to do more of the work he was not capable of and pay them again according to some scale of value that would outrage Satan himself and when those people wanted a little of what he wanted, some apples for their Christmas, and took some, he dismissed them with a flutter of the fingers, because they were thieves, and nobody knows thieves and thievery better than he did.
>
> (202–3)

By locating a critique of disaster capitalism within a history of colonialism and imperialism in the circum-Caribbean, the novel implicates Valerian's philanthropy and neoliberalism in the disruption of an otherwise idyllic island setting. Son extends his criticism of the retired candy magnate by referring to Valerian as "one of the aliens, the people who in a mere three hundred years had killed world millions of years old" (269). Acknowledging Valerian as an alien, outsider, or interloper represents a turning point in Son's evolutionary move toward a self-defined position as Jadine's lover aligns himself with the indigenous island population in a disruption of the colonial gaze and its psychologically rupturing effects.

Intra-feminine Communities

Tar Baby takes up issues of maternal loss through an engagement with Africa and its unrecognized role in shaping European culture. In her appraisal of American and Western culture, for example, the award-winning author refuses to acknowledge a construction of Blackness that would separate it from the classics; nor is she willing to ascribe authority to the Greco-Roman tradition in ways that would suggest its preeminence in hierarchal fashion over raced and gendered forms.[13] Morrison's assertions regarding the self-contradictory nature of Africanisms in Early American literature and culture shed much-needed critical light on the role that Son plays as an embodiment of Blackness in unsettling hierarchal social arrangements present within the Street household. For her, Blackness "can be evil and protective, rebellious and forgiving, fearful and desirable—all of the self-contradictory features of the self. Whiteness, alone is mute, meaningless, unfathomable, pointless, frozen, veiled, curtained, dreaded, senseless, implacable. Or so our writers seem to say."[14]

Son disarms Valerian through a series of performances that allow the uninvited houseguest to mediate the power dynamics within the Street household while advancing a love interest in Jadine. As a figure for the many problematical readings of Blackness in a New World setting, Son defies the essentialist enterprises with which he is confronted. Jadine's itinerant lover achieves conscious self-hood within the darkened vision of Mary Therese, and only then in relation to the Manichaean tensions associated with a colonial past. Her envisioning of Son as a reincarnation of one of blind horsemen who people the island's countryside destabilizes an otherwise linear history, even as it aligns Son with the maroon community in a manner suggestive of Son's ability to evade the semiotic structures that seek to delimit his complex identity as a son of Africa.

Insinuations of Africa as metonymic presence are powerfully at work with the many intra-feminine communities appearing as a refiguration of maternal absence or the reality of the unseen. Mary Therese Foucault, the novel's quintessential mother-figure, presides over the linkages involving erased and reconfigured identities in her multiple associations with maternity, Greco-Roman mythology involving sight, seeing, and blindness, and structures of dominance and surveillance. As an embodied Eshu Elegbara, guardian of crossroads and entrances, she is tasked with the responsibility for ushering Son outside hierarchal arrangements governing life in the Street household and back to a mythic past. Therese operates outside of the dialectical tensions surrounding whiteness and Blackness. Her perception or misperception of America as a dystopic world teetering on the brink of chaos and ruin summons a poetics of futurity involving the gender indeterminacy essential to a fluid Black Atlantic subjectivity. She reenvisions America as a place

> where everybody on the television set was naked and that even the priests were women. Where for a bar of gold a doctor could put you into a machine and, in a matter of minutes, would change you from a man to a woman or a woman to a man. Where it was not uncommon or strange to see people with both penises and breasts.
>
> (151)

Not only does her blindness herald a spiritual vision that disrupts a colonizing gaze, it also serves as the locus for the construction of a counterhegemonic positioning essential to the postapocalyptic world emerging at the novel's end. That her breasts continue to give milk prompts an appraisal of Therese as a transcendent mother-figure existing apart from essentialist identity constructs. Letitia L. Moffit associates Therese's spiritual vision with the novel's complex rendering of character. She asserts that "we are never limited to a single viewpoint; being privy to their personal histories, we are allowed to see that the characters have depths that exceed the stereotypes they create and are forced into."[15] Judylyn Ryan points out regarding the spiritual vision empowering Therese that "this transformed blindness or second sight, to return to the language of DuBois's analysis, is a primary feature in the strategies African peoples have devised to survive and overcome the fertile brutality of European/Euro American imperialism in the 'New World.'"[16]

Intra-feminine communities present themselves as possible solutions to maternal absence in ways that summon the role of "other-mothers" as enabling figures in Africana literature and culture. In *Tar Baby*, such communities are closely associated with nature as Morrison attempts to reinscribe the feminine as a site of dynamic self-construction. Margaret's conflicted relationship with her only son, Michael, underscores the challenges of motherhood divorced from the nurturing impulse that Therese exhibits. Although Michael never appears in the novel, he hovers in the background as a shadowy figure who reminds the reader of Jadine's disavowal of the ethnic heritage laying claim to Son's identity as an embodied Son of Africa. The relationship between Ondine and Margaret offers the strongest possibilities for framing female bonds across racial lines, but the conflicts between the two women threaten to disrupt their union. Communities of women converge in Jadine's confrontation with the night women in Eloe whose protruding breasts remind her of her rejection of a domestic identity. Son echoes this notion during his tirade relegating Jadine to the role of mammy in her decision to marry Ryk. Ondine reminds Jadine of the young woman's motherless-ness prior to Jadine's return to Paris.

Jadine not only loses her mother, she is also intent on distancing herself from any semblance of motherhood. Eloe emerges a starting point for Jadine's reconnection with Black folk culture and a site where she and Son might establish a harmonious relationship. But Jadine is motivated by an evasion of the excessive primitivism of his rural Florida upbringing. The African woman in yellow that Jadine encounters in a Parisian supermarket, the swamp women, and the night women in Eloe with protruding breasts are menacing, not because they offer a reminder of a diasporic past, but because they embody an unmediated raced and gender subjectivity.

"He Believed He Was Safe": Otherworldly Encounters in the Briar Patch

The novel's opening line, "He believed he was safe," announces a concern with the contradictory impulses embedded in contemporary discourses of race, gender, and sexuality that mediate against a harmonious relationship between Son and Jadine. Morrison's reinscription of the classic tar baby tale prompts her to center narrative action in a space of linguistic indeterminacy, one that lends itself to a reading of *Tar Baby* as "a love story, then. Difficult, unresponsive, but seducing woman and clever, anarchic male, each with definitions of independence and domesticity, of safety and danger that clash."[17] Harmony within their relationship can exist only by dismantling the power dynamic inherent in colonial inscriptions or by eliding the oppressive gaze and its fragmenting effects. Morrison sets the reader-audience up for a departure from temporal history through a focus on a prelapsarian realm surviving a succession of catastrophes designed to realign the natural and social environment along altogether different lines. L' Arbe de la Croix, home to the expatriate Street Family, signals the imposition of colonial structures of dominance in the otherwise untouched world of nature, an organic setting where butterflies, champion daisy trees, rivers, and streams bear the marks of capitalist influences in the Francophone Caribbean. Over time, nature grows accustomed to the shock and awe effects of human intervention, adapting to the disturbances of humanity by shifting course, altering itself in response to imperialist undertakings in a New World setting.

Tar Baby finds its resolution, or rather its enriching complexity, in the closing account of Son's journey back to Isle de Chevaliers, a move signaling the transformative potential associated with an affirmation of a folk sensibility. The rift between Valerian and Margaret continues following the explosive Christmas dinner and culminates with his retreat to the greenhouse, a space of artificial containment reminding the reader of colonial and imperialist interventions in the Francophone Caribbean. Unlike Sidney and Ondine who manage to sustain marital harmony throughout their sojourn abroad, the Streets are a mismatched couple unable to forge ahead toward a blissful conjugal state. Jadine returns to the island, but only in an effort to retrieve the fetishized sealskin coat symbolizing her disregard for nature.

Son, alone, emerges as the best possibility for embracing a self-defined identity. That the novel's resolution occurs in terms of the continued tension between Son and Jadine implies the role of Blackness and its transformative potentiality for a postapocalyptic culture. Trudier Harris astutely observes that "Son, who proves to be most sensitive to the natural order of things, has the greatest potential to restore harmony and eliminate strife."[18] The arrival at the rear of the mystical island constitutes a reversal of the Middle Passage in summoning projects involving a redemptive return to Mother Africa. But the space to which Son returns resists utopian significations, as Therese leads him to the ugly part of the island in affirmation of the ambivalent relationship between a postcolonial subjectivity and places of genealogical origins.

Not surprisingly, Therese guides Son away from an entrapment within a European imaginary so as to ensure his move toward a futuristic world located outside the novel's temporal framework, a world where established meaning loses all validity. Son's oneness with the natural environment signals an end to the tension between his allegiance to Jadine and his destiny as a reembodied horseman, between the past and future. In the hampered vision signaling a move outside of colonial and neocolonial structures of dominance and control, Son becomes "Small boy" through a gesture of un-naming/re-naming with implications for an a-temporal constituency signaling restored maternal reconnections (305). Anissa J. Wardi's reading of the novel's ambivalent ending attends to the role of nature or the natural environment as a locus for memory and history. "Although ancestral bodies of the horsemen are absent," she points out, "the natural world is a conduit to the past through bodies of water—swaps, bayous, and wetlands."[19] Evelyn Schriebert situates her reading of the novel's ending within a conversation surrounding the house/home antagonism and the social stratifications associated with the plantation hierarchy of the Street household. She rightly observes that Son moves outside the realm of master–slave relations in his journey toward self-identity.[20]

Therese's blindness, no less than the dense fog hampering Son's vision, centers narrative action within the dislocations of the Black Atlantic voyage in ways that affirm Son's fluid identity as a border-crosser. As Trudier Harris suggests, "The tales of the blind horsemen, who had hidden from their enslavers and now ride freely through the hills of Isle de Chevaliers, carry the same connotations for spiritual rebirth for Son as the tales of the flying Solomon carry for Milkman Dead."[21] Keith Byerman asserts that "*Tar Baby* marks the final step of immersion into the black folk world. Son achieves this truest nature by becoming one, not with the tellers of the tales, ... but with the tales themselves."[22] Craig Werner relies upon the polyrhythmic nature of jazz in a reading of the novel's closing scene when he suggests that Son forgoes predictability in order to embrace "free play."[23] His insights direct attention to the novel's linguistic structures and their implications for a radically transformed self and society.

Like the wily rabbit of folklore fame, Son elides negative significations through a folk sensibility that acknowledges both whiteness and Blackness while refusing to capitulate to either designation. He therefore comes to embody a fluid constituency essential to survival in an increasingly cosmopolitan setting. Not only does the circum-Caribbean betray a turbulent history involving slavery and colonization, it also holds the possibilities of an imaginative, if not literal, return to a diasporic home, a highly speculative journey leading to a recovery of a lost ancestral past closely associated with Mother Africa. Son's storied return to Isle de Chevaliers defies the mandates of disaster capitalism with its insistence upon a linear history that would pose a separation between past, present, and future, even as he embraces the past as a locus for alternative worlds emerging in the aftermath of catastrophe and ruin.

"Bodies Tell Stories": Jesmyn Ward's *Salvage the Bones*

Apocalypse across the Waters

Jesmyn Ward's *Salvage the Bones* locates itself in a historical context involving Hurricane Katrina, refigured as an apocalyptic event of biblical proportions and a natural disaster with far-reaching social, economic, and cultural implications for the Mississippi and Louisiana Gulf regions. Aside from the toll the hurricane exacts in wreaking havoc on the region's natural and environmental resources along with its infrastructures, not to mention the devastating effects of the storm on human capital and institutional systems, Ward concerns herself with the interlocking influences of race and class oppression resulting in Katrina's disproportionate effects in the lives of Black and brown communities, including the Batiste Family whose efforts to prepare for the storm's arrival are no less compelling than the family's resistance against an onslaught of personal and communal tragedies plaguing the region as a whole. Ward is intent on retelling the events surrounding the massive storm, but she is equally as invested in disclosing the structural inequities that have led to conditions making storm residents vulnerable to a range of calamities and disasters affecting communities of color worldwide.

Ward's reliance upon the perspective of Esch Batiste, a young, unwed pregnant teen, as a lens for a narrative engagement with the moments before, during, and after the storm underscores the novel's concerns with temporal history and its implications for the transformed social arrangement emerging in Katrina's catastrophic wake. Although the Batiste Family's survival and that of the Bois Sauvage community at large directs attention to the resilience on the part of storm survivors, it is the novel's youthful narrator whose rise from Katrina's floodwaters summons in strikingly mythological terms the role that women of color are to assume in the construction of a radically transformed future, not only for the Batiste Family, but the entire trans-Atlantic region.

Ward's second novel signals a concern with the diasporic wanderings of the Black Atlantic through a focus on an interconnecting network of journeys leading to and from Bois Sauvage, a poor, Black, segregated Mississippi town. Like similar communities in the rural South, the town is separated from neighboring areas by an invisible boundary marking the race and class distinctions that keep the Batiste Family in a state of poverty. Daddy's reliance upon the sale of scrap metal as a means of supporting the family, the grandfather's selling of land from the Pit for income, and the ramen noodles that the family relies upon underscore the ways in which racism and profound poverty lead to a lack of resources preventing residents from evacuating the region or adequately preparing for the storm. Only Daddy seems to be aware of the potentially catastrophic nature of the approaching storm, likely because of past experiences in living through a succession of hurricanes and other tragedies, and he assumes a central role in organizing the family's storm preparations until a freak injury sidelines his efforts. As a contemporary embodiment of the Old Testament Noah, Daddy issues storm warnings that go unheeded, at least until his injury prompts the Batiste children to take on the responsibilities for storm preparations. Christopher Clark discusses how the Batistes inhabit a hidden place that summons the South's racist history and the institutional neglect of poor, sick, elderly, and minoritized communities. By setting the novel in Mississippi, Clark observes, Ward draws attention to the impacts of Katrina that expanded beyond New Orleans. For him, "The rising waters that engulf the landscape figuratively drown it in the past, and the throwaway bodies left behind recall other victims of racial violence."[24]

Bois Sauvage's landscape featuring bodies that are marked, scarred, vanished, and dismembered announces a concern with a turbulent history involving slavery and colonization. Mama's recollections of bodies strewn across the region in the wake of Hurricane Camille summon the Middle Passage and the perilous trans-Atlantic journey, the traumatic moments of the Black experience in a New World setting. Conditioned by her reading of Greek mythology, Esch associates water with death. "Medea's journey took her to the water," Esch recalls in her reimagining of the classical figure's voyage in the quest for the golden fleece, "which was the highway of the ancient world, where death was as close as the waves, the sun, the wind."[25] But the postapocalyptic imaginary that informs the novel prompts a re-reading of the trans-Atlantic journey in relation to a multidirectional passage leading to fanciful worlds of female empowerment existing outside the boundaries of linear history and the tragic cosmology governing life in the Delta region. Water and bodies of water in the form of marshes, bayous, wetlands, rivers, swamps, and tributaries signal the viability of memory and history in the terms that Anissa J. Wardi announces, underscoring the roots and routes linking the southeast United States, the circum-Caribbean, and Africa in a complex network of interconnected waterways.[26] With its multiple significations in the Black narrative, water insinuates the a-temporal cosmology informing the novel as a whole in framing the close relationship between residents of the region and the landscape, and between the human and nonhuman community. Much of the novel involves Esch's attempts to mediate between inscriptions of a gendered identity from the past, her understanding of her own sexuality in the present, and the role she will play once she becomes a mother in the future.

The Pit is a hard-scrabble setting that directs attention to the social and economic conditions confronting local residents and the contradictory role the landscape assumes. While the Pit lends itself to recreational activities on the part of the Batiste children, the large hole surrounding the family's property is likely the cause of the infections that the children develop routinely or the worms plaguing Skeetah's prized pit bull, China. With each appraisal or re-appraisal of the space, the region is transformed, relocated outside the center of established meaning and enmeshed in parallel narratives evolving from and leading to issues surrounding border-crossing as a paradigmatic move across nations, cultures, and worlds. The journey in and out of Black Bois Sauvage assumes ritual dimensions in its implications for the transformative possibilities awaiting at the novel's unresolved ending, whether the passage involves death, the move to a largely white enclave, or, possibly, a recovery of a diasporic past. The novel's ending with Skeetah's worried vigil as he awaits China's return situates the encounter with newness within a discursive space signaling at once both the beloved pit bull's hoped-for return and the anticipated homecoming on the part of the émigré along with an authorial concern with bodies lost and found.

Reinscribing the Encounter between Self and "Other"

Salvage the Bones features a series of corresponding stories that diverge, intersect, and eventually reconverge around domestic space or conjugal relations involving associations between humans and nonhumans or animals. Esch's conflicted relationship with Manny constitutes the novel's emotional center, but it is a center that exudes outward to include other, equally as fraught, interactions—from Daddy's courtship with Mama to Skeetah's interactions with China to China's mating with Kilo. Medea, an inspiriting maternal influence who embodies the dialectical tensions of motherhood, figures as a resolution to, if not a complication of, the changing cultural landscape featuring gender roles and sexualities. Perhaps best known for her role in helping Jason acquire the golden fleece, Medea is at once a sorceress, enchantress, mother, and vengeful lover—an enigmatic persona who defies positive categorization in a prefiguration of an intersectionality that offers a resolution to the identity crisis confronting Esch in relation to Manny. Esch not only reinvents narrative accounts of Medea after reading *Edith Hamilton's Mythology*, the protagonist also modernizes "other cultural constructions of motherhood" in an effort to fill in the gaps associated with the raced, gendered subject in canonical texts.[27] In a similar fashion, Ward relies upon her own experiences and those of Mississippi Gulf residents in reinscribing the events surrounding Katrina "with the hope that she can offer a counter-representation of a community that has not been accurately portrayed in canonical white literature."[28] This includes representing the ways in which impoverished communities throughout the region attempted to prepare for the storm so as to undermine prevailing discourses of passivity and indifference on the part of the people who stayed.

Ward attends to issues surrounding the misrepresentation or erasure of communities of color through the creation of complex, self-defined characters who defy positive categorization. Such a strategy liberates the raced, gendered subject from the objectifying representations present in Katrina discourses and mass media reportage in framing an altogether new subjectivity unencumbered by existing semiotic structures. Skeetah unsettles stereotypic portrayals of young Black males engaging in dog fighting with his devotion to China and plans to use money from those fights to pay for Randall's attendance at basketball camp. Skeetah emerges as a sympathetic figure whose affection for China mirrors Daddy's protective role within the Batiste Family. Esch, too, contradicts negative portrayals of young, Black, pregnant, unwed teenage girls in her decision to become a mother, choosing to be a single parent rather than resorting to abortion.

Mary Ruth Marotte argues that the corresponding narratives of China, Esch, and Katrina reveal "how even as death and destruction loom, life inevitably grows. These pregnancies, drawn against the backdrop of Hurricane Katrina, figured here as maternal in several scenes, become parallel disasters to the storm. Ward presents a conflation of creation and destruction that ultimately inspires familial cohesion."[29] Esch reimagines her conflicted relationship with Manny in ways that gesture toward the shifting nature of social or interpersonal interactions in response to the structural and institutional upheavals that Katrina occasions. Tropes of doubling announce the dualistic split between self and "other" prompting an association between Esch's changing role within the family and the community and the cultural landscape seeking to define her evolving identity. The scene in which Esch conflates her morning sickness with Daddy's nausea after one of many drinking binges constitutes a gender-bending play of difference uniting young girl with her father. In yet another instance of erased and reconfigured identities, Esch reinvents her relationship with Manny in response to his sexual aggression while the two are naked in the Pit. Manny considers Esch as a sexual conquest, but her longing for "the other Manny" prompts her to conjure images of a loving relationship involving mutual affection (56).

Self-reflexive encounters within and outside of Black Bois Sauvage direct attention to Ward's concern with the invisibility of storm survivors and society's unwillingness to acknowledge the humanity of Katrina survivors. Christopher Clark asserts that "southern myths work alongside Katrina discourse to erase individuals' identities and histories."[30] The white storeowner outside Black Bois Sauvage fails to acknowledge Esch when she accompanies Big Henry into town for dog food. Esch longs for affirmation from Manny, who is at first unaware of her pregnancy, and for much of the novel, she tries to conceal her pregnancy by wearing male clothing or loose-fitting garments and attempting to suppress the bodily symptoms of pregnancy, including morning sickness, tender breasts, and frequent urination. Only later does Daddy notice Esch's bulging stomach, evidence of her gendered identity in an all-male space.

The novel's investment in parallel stories involving varied and shifting representations of love heralds transformed familial and communal relations emerging in Katrina's wake. In a rendering of a utopian society where artificial boundaries no longer exist, Skeetah enjoys a relationship with his prized pit-bull bordering on a romance. Not only does he sleep in the shed with her, he risks his safety and that of his siblings in stealing wormer when China is ill. But the bond between the young boy and China evolves from one suggestive of romance to filial love when Skeetah pilfers scrap wood from his grandparents' dilapidated home in order to build a kennel for China and her puppies, mimicking Daddy's efforts while building a home for Mama.

Blurred lines between familial and romantic love underline the novel's investment in changing gender identities as well as the adaptability of storm survivors in the face of catastrophe and ruin. Esch's musing on the circumstances surrounding a tragic car accident involving male abandonment of the anonymous woman in the ditch offers a critique of conflicted love relations within and outside the novel's temporal framework, including Medea's relationship with Jason, the courtship between Mama and Daddy, and China's mating with Kilo. In each instance, women are most imperiled in such arrangements as they find themselves imprisoned within prevailing discourses of masculine privilege and female subordination.

Erased boundaries between familial and romantic love also hint at the posthuman or transhuman arrangements that offer a resolution to the conflicted gender relations that doom Esch's relationship with Manny. Skeetah's bond with China offers insight into the contradictory gender roles Esch confronts as she prepares to become a mother. Expectations involving passivity and agency, love and hate, weakness and strength are under constant scrutiny, and, especially in the young boy's shifting connection with his prized pit bull. China resists coupling with Rico's dog, Kilo, another pit bull renowned for his fierceness. China "hated the submission of it," as if in defiance of an acquiescent role (95). When Skeetah attempts to give her Ivomec, however, China's passivity counters the aggression she exhibits in fights with other dogs from the Pit. China's ferocity in her contest with Kilo, who fathers her five puppies, offers evidence of maternal strength. Although Randall's persistent questioning of Skeetah's intentions of allowing China to fight after she becomes a mother summon discourses surrounding femininity and power, China's victory points to the resilience that Esch will undoubtedly exhibit in the new role she will assume as a mother. Manny considers weakness as being an inevitable consequence of being female, but Skeetah's response refuses to acknowledge a difference between maternal strength and love. "To give life"—Skeetah bends down to China, feels her from neck to jaw, caresses her face like he would kiss her; she flashes her tongue—"is to know what's worth fighting for. And what's love" (96).

"What's Love Got to Do with It?": Maternal Metaphors of Empowerment

Ward's fictionalization of the circumstances surrounding Esch's pregnancy and the young girl's conflicted relationship with Manny reveals Katrina's signifying role as a rupturing moment linked inextricably with associations between erased and reconfigured identities in the service of a postapocalyptic culture emerging in the storm's uncertain aftermath. Esch prepares to become a mother in a contemporary setting where gender roles and sexualities are under constant negotiation and renegotiation in ways that hold the promise of redefined domestic and social arrangements, a New World Order featuring the mother or motherhood as a locus for transformed social relations. *Salvage the Bones* joins with other texts included in the present study in raising important questions about the mother or motherhood as a crucial link in the articulation of a Black Atlantic identity: If the mother offers the clearest path back in recovery of a lost diasporic heritage, what are the implications of maternal absence in terms of transcultural passage in the journey toward a postapocalyptic culture? Ward addresses this issue through the creation of Mama as a fluid semiotic space, a site of linguistic indeterminacy signaling the promise of an alternative reality arising in the storm's devastating wake. Not only is she a catalyst for the dynamic self-construction laying claim to Esch's evolving subjectivity as a young, Black female, as a figure for a lost, maternal past, she also offers a reminder of the viability of ritual practices, beliefs, and customs linking Gulf residents with a diasporic past. Mama is as much of an influence in the lives of her husband and children after her death as she was during her lifetime. While Junior has no recollections of Mama and must rely upon stories from family members, as the only female in the family, Esch arises as the closest connection with the maternal. Esch's remembrance of Mama directs attention to the viability of memory and the ways that recollections of past events continue long after the events themselves are over. "For a moment, Mama is there next to him on the sofa, her arm laid across his lap while she palms his knee, which is how she sat with him when they watched TV together. I wonder if that is phantom pain, and if Daddy will feel his missing fingers the way we feel Mama, present in the absence" (247).

Esch's journey into motherhood is not only bound narratively with the disruption that Katrina occasions as, in Daddy's pronouncement, "*like the worst ... A woman,*" the protagonist's introduction to what it means to be a mother also translates the semiotics of maternity into narrative freedom in redefining herself in relation to an indistinct gendered past (124). Katrina therefore figures as metonymic presence bound with the mother and tied inextricably with linguistic structures involving naming as an emancipatory gesture that liberates the postslavery subject from objectifying discourses emanating from the dominant society. Katrina figures as at once both a source of unrelenting disaster and calamity in the terms that Naomi Klein puts forth and a catalyst for transformed societal and institutional structures in response to devastation and loss. Junior, the youngest of the Batiste children and the child who is born as Mama dies, offers evidence of the role of memory and forgetting in the life of the postslavery subject. He serves as a locus for receipt of transgenerational memories of the mother in all of her complexity. It is Junior who has no memories of the mother and offers the strongest possibilities for a redefined identity in relation to a vanished maternal heritage:

> Sometimes I wonder if Junior remembers anything, or if his head is like a colander, and the memories of who bottle-fed him, who licked his tears, who

mothered him, squeeze through the metal like water to run down the drain, and only leave the present day, his sand holes, his shirtless birth chest, Randall yelling at him: his present washed clean of memory like vegetables washed clean of the dirt they grow in.

(91–2)

Esch's entrance into motherhood is a ritual passage that is predicated upon a remembered past with the mother or motherhood as a sign that is reinterpreted, reinvented, read anew in relation to the protagonist's shifting subjectivity. The process of becoming a mother constitutes a ritual border-crossing prompting a critique of discourses surrounding maternity, sexuality, and gender roles. Mary Ruth Marotte astutely observes that maternity is associated with loss prior to China's delivery of the five puppies and how watching China give birth empowers Esch as a mother.[31] This empowerment through maternity becomes a means of strength for Esch that carries her family through their collective rebirth in Katrina's wake. Patricia Hill Collins mentions the contradictory expectations imposed upon Black women as a central focus in Black feminist thought. She correctly asserts that African-American women are united by a concern with self-definition as a means of reclaiming a subjectivity existing apart from the denigrated grouping in which all Black women are positioned. Hill Collins describes Black women's lives as "a series of negotiations that aim to reconcile the contradictions separating our own internally-defined images of self as African-American women with our objectification as the Other."[32]

Narrative accounts of the courtship between Daddy and Mama point to Mama's sensuality, her undeniably sexualized appeal apart from the role she later assumes as wife and mother. Laura Fine offers a reading of the novel that takes into account the ways in which Ward disrupts stereotypes of the strong Black woman. Rather than considering Mama as an uncritical fictional rendering of the Black woman who possesses indomitable strength and resilience, Fine points out that sexuality is part of Mama's force.[33] As a complex figure who resists positive categorization, Mama serves as a locus for Esch's formation of a self-defined identity apart from externally imposed notions of race and gender.

Mama's complexity is apparent in Esch's reimagining of the vague circumstances of her parents' courtship and marriage. The father tells Mama that he loves her (104). Mama relates the story of how she hit Daddy in the chest so hard he lost his breath (141). Mama dances sensuously at the Oaks, a blues club (93). Her dancing is reminiscent of China's dancing posture with Skeetah while he administers the worm medicine. "China is hopping on her hind legs.

What tore through the gray dog yesterday is now a woman approaching her partner on the floor of the Oaks, the first lick of the blues guitar sounding from the jukebox, a drink in her hand" (101).

Esch's evolution is the most complex as her identity shifts in response to a changing social and environmental landscape. She shares a transcendental oneness with China, Medea, and Katrina in her attack on Manny. The scene detailing the sexual encounter between Manny and Esch reveals her evolving subjectivity:

> When I can breathe, I leave the stall to splash cold water on my face, but my eyes still look red, my eyelids swollen in the funhouse mirror. And then I think that Manny saw me, and that he turned away from what I carry, pulling his burnt gold face from my hands, and then I am crying again for what I have been, for what I am, and for what I will be, again.
>
> (147)

Esch's journey toward motherhood involves at once both an affirmation of Mama and a disassociation from the mother in the move toward a complex self-identity. Esch tries to decipher the mother's gesture prior to dying in childbirth. "Shaking her head. Maybe that meant no. Or *Don't worry—I'm coming back*. Or *I'm sorry*. Or *Don't do it. Don't become the woman in this bed, Esch*, she could have been saying. But I have" (222).

Mama's insistence upon the viability of the maternal presence situates narrative action in a historical and cultural context privileging the feminine as a locus for dynamic self-construction. During one of many egg-gathering scenes, Mama reminds the reader that *"The cock, he always running off being a bully*, she said. *But the mama, the mama always here See?"* (199). The theft of the white farmer's wormer implies the process of ungendering in its insinuation of intermediacy as a locus for limitless identity construction apart from the discourses of femaleness. Esch's clothing—a black T-shirt and a pair of black basketball shorts—allows her to conceal her pregnancy. Although she is a fast runner, she is slowed when the Batiste children attempt to flee from the white farmer and his dog, Twist. Gold figures throughout the novel as a trope gesturing toward the association between the Batiste children's escapades and the classical story of Jason's search for the golden fleece.[34] Esch assumes the role of Medea, a benevolent, protective persona who lends her supernatural powers in enabling her lover to attain his goals as Ward contemporizes the classical story of adventure on the high seas. China attacks the farmer's dog, Twist, proving to be violent defender of her owner. Although Esch deals with the symptoms of pregnancy—swollen breasts, frequent urination, and clumsiness—she runs away along with her brothers, a little slower than usual, but none-the-less agile enough to escape the farmer's wrath.

Looking back while Moving Forward: Encounters with Newness after the Storm

The Batiste Family's emergence from Katrina's floodwaters occurs in relation to a radically transformed society where the terms of a raced, gendered, sexualized self are redefined. The postapocalyptic imaginary presenting itself at the novel's end features a unified familial and communal setting existing in the face of disaster and ruin. Although the family's home is destroyed, the bonds that have sustained them through successive tragedies remain intact. It is the novel's relation with metonymic presence through the discourses surrounding motherhood that offers evidence of the transformative potential of a postapocalyptic culture. Esch vows to "tell the story of Katrina, the mother that swept into the Gulf and slaughtered" in assuming the role of griot or storyteller in a gesture marking the continuation of cultural traditions from the past in shaping the yet-to-be realized future (255). That Esch intends to name her unborn child after the mother, whose name is Rose Temple Batiste (aka Mama), if the baby is a girl, is an emancipatory mnemonic gesture summoning a gendered past. Naming the child Jason if he is a boy would link the child with Esch's brother, Jason Aldon Batiste (aka Skeetah) as well as Jason from classical mythology in pointing the narrative in multiple directions simultaneously, thereby destabilizing an otherwise linear narrative with its tragic cosmology in favor of a utopian world existing within and apart from temporal history.

"The Twelfth Day: Alive" mediates against notions of a clean slate on the part of disaster capitalism through an affirmation of a past kept alive through memory and the rituals surrounding the family's agrarian homestead. Big Henry's announcement that "this baby got plenty daddies" signals the novel's investment in a new societal arrangement arising in Katrina's aftermath, a world featuring redefined family and social relations (255). Ward's novel returns us to a restructured home and community—a space that is ravaged by the storm but spiritually whole. The novel becomes a narrative celebration of survival in the face of disaster and ruin, an affirmation of the communal bonds and ritual practices that enable marginalized communities not only to endure multiple catastrophes, but rebuild.

Beyonce's *Lemonade*: Exploring the Roots of Blackgirl Magic

Gender, Nature, and Diaspora in a Postapocalyptic World

Beyonce's *Lemonade* also takes up issues of domestic relations in the wake of Hurricane Katrina, but in the context of the journey from betrayal to healing and forgiveness following an episode of marital infidelity. The 2016 album situates itself against a backdrop of a storm-ravaged New Orleans, a space invigorated by the sights and sounds, the vibrant rituals and cultural traditions of the Louisiana Gulf region. As a visual tour de force and a kaleidoscopic celebration of Black womanhood, the wildly popular sixth studio album by the talented performer is as devoted to a retelling of a scorned wife's recovery from the pain of her husband's unfaithfulness as it is with a commemoration of the endurance of local residents in the face of tragedy and loss. The album links the individual and collective experiences of Black women with the survival of the community at large through a series of parallel narratives that draw upon the rich traditions of the region in ways that signal the role that Black women and men together can play in ushering in a utopian future.

Much of the album's power issues from close attention to the everyday reality of residents of the Louisiana Delta who survive the massive storm. However, Beyonce is not just concerned with the environmental and human toll that Katrina exacts; she shares with Jesmyn Ward an interest in recapturing the heritage that points to the existence of the synergistic customs, practices, and ritual beliefs that have allowed African-Americans to persist in the face of successive disasters. Scenes featuring the syncopated rhythm of a second-line jazz funeral procession, a lively sermon in a traditional Black church, an assortment of brightly colored wigs in a beauty supply shop, women adorned with tribal face paint aboard a city bus, and street scenes of children at play appear alongside images of a storm-ravaged lower Ninth Ward. Consistent with the album's vernacular origins in storytelling, *Lemonade* blends the celebratory moments of everyday life with the tragedies of an epic category five storm that wreaked havoc on the region and its inhabitants. The album mixes a past involving the pulsating tempo of Black culture with the ongoing struggles of African-Americans in the creation of an a-temporal, multidimensional work of expressive culture that defies the otherwise tragic contours of a linear history and speaks futuristically to the possibilities for communal healing and recovery in twenty-first-century America.

The semi-autobiographical album conveys a disjointed history resonant with the diasporic wanderings on the part of Black Atlantic subjects by drawing upon the shared domestic tragedies of Black womanhood, including issues of child loss, efforts to cope with European standards of beauty, problems with conventional gender roles and expectations, the challenges of unbridled female sexual expressivity, and threats to Black masculinity through state-sanctioned police violence—the myriad issues engaging the interests of writers whose works this study interrogates. Addressing matters such as these prompts a conceptualization of the work as not just an expose of possible marital strife on the part of the Carter's or even the alleged infidelity that Tina Knowles experiences. Instead, *Lemonade* implies a broad, communal dilemma engulfing Black women and men across a diasporic geography.

Emphasis on water and bodies of water insinuate the Gulf region as a liminal border space between nations, cultures, and worlds. *Lemonade* extends the conversation surrounding water as a trope for memory, history, and culture to include Judeo-Christian associations with baptism, birth, rebirth, judgment, and impending secular doom. The scene with Beyonce atop a police car sinking into flood waters prompts a connection between the social unrest following police shootings of unarmed Black males and issues of divine retribution for racialized violence, even as the evocative scene conjures folkloric stories of Mama Wata or Mother Water, mythical sea-goddess whose inspiring influence is at times benevolent; at other times, destructive.[35] Beyonce becomes a transcendent spirit-goddess at one with the unremitting waters of the Gulf, a detached witness to or perhaps a catalyst for the watery judgment imposed upon aggressive forces of police control.

"Love Drought," among the most mystical songs in the album, draws upon a marshy setting that closely resembles Ibo Landing, an interstitial space recalling the Middle Passage as a site of liminal bodily constituency on the part of Black Atlantic subjects during and after slavery.[36] The melody extends the multilayered significations of Black identity in the performer's representation as a mythological figure—an embodied New World Eshu Elegbara—in relation to a group of Black and brown women as she presides over linkages involving dissolved and reconfigured identities. Beyonce leads a line of women dressed in white, bound together by a rope as the group walks in unison toward the horizon, arms lifted as if in suppliant fashion, while the performer intones softly, "we could make it right now/we can end this love drought."[37] Song lyrics and the powerful visual imagery of a group of women tethered by a single rope link romantic love with slavery in a manner that is at once both historically relevant and futuristically suggestive in its implications for male–female relations, gender constructions, and passionate love. In *Their Eyes Were Watching God*, Zora Neale Hurston's classic novel of the Black woman's experience, Nanny counters Janie's romanticized longings for marital bliss with a history lesson that locates the tension in male–female relationships within the context of slavery and hierarchal social arrangements prompting notions of Black women as mules of the world. The weary ex-slave considers romantic love as "de very prong all us black women gits hung on. Dis love! Dat's just whut's got us uh pullin 'and uh haulin' and sweatin 'and doin' from can't see in de mornin' till can't see at night."[38]

But if conflicted male–female liaisons are a painful legacy of the political and economic conditions responsible for the interlocking systems of race, class, and gender oppression, then healing can occur only through a willingness to name the source of that oppression, to reclaim the forgotten margins as a site of intersectional empowerment. *Lemonade* gestures toward this resolution through a reliance upon posthuman constructions that signal an erasure of artificial boundaries between humans and nature, physical and spiritual, between Hurricane Katrina and Beyonce as an embodiment of an intersectional self. Kristen Lillvis attends to the ways in which the Black Atlantic journey lends itself to the construction of a posthuman Blackness that elides established identity constructs.[39] "Love Draught" features such a subjectivity with an association between women and the realm of nature or the natural environment, between the female body and the untouched marshy wetlands—a world existing apart from and resistant to the bureaucratic structures of urbanized New Orleans. As if to signal the radically transformed society in Katrina's aftermath, "Freedom," with its signifying allusion to the emancipatory gestures on the part of a nation of enslaved subjects emerging from the shackles of bondage, turns on a group of women poised on tree branches watching Beyonce perform. Not only does the scene imply the existence of a folkloric realm reminiscent of *Tar Baby*'s rendering of the mystical swamp women who inhabit Sein de Veilles, it also conveys a vital oneness between human and nonhuman communities with the natural world figuring as a sentient space of unbridled female expressivity.

Lemonade's insistence upon an unsettling of temporal history through a reliance upon a series of corresponding narratives announces a concern with the metaphysical journey on the part of marginalized subjects from tragedy to triumph, or at least a vision of a radically transformed future. One is reminded of Ntozake Shange's colorful rendering of the Black woman's multifaceted experiences in the celebrated choreopoem, *For Colored Girls*. The poem culminates with a scene of communal affirmation among a group of dispossessed women who "found god in myself/& I loved her/I loved her fiercely."[40] *Lemonade* offers a spirited clap back to that declaration with, "God is God. I am not." Much like the slave narrative with its paradigmatic move from South to North, rural to urban, the album follows the historical pattern of migration characterizing Black life in the modern era and the associated demographic shift from agrarian to capitalist–industrial setting, from bondage to freedom. Whether the husband's sexual dalliances are a consequence of the fragmented family and communal structures present in urban realism fiction is a matter of conjecture. What is apparent is Beyoncé's refusal, like the resilient women who people the pages of Gloria Naylor's *Bailey's Cafe*, to remain acquiescent in the face of male domination and control.

A movement from scenes rendered in black-and-white or sepia to those involving color conveys the temporal stakes involved in the scorned wife's journey toward an empowered position. Scenes from the album that feature a multigenerational assembly of Black women clad in all-white attire recall the southern belle as cultural icon. With its nineteenth-century associations involving slavery and the ensuing hierarchal social arrangements relegating Black women to the position of objectified "other," the plantation and front porch figure ambiguously as sites of raced, gendered inscriptions of Black womanhood and a locus of female empowerment. Patricia Hill Collins traces the controlling images governing Black female sexual ideology to slavery and what she aptly describes as "the relationship between notions of differences in either/or dichotomous thinking and objectification."[41] "In either/or dichotomous thinking," Hill-Collins notes, "difference is defined in oppositional terms. One is not simply different from its counterpart; it is inherently opposed to its 'other.'"[42] *Lemonade* seeks to trouble the controlling narratives surrounding Black women's identities by featuring unconventional images of Black femininity.

Alien Encounters: The Wild Woman as Cultural Icon

Like the album as a whole, "Hold Up" and "Six Inch (Heels)" gesture toward conjure, magic, and the supernatural in the creation of an otherworldly visual performance reliant upon the genre conventions of the speculative. Teresa Washington's concept of *Aje* or woman-power as a quintessential essence defining a femininity based in an Africanist epistemology points to the existence of a close, dialogic relationship between *Lemonade* and works in Black women's literary and expressive culture.[43] Symbolic acts of rhetorical doubling, twinning, or mirror-imaging underscore the album's investment in vernacular structures signaling a new corporeality in opposition to conventional representations of

Black womanhood. Beyonce's surprising claim in "Hold Up" that "I can wear her skin over mine," presumably an expression of the scorned wife's ability to appropriate the identity of the other woman, recalls the soucouyant of African-Caribbean fame, renowned for her blood-sucking, shape-shifting abilities. Here, the soucouyant is refigured as a trope for an intersectionality that defies essentialist identity constructs. Although Jadine Childs expresses a similar intent in *Tar Baby* when she mentions that she wishes she could get out of her skin and be only the person inside, the Parisian fashion model is only moderately successful at mediating the various identities of contemporary Black womanhood. Shange's choreopoem is once again relevant in an appraisal of the shifting subjectivity that Beyonce exhibits. In her willful defiance of established gender conventions, the mysterious woman in "Six Inch (Heels)" bears a striking cultural resemblance to Sechita or the Lady in Green, also known as the Egyptian goddess of creativity associated with Delta dust and Creole culture, in Shange's choreopoem. Shange mentions that she studied the mythology surrounding women from Antiquity to the present in the construction of female character.[44] The declaration on the part of Shange's embattled Lady in Yellow that "my love is too delicate to have thrown back on my face," echoed in turn by the other women but with a slight variation, could easily have been Beyonce's twenty-first-century mantra.[45]

"Hold Up" and "Six Inch (Heels)" exist in dialogic relationship in terms of issues surrounding the invisibility of the Black female subject and the need to construct self-authenticating images of Black femininity. Whereas "Hold Up" allows Beyonce to assert, "Why can't you see me? Everyone else can," "Six Inch (Heels)" offers a possible response to the pointed question of the Black woman's struggle for recognition within the domestic and social structures of contemporary society and the larger society's unwillingness to acknowledge the humanity of storm survivors. *Lemonade* seeks to counter a temporal history prompting Malcolm X's assertion that "the most disrespected woman in the world is the black woman" through a focus on the lively traditions, customs, and ritual practices of a gendered heritage. The scene of a triumphant Beyonce reclining on top a police cruiser sinking into Katrina's flood waters can be read as a cautiously optimistic sign of the end of social system that devalues Black bodies as well as a tribute to the indomitable spirit of Black women. As a contemporary southern daughter, baptized, reborn, and willing to forgive, Beyonce, we assume, will emerge from Katrina's flood waters unscathed.

"Six Inch (Heels)," arguably the song with the most elusive meaning, involves a complex play of rhetorical doubling as Beyonce spins a fanciful tale about a mysterious, badass woman, possibly an alter ego or second self, who dares to challenge the domestic role ascribed to marginalized women when the woman "murdered everyone and I was her witness." Rather than recoiling from the mysterious woman's violent acts, Beyonce pays homage to her as a likely inspiring influence or foremother, immortalizing the woman's fierce behavior in song. As one of many wild women appearing in the performance, the mysterious woman in red replaces the revered southern belle as a cultural icon. That the woman is down in Mexico gestures toward the album's investment in cross-cultural or transnational representations of dispossessed women, a global sisterhood uniting women of color in a peculiar confraternity defying conventional gender roles and sexualities. Not only is the mysterious woman in red nameless as she operates outside semiotic structures of white, male authority, we learn that she works for the money, possibly through prostitution, aligning her with the misfit women who take up residence at Eve's boardinghouse/bordello in *Bailey's Cafe*.

A disembodied voice that both is and is not "Beyonce" weaves itself in and out of the album, linking an otherwise fragmented collection of stories together as one coherent visual enactment. It is this voice that announces the Black woman's multiple, overlapping subjectivities serving as a locus for a new societal arrangement issuing from the postapocalyptic imaginary emerging at the album's triumphant end. The query, "What are you gonna say at my funeral now that you've killed me?," occurring after the rejected wife has reached the nadir of her hurt, prompts an association between Beyonce's emergence from the mind-numbing effects of her husband's betrayal and the uncertain promise of social and environmental revitalization as the Gulf region emerges from disaster in Katrina's aftermath.

"Pray" opens the album with a ghostly voice labeling Beyonce's father as a magician. That the father never appears suggests his role as an abstraction; he has no identity apart from his position as a refiguration of male infidelity. Issues surrounding transgenerational masculine betrayal converge as Beyonce descends into water, enacting one of many scenes implying rebirth in the wake of Hurricane Katrina as well as a transcendental oneness between the female body—objectified, sexualized, traumatized, and healed—and the realm of nature. "Daddy Lessons" extends the conversation surrounding masculinity with pictures of Black males while Beyonce muses on her relationship with her father. The question, "why are you afraid of love?," resonates with the album's attempt to fathom the reasons prompting male unfaithfulness, and the question becomes one that the album raises yet fails to answer.

Reclaiming Inspiriting Motherly Connections

Lemonade fashions a myth of origins that undermines an oppressive history involving what Patricia Hill Collins aptly describes as the controlling images of Black womanhood and female sexuality. According to Hill Collins, objectifying stereotypes involving the Mammy, Matriarch, or Jezebel are part of an ideology of domination serving as instruments of power on the part of elite white men and their associates.[46] Whereas Morrison relies upon the myth of the blind horsemen and Ward turns to classical mythology, Beyonce situates her work in vernacular structures involving myths of resilient female personae whose complex subjectivities counter the psychic violence of economic and political conditions giving rise to an interlocking system of race, class, and gender oppression. Such myths are not only based in a diasporic cultural and spiritual epistemology, they also serve as a locus for the critique of claims on the part of disaster capitalism and its proponents that marginalized cultures have no viable past or that indigenous customs are readily expendable.

After all, *Lemonade* boasts of folkloric beginnings in a family recipe that Miss Hattie, Jay-Z's ninety-year-old grandmother, passes down intergenerationally.[47] That recipe becomes a metaphor for the dynamic process of self-construction issuing from, but not limited to, the singular roles ascribed to Black women throughout a temporal history. Beyonce is not hesitant to remind us that she is a product of her mother's Texas, Louisiana, Creole, French, and Native American culture and her father's Alabama upbringing, resulting in the creation of a creolized "Texas-bama" daughter of the South. For her and countless other Black writers, artists, and performers, the South is much more than a geographical locale; it is a ritual site lending itself to an intersectional identity existing apart from the controlling narratives of the dominant society. The album evolves from an intermediate space involving a disjuncture between the myriad personae that Beyonce reembodies and her creolized subjectivity as Beyonce Giselle Knowles Carter, with "Sasha Fierce" as an alter ego. That space becomes a fluid site of self-representation allowing her to elide an objectifying gaze.

Lest we forget about Katrina as an apocalyptic moment or the postapocalyptic imaginary informing the album in full, water and fire figure as recurrent tropes, ambiguous in their import, constituting either a threat or a promise, a cause or a consequence of unrelenting social and environmental ills continuing to exert an influence well into the twenty-first century. In what is arguably the most memorable scene in the album, "Formation" features a young boy dancing in front of a phalanx of armed, uniformed police officers who suddenly raise their hands in unison in an ironic gesture of surrender.[48] One is reminded as well of the scene evolving out of the Carters' domestic strife with a vengeful, bat-wielding Beyonce wearing a revealing yellow dress striking a fire hydrant after discovering her husband's unfaithfulness.[49] The flames and ensuing deluge that inundate the bustling streets of New Orleans bring to mind Katrina's merciless flood waters in a conflation of the massive storm, the biblical account of the end of the world, and Beyonce herself. What is worse, the album queries in rhetorical fashion: "looking jealous and crazy or being walked out on?" "Hold Up" reminds us that there is something equally as terrifying as a category five hurricane: a rejected Black woman, baseball bat in hand, who is both jealous *and* crazy.

"Daddy Lessons" lends emphasis to the album's suggestion of the mother as a fluid semiotic construct with, "women, like your mother, cannot be contained." As if to affirm the transformative power issuing from an identification with mothers or motherhood on the part of politically awakened and sexually liberated Black women, "Sorry" features Beyonce seated comfortably in an antebellum plantation, enjoying that space in leisurely fashion, not as a stereotypical Mammy-figure at the beck and call of a white retainer, but as a self-possessed woman groomed for and entitled to a life of luxury while a scantily clad Serena Williams twerks in the foreground unashamedly. Beyonce tells her absconding lover, "I ain't thinking 'bout you," reminding him and us that she has moved on with her life. In what has become a rallying cry for contemporary Black women confronting externally defined standards of beauty, she tells her unfaithful husband to "call Becky with the good hair." In "Formation," in many respects a manifesto on behalf of awakened Black women, Beyonce unsettles discourses surrounding the blonde-haired, blue-eyed southern belle promoted through the Cult of True Womanhood by celebrating her Negro nose and her baby's curly hair—specifically Black beauty standards. Her audacious claim that she "just might be a black Bill Gates in the making" races and genders the American business magnate and Microsoft founder in ways that situate Black women as insiders, not only within the walls of the southern plantation, but also within a bustling capitalist–industrial–technological system existing no longer as the exclusive purview of powerful white males.

Reracing the Past and Ungendering the Future: Moving Forward after the Storm

Entrenched in the performance mode and steeped in an African folkloric tradition involving a range of female personae, the visual album makes its claim for the humanity of Black women and, by extension, communities of color across the African diaspora through an emphasis on ordinary individuals and the spaces of everyday life. The work offers a critique of Katrina discourses that would posit the notion that hurricane survivors are bereft of an identity or past or that they are unwelcome refugees or wards of the South instead of conscious contributors to a vibrant transnational culture. Through an emphasis on female bonds across the diaspora and a reliance upon storytelling, the album is a visual enactment of what feminist theorists describes as a counterhegemonic discourse that undermines the dominant narratives of Black female passivity in the face of oppression.[50] In her stellar performance of a range of female personae—from a vengeful, baseball bat-wielding, middle finger-pointing scorned lover, to a self-assured, financially independent woman with her own money, to a loving wife, mother, daughter, and granddaughter—Beyonce runs the gamut of Black female intersectional subjectivities in defiance of a temporal history with its static portraits of Black femininity in literature and popular culture.

bell hooks offers an informed, albeit mixed, appraisal of the album as a visual enactment of what she refers to rather derisively as Beyonce's fantasy feminism. hooks writes:

> It is the broad scope of *Lemonade*'s visual landscape that makes it so distinctive—the construction of a powerfully symbolic black female sisterhood that resists invisibility, that refuses to be silent. This in and of itself is no small feat—it shifts the gaze of white mainstream culture. It challenges us all to look anew, to radically revision how we see the black female body. However, this radical repositioning of black female images does not truly overshadow or change conventional sexist constructions of black female identity.[51]

For the assortment of marginalized women whose dramatic stories of tragedy and triumph are featured, the future is not only Black, but female and bound inseparably with the liberation of the larger post-Katrina society. "Forward," with its futuristic gesture toward a utopian world order featuring Black and brown women, young and old, asks, "how do we lead our children to the future?" The song looks forward and back simultaneously, merging the future with the past in the creation of a fantastic world returning us to issues surrounding the nature of what *Beloved*'s battered ex-slave Paul D would refer to as love that is too thick: frustrated, betrayed, thwarted, denied, but expressed without measure.[52] Scenes of Black mothers holding photographs of their slain sons point to the historic challenges of maternal love in a racially polarized America along with the album's concern with the collective need to heal from the wounds of state-sponsored police violence. Envisioning a new social order arising in the aftermath of calamity and ruin, Beyonce speaks of women in childbirth, invoking the trope of the unborn child as a metaphor for futuristic potentiality when she says, "I see your daughters in childbirth."

As an affirmation of the power of unconditional love and forgiveness, "Sandcastles" features home videos highlighting loving interactions with family, including scenes with Jay-Z and Blue Ivy. Beyonce sings, "Show me your scars and I won't walk away," as if to summon utopian constructions of a domestic arena informed by African or American-Indian cultural practices as the basis for transformed societal arrangements. "All Night" extends the idealized portrait of domestic bliss with a focus on scenes from the Carters' wedding as well as those from Tina Knowles's second marriage. Unlike Morrison's *Tar Baby*, however, the album places the responsibility for resisting patriarchal domination squarely on the shoulders of Black women. And *Lemonade*'s implications that female violence is an acceptable response to masculine betrayal, like those in Ward's *Salvage the Bones*, simply replace a system of male domination with one in which women become perpetrators of cruelty, hostility, and aggression. Any solution to the problem of conflicted male–female relationships that positions women as mirror images of their male oppressors does not represent positive change in the terms opponents of disaster capitalism would advocate; women who engage in violent acts merely replicate the domineering, shock-and-awe social and economic structures responsible for the subjugation of marginalized cultures. bell hooks finds the album's solution to male–female conflict unsatisfying because of the seeming validation of female aggression. "It is only as black women and all women resist patriarchal romanticization of domination in relationships can a healthy self-love emerge that allows every black female, and all females, to refuse to be a victim," hooks asserts. "Ultimately *Lemonade* glamorizes a world of gendered cultural paradox and contradiction. It does not resolve."[53]

If the album falls short in denouncing the violent structures of dominance, scenes of same-sex-loving couples alongside pictures of the Carter's points to an expanded conceptualization of domestic relations featuring members of the LGBTQ community, extending the album's engagement with romantic love beyond the perimeters of heterosexuality and a cisgendered norm. *Lemonade* does not disavow male–female relations in the service of a gay-lesbian agenda; rather, the album presents same-sex love as a viable option for futuristic social constructions. The New World Order coming into existence is not only Black and female, but markedly queer, at least in its presentation of a range of sexualities, following the line of scholarly argumentation that Chapter 3 of this study advances. Like the unpredictable waters of the Atlantic, Katrina's incessant flood waters recede only to reveal a futuristic social order resistant to the mandates of a capitalistic bureaucracy or disaster capitalism, a world holding forth the promise of a society poised on the brink of radical change.

Beyonce aligns herself with Toni Morrison and Jesmyn Ward in addressing concerns surrounding the challenges and possibilities for romantic love in the era of the "post." The trio of writers and performing artists issue a clarion call for individual and communal healing in the face of race, class, gender, and sexual oppression with a radically reconstituted domestic arena serving as a locus for the creation of a mythology of Black femininity that seeks to undermine the controlling mandates of white supremacist ideology. While the bureaucratic structures of the larger society insist upon a clean slate as a means of disrupting indigenous cultural practices and realigning society in ways that privilege a hierarchal ordering, in works by Black women, disaster engenders hope for new beginnings arising in the aftermath of ruin. Jay-Z's all-wise grandmother who touts her lemonade recipe as a life lesson for personal empowerment brings this study's concerns full-circle, returning discursively to a focus on domestic space and gender relations along with the folklore that informs Black culture. For her as well as the countless other Black women, home is a site of trauma and healing, a space of pain and exciting opportunity, a place where disparate experiences have the potential to converge in the creation of something at once both old and new. *Lemonade* posits the notion that the domestic arena is or at least has the potential to be a space without borders, a site that Homi Bhabha would label as "a space of intervention in the here and now," even as the work endeavors to map the territory leading to restored loving relations as a foundation for a postapocalyptic society that outlasts the disruptive imperatives of the dominant culture.[54]

Notes

Chapter 1

1 The album cover for Ebony Bones's *Behold, a Pale Horse* discloses a concern with a postapocalyptic imaginary in Black female popular culture.
2 Mark Dery, "Black to the Future: Interviews with Samuel R. Delany, Greg Tate, and Tricia Rose," in *Flame Wars: The Discourse of Cyberculture*, ed. Mark Dery (Durham, NC: Duke University Press, 1994), 180.
3 Eshun Kodwo, *More Brilliant than the Sun: Adventures in Sonic Fiction* (London: Quartet Books, 1999); Tricia Rose and Andrew Ross, eds. *Microphone Fiends: Youth Music and Urban Culture* (New York: Routledge, 1994); Greg Tate and Arthur Jafa, "La Venus Negre," *Artforum*, 30, 5 (1992), 90–3; Jonita Davis, "How Black Women Are Reshaping Afro-Futurism," *Yes!Magazine*. April 24, 2020; and Ytasha L. Womack, *Afro-Futurism: The World of Black Sci Fi and Fantasy Culture* (Chicago, IL: Lawrence Hill Books, 2013).
4 See Marleen Barr, ed. *Afro-Future Females: Black Writers Chart Science Fiction's Newest New Wave* (Columbus: Ohio State University Press, 2008); Rebecca J. Holden and Nisi Shawl, eds. *Strange Matings: Science Fiction, Feminism, African-American Voices, and Octavia E. Butler* (Seattle, WA: Aqueduct, 2013); Kristen Lillvis, *Posthuman Blackness and the Black Female Imagination* (Athens: University of Georgia Press, 2017); Ingrid Thaler, *Black Atlantic Speculative Fictions: Octavia E. Butler, Jewell Gomez, and Nalo Hopkinson* (New York: Routledge, 2010); Ytasha L. Womack, *Afro-Futurism: The World of Black Sci Fi and Fantasy Culture* (Chicago, IL: Lawrence Hill Books, 2013).
5 Mae Gwendolyn Henderson, "Speaking in Tongues: Dialogics, Dialectics, and the Black Woman Writer's Literary Tradition," in *African-American Literary Theory: A Reader*, ed. Winston Napier (New York: New York University Press, 2000), 348–68.
6 Ibid., 358.
7 Hortense Spillers, "Mama's Baby, Papa's Maybe: An American Grammar Book," in *Within the Circle: An Anthology of African American Literary Criticism from the Harlem Renaissance to the Present*, ed. Angelyn Mitchell (Durham, NC: Duke University Press, 1994), 454–81.
8 Kimberlé Williams Crenshaw, "Mapping the Margins: Intersectionality, Identity Politics, and Violence against Women of Color," in *The Public Nature of Private Violence*, eds. Martha Albertson Fineman, Rixanne Mykitiuk (New York: Routledge,

1994), 93–118. Jennifer Nash reframes Black feminism's engagement with intersectionality by challenging constructions of a fixed identity underlying constituent aspects of Black femininity. See *Black Feminism Reimagined: After Intersectionality* (Durham, NC: Duke University Press, 2019).

9   Octavia Butler, "Interviewing the Oracle: Octavia Butler," interview by Kazembe Balagun *The Indypendent*. March 3, 2019. https://indypendent.org/2006/01/interviewing-the-oracle-octavia-butler/.

10 Ibid., 238.

11 Frantz Fanon, *Black Skin, White Masks* [*Peau noire, masques blancs*, 1952], translated by Charles Lam Markmann (New York: Grove Press, 1967).

12 Recent studies offer useful insights in a reappraisal of the trans-Atlantic journey and its implications for speculative genre conventions: Avery F. Gordon, *Ghostly Matters: Haunting and the Sociological Imagination* (Minneapolis: New University of Minnesota Press, 2008); Saidiya Hartman, *Lose Your Mother: A Journey along the Atlantic Slave Route* (New York: Farrar, Straus, and Giroux, 2007); and Lisa Woolfolk, *Embodying Slavery in American Culture* (Urbana: University of Illinois Press, 2008).

13 James Berger, *After the End: Representations of the Post-Apocalypse* (Minneapolis: University of Minnesota Press, 1999), 7. Although other, more recent, titles disclose a growing scholarly interest in postapocalypticism in fiction, television, and film, the present study involves a singular focus on the ways in which contemporary Black women novelists respond to crises and disaster. See Heather Hicks, *The Post-Apocalyptic Novel in the 20th Century: Modernity beyond Salvage* (Camden: Palgrave Macmillan, 2016); Barbara Gurr, ed. *Race, Gender, and Sexuality in Post-Apocalyptic TV and Film* (Camden: Palgrave Macmillan, 2015); Teresa Heffernan, *Post-Apocalyptic Culture: Modernism, Postmodernism, and the 20th Century Novel* (Toronto: University of Toronto Press, 2008); and Claire Curtis, *Postapocalyptic Fiction and the Social Contract* (Washington, DC: Lexington, 2010).

14 James Baldwin, *The Fire Next Time* (New York: Dial Press, 1963), 119. Baldwin's assessment of the 1943 race riots in Detroit and New York as an instance of social catastrophe is consistent with the tendency toward a secularization of apocalypse in relation to unresolved racial tensions. For other inferences involving the secularization of apocalypse in Baldwin's writing, see the title essay in *Notes of a Native Son* (New York: Bantam, 1955).

15 Keith Byerman, *Remembering the Past in Contemporary African American Fiction* (Chapel Hill: University of North Carolina Press, 2005), 3.

16 Ibid., 179.

17 Toni Morrison, "Home," in *The House That Race Built*, ed. Wahneema Lubiano (New York: Random House, 1998), 3–12.

18 Toni Morrison, "An Interview with Toni Morrison," interview by Christina Davis, in *Conversations with Toni Morrison*, ed. Danielle Taylor Guthrie (Jackson: University Press of Mississippi, 1994), 224–5.
19 Ibid., 225.
20 Susanna Morris, "Black Girls Are from the Future: Afrofuturist Feminism in Octavia Butler's *Fledgling*," *Women's Studies Quarterly*, 40, 3/4 (2012), 146–66.
21 Whereas Maxine Lavon Montgomery's *The Apocalypse in African American Fiction* (Gainesville: University Press of Florida, 1996) interrogates the ways in which US Black novelists reframe biblical and media images of the end of the world in the creation of utopian worlds of Black freedom and empowerment, *The Postapocalyptic Black Female Imagination* attends to reimagined gender and sexual identities emerging in the aftermath of catastrophe in fiction and expressive culture by Black women in a US and Anglo-Caribbean geography. Although apocalypticism runs the risk of sliding into postapocalypticism, the current project constitutes a fundamental reconceptualization of the central argument that I put forth in the previous book by locating itself within a diasporic imaginary involving catastrophe and the futuristic worlds that ensue.
22 Michelle D. Commander critiques the mythmaking involved in imagining Africa as a utopian site of return for African-Americans in the post-civil rights United States and postcolonial African Diaspora. See *Afro-Atlantic Flight: Speculative Returns and the Black Fantastic* (Durham, NC: Duke University Press, 2017). Tuire Valkeakari interrogates Anglophone African diasporic fiction in relation to a reimagining of an African homeland. See *Precarious Passages: The Diasporic Imagination in Contemporary Black Anglophone Fiction* (Gainesville: University Press of Florida, 2017).
23 Lillvis, *Posthuman Blackness*, 83; Kodwo Eshun, "Further Considerations on Afro-futurism," *New Centennial Review*, 3, 2 (2003), 300; Tate and Jafa, "La Venus Negre," 90–3; and Calvin L. Warren, "Black Nihilism and the Politics of Hope," *CR: The New Centennial Review*, 15, 1 (Spring 2015), 215–48. Web. May 31, 2015.
24 Russell Porter deploys a critical methodology attendant to language use in attending to postapocalyptic interventions on the part of hip-hop artists. For him, "hip-hop's time is post-apocalyptic": "hip-hop's triad of graffiti, dance, and rap are post-apocalyptic arts, scratches on the decaying surfaces of post-industrial urban America." I am referring to *Spectacular Vernaculars: Hip-Hop and the Politics of Postmodernism* (New York: State University of New York Press, 1995), 8. Anthony Obst traces apocalyptic themes in 1990s' hip-hop in the insightful "How Doomsday Rhetoric Scorched the Earth of Rap's Underground," Red Bull Music Academy Daily. March 27, 2019.
25 Lisa Yasek, "Afro-futurism, Science Fiction, and the History of the Future," *Socialism and Democracy*, 20, 3 (2006), 47. Web. June 6, 2019.

26 Sofia Samatar, "Toward a Planetary History of Afrofuturism," *Research in African Literatures*, 48, 4 (2017), 175–91. Web. June 13, 2019.
27 Okorafor's *Who Fears Death*, a postapocalyptic narrative set in futuristic Sudan, is being translated into an HBO series produced by *Game of Thrones* creator, George R. R. Martin. It is also worth noting that the best-selling Nigerian-American author has lent her talent in writing *The Black Panther* series for Marvel Comics with the creation of Shuri, the film's tough-minded, outspoken science nerd who is reminiscent of Binti. Although Okorafor is perhaps the most widely known and critically acclaimed African author of Afro-futurist fiction and her fiction relies upon epistemes of African diasporic cultures, the Middle Passage, and colonialism/postcolonialism, full interrogation of her work is beyond this study's US and Anglo-Caribbean disciplinary and geographic reach.
28 bell hooks, *Yearning: Race, Gender, and Cultural Politics* (Boston, MA: South End Press, 1990), 145.
29 Jacques Derrida, *Writing and Difference* (New York: Routledge, 2001), 278.
30 Lamonda Horton Stallings, *Mutha Is Half a Word: Black Performance and Cultural Criticism* (Columbus: Ohio State University Press, 2007), 9.
31 Ibid., 11.
32 See Calvin L. Warren, *Ontological Terror: Blackness, Annihilation, and Emancipation* (Durham, NC: Duke University Press, 2018). Toni Morrison theorizes Blackness in relation to whiteness, using early American textual spaces as a locus for interrogating the Africanist presence in American Literature and Culture. See *Playing in the Dark: Whiteness and the Literary Imagination* (Cambridge: Harvard University Press, 1992).
33 George Lipsitz, *Dangerous Crossroads: Popular Music, Postmodernism, and the Poetics of Place* (London: Verso, 1994), 19, 20; and hooks, *Yearning*, 145–53.
34 Kwame Anthony Appiah, "Is the Post- in Postmodernism the Post- in Postcolonial?" *Critical Inquiry*, 17, 2 (1991), 348. Web. February 13, 2019.
35 Ibid., 346–8.
36 Homi Bhabha, *The Location of Culture* (Abingdon: Routledge, 1994), 7.
37 George Lipsitz, "We Know What Time It Is: Race, Class, and Youth Culture in the Nineties," in *Microphone Fiends*, eds. Tricia Rose and Andrew Ross (New York: Routledge, 1994), 17–28. Lipsitz outlines the contradictory impulses associated with what he describes as the "crossroads of commerce and culture" in relation to the 1992 Los Angeles social unrest following the acquittal of white police officers in the beating of Rodney King and xenophobic attacks upon members of racial and ethnic groups. For him, "The crossroads we confront contain both residual and emergent elements; they encompass both dangers and opportunities." My reading of representative works by Black women attends to the transformative possibilities of the crossroads as a locus for the creation of a self-defined reality apart from past inscriptions. See *Dangerous Crossroads*, 19.

38. Ibid., 33.
39. Lipsitz, *How Racism Takes Place* (Philadelphia, PA: Temple University Press, 2011).
40. Derrida, *Writing and Difference*, 98.
41. Bhabha, *The Location of Culture*, 15, 6.
42. Andrew Cuomo, [CNN Press Conference], April 19, 2020.
43. Edwidge Danticat, Tavis Smiley, "Writer Edwidge Danticat," Public Broadcasting Station. Web. November 12, 2019. http://www.pbs.org/wnet/tavissmiley/interviews/edwidge-danticat/.
44. Kinetra Brooks offers a useful definition of zombie apocalypse in "The Importance of Neglected Intersections: Race and Gender in Contemporary Zombie Texts and Theories," *African American Review*, 47, 4 (Winter 2014), 461–75. Although Brooks attends to raced, gendered tropes of zombie-ism in filmic productions or visual culture, her insights are relevant to representations of the zombie in literary texts by Black women.

Chapter 2

1. Recent scholarship directs attention to constructions of Black girlhood and historical attribution of adult characteristics and behaviors to young Black females. See the groundbreaking study by Rebecca Epstein, Jamila J. Blake, and Thalia Gonzalez, "Girlhood Interrupted: The Erasure of Black Girls' Childhood," Georgetown Law School, Center on Poverty and Equality. Web. June 2017. Useful in its implications for literary and cultural criticism, this study seeks to interrogate the dominant paradigms about Black femininity and the "adultification" of Black girls.
2. Christopher N. Okonkwo, *A Spirit of Dialogue: Incarnations of Obanje, the Born-to-Die, in African American Literature* (Knoxville: University of Tennessee Press, 2008).
3. Saidiya Hartman, *Lose Your Mother: A Journey along the Atlantic Slave Route* (New York: Farrar, Straus, and Giroux, 2007).
4. Octavia E. Butler, *Fledgling* (New York: Grand Central Publishing, 2005), 123. Subsequent references to this edition are included parenthetically.
5. Toni Morrison, "Home," in *The House That Race Built*, ed. Wahnema Lubiano (New York: Random House, 1998), 10. Much like Shori, the youthful heroine in Nnedi Okorafor's *Binti* confronts an estrangement from home and family resonant with the dislocating experience of the Middle Passage. Both coming of age texts find their resolution in the attainment of an adult constitution located outside traditional constructions of a gendered subjectivity.
6. Patricia Hill Collins, *Black Feminist Thought: Knowledge, Consciousness, and the Politics of Empowerment* (New York: Routledge, 1991), 67–90.

7   Lamonda Horton Stallings, *Funk the Erotic: Trans Aesthetics and Black Sexual Cultures* (Champaign: University of Illinois Press, 2015), 131–2.
8   Kristen Lillvis, *Post Human Blackness and the Black Female Imagination* (Athens: University of Georgia Press, 2017), 81.
9   Ibid., 82.
10 Frantz Fanon, *White Skin, Black Masks* (New York: Grove Press, 1967), 112.
11 Toni Morrison, *Playing the Dark: Whiteness and the Literary Imagination* (Cambridge: Harvard University Press, 1992), 46
12 Toni Morrison, *The Origin of Others* (Cambridge: Harvard University Press, 2017), 6.
13 Ibid., 55.
14 Ibid., 15.
15 Rob Gates, "Fledgling by Octavia Butler," *Strange Horizons*. March 6, 2006. Web.
16 Ali Brox, "'Every Age Has the Vampire It Needs': Octavia Butler's Vampiric Vision in Fledgling," *Utopian Studies*, 19, 3 (2008), 401.
17 Shari Evans, "From 'Hierarchal Behavior' to Strategic Amnesia: Structures of Memory and Forgetting in Octavia Butler's Fledgling," in *Strange Matings: Science Fiction, Feminism, African American Voices, and Octavia E. Butler*, eds. Rebecca J. Holden and Nisi Shawl (Seattle, WA: Aqueduct Press, 2013), 237.
18 See Michelle D. Commander, *Afro-Atlantic Flight: Speculative Returns and the Black Fantastic* (Durham, NC: Duke University Press, 2017); Hartman, *Lose Your Mother*; Hortense Spillers, "Mama's Baby, Papa's Maybe: An American Grammar Book," in *Within the Circle: An Anthology of African American Literary Criticism from the Harlem Renaissance to the Present*, ed. Angelyn Mitchell (Durham, NC: Duke University Press, 1994), 454–81; and Tuire Valkeakari, *Precarious Passages: The Diasporic Imagination in Contemporary Black Anglophone Fiction* (Gainesville: University Press of Florida, 2017).
19 Jacques Derrida, *Writing and Difference* (New York: Routledge, 2001), 278.
20 Lillvis, *Posthuman Blackness*, 86.
21 Rosi Braidotti, *The Posthuman* (Cambridge: Polity Press, 2013), 3–5.
22 Melissa J. Strong situates her interrogation of Shori's compound identity within the discursive framework of cultural hybridity. See "The Limits of Newness: Hybridity in Octavia E. Butler's *Fledgling*," *FEMSPEC: An Interdisciplinary Feminist Journal Dedicated to Critical and Creative Work in the Realms of Science Fiction, Fantasy, Magical Realism, Surrealism, Myth, Folklore, and Other Supernatural Genres*, 11, 1 (2011), 27–43.
23 Pramod K. Nayar, "Vampirism and Posthumanism in Octavia Butler's Fledgling," *Notes on Contemporary Literature*, 41, 2 (2011). Web.
24 bell hooks, *Black Looks: Race and Representation* (Boston, MA: South End, 1992), 21–39.
25 Strong, "The Limits of Newness," 32.

26 Susanna M. Morris, "Black Girls Are from the Future: Afrofuturist Feminism in Octavia E. Butler's Fledgling," *Women's Studies Quarterly*, 40, 3/4 (2012), 152.
27 Nayar, "Vampirism and Posthumanism," 36.
28 Donna McCormack, "Living with Others Inside the Self: Decolonising Transplantation, Selfhood, and the Body Politic in Nalo Hopkinson's Brown Girl in the Ring," *Medical Humanities*, 42, 4 (2016), 255.
29 Ibid., 253.
30 Gregory Jerome Hampton, "Vampires and Utopia: Reading Racial and Gender Politics in the Fiction of Octavia Butler," *Changing Bodies in the Fiction of Octavia Butler: Slaves, Aliens, and Vampires*, ed. Gregory Jerome Hampton (New York: Lexington Books, 2010), 111.
31 Judith Halberstam and Ira Livingston, eds. *Posthuman Bodies* (Bloomington: Indiana University Press, 1995), 14.
32 Hampton, "Vampires and Utopia," 16.
33 McCormack, "Living with Others Inside the Self," 254.
34 Morris, "Black Girls Are from the Future," 147.
35 Jordan Peele's Science Fiction thriller, *US*, interrogates issues of doubling and identity construction in relation to whiteness and Blackness. The movie's core concerns intersect with issues of Black, female subjectivity in Butler's novel.
36 See Hayden White, *Meta-History: The Historical Imagination in Nineteenth Century Europe* (Baltimore, MD: Johns Hopkins University Press, 1975).
37 Houston A. Baker, Jr., *Workings of the Spirit: The Poetics of Afro-American Women's Writing* (Chicago, IL: University of Chicago Press, 1991), 75–6.
38 Elena Clemente Bustamante, "Fragments and Crossroads in Nalo Hopkinson's *Brown Girl in the Ring*," *Spaces of Utopia*, 4 (2007), 12.
39 Sheree Thomas, ed. *Dark Matter: A Century of Speculative Fiction from the African Diaspora* (New York: Warner Books, 2000), xiv.
40 See Homi Bhabha, *The Location of Culture* (New York: Routledge, 1994); and Ana Maria Alonso, "Borders, Sovereignty, and Racialization," in *Companion to Latin American Anthropology*, ed. Deborah Poole (Oxford: Blackwell, 2008).
41 Bill Ashcroft, Gareth Griffiths and Helen Tiffin eds. *Post-colonial Studies: The Key Concepts* (New York: Routledge, 1998), 119.
42 Hopkinson, "Science Fiction versus Science Fact."
43 Quote form *TV Ontario Channel* Interview.
44 Nalo Hopkinson, *Brown Girl in the Ring* (New York: Grand Central, 1998), 200. Subsequent references to this edition are included parenthetically.
45 Hopkinson's fictional description of the riots recalls the 1990 Yonge Street Riots that erupted in Toronto following an incident involving the police shooting of an unarmed Black man and racial tensions in other urban mid-western cities. Set in 2049, "Brown Girl Begins," the cinematic work based on Hopkinson's novel, offers a graphic portrait of the inner city as a wasteland following decades of social unrest and unjust economic policies.

46 Hill-Collins, *Black Feminist Thought*, 119.
47 Hopkinson deploys the circle game as a trope for the various choices confronting Ti-Jeanne as a young Black woman in contemporary America. See the author interview following "Brown Girl Begins." Rebecca Romdhani reads the circle game in terms of its implications for a cosmic circle in "Zombies Go to Toronto: Zombifying Shame in Nalo Hopkinson's *Brown Girl in the Ring*," *Research in African Literature*, 46, 4, *What Is Africa to Me Now?* (Winter 2015), 72–89.
48 Reference to the rose summons legend and lore surrounding Eruzuli(e), African-Caribbean goddess of love and beauty, with the figure's insinuation for rhetorical doubling, revision, and mimesis. The presence of the rose signals the novel's investment in vernacular structures as a locus for the transformed social arrangement arising at the novel's end.
49 Elena Clemente Bustamante, "Fragments and Crossroads," 21–2.
50 *TV Ontario Channel* Interview.
51 Edwidge Danticat, *Create Dangerously: The Immigrant Artist at Work* (New York: Random House, 2010), 129.
52 Zora Neale Hurston, *Tell My Horse* (Berkeley, CA: Turtle Island, 1981), 141.
53 Maya Deren, *The Divine Horsemen: The Living Gods of Haiti* (Kingston, NY: McPherson, 1983), 94.
54 Bustamante, "Fragments and Crossroads," 21.
55 Horton Stallings, *Funk the Erotic*, 34–5.
56 Giselle Liza Anatol, *The Things That Fly in the Night: Female Vampires in Literature of the Circum-Caribbean and African Diaspora* (New York: Rutgers University Press, 2015), 14.
57 Ibid., 2.
58 Romdhani, "Zombies Go to Toronto," 81.
59 Hill-Collins, *Black Feminist Thought*, 119.
60 See Danticat, *Create Dangerously*, 65; Hartman, 155–7; and Zora Neale Hurston, *Tell My Horse* (Berkeley, CA: Turtle Island, 1981), 206.
61 Bustamante makes this point as well in "Fragments and Crossroads," 23. The contemporary saga of cultural clashes with the alien "other" is couched in apocalyptic terms in the Rastafari song by Jamaican Reggae group, the Melodians, with "Rivers of Babylon" as the "A" side to a single based on Psalms. The various iterations of clashes with the foreigner attest to the portability of stories of alien encounters and apocalyptic dimensions of such stories.
62 Bhabha, *The Location of Culture*, 4.
63 Romdhani, "Zombies Go to Toronto," 81.
64 Ibid., 81. Romdhani reveals that Oshun is Yoruba goddess of beauty, love, order, fertility, and prosperity. Also known as Yemaya, she is renowned for her cooking skills. She is also Mother of the African sweet or fresh waters. Yemaya or Emanjah is a leader of other river deities, often depicted as a mermaid, protector of women and children, and a guardian of secrets.

65 Laura Salvini, "A Heart of Kindness: Nalo Hopkinson's 'Brown Girl in the Ring,'" *Journal of Haitian Studies*, 18, 2 (Fall 2012), 186.
66 Ibid.
67 Review of *Brown Girl in the Ring. Publisher's Weekly*. Web. July, 1998.
68 Salvini, "A Heart of Kindness," 86.
69 Maxine Lavon Montgomery, "Putting together the Fragments: A Conversation with Edwidge Danticat," in *Conversations with Edwidge Danticat*, ed. Maxine Lavon Montgomery (Jackson: University Press of Mississippi, 2017), 208.
70 Robyn Cope, "'We Are Your Neighbors': Edwidge Danticat's New Narrative for Haiti," *Journal of Haitian Studies*, 23, 1 (2017), 98.
71 Rachel Martin, "Haitian Youth Illuminated in 'Sea Light,'" in *Conversations with Edwidge Danticat*, 151.
72 Danticat, *Create Dangerously*, 94.
73 Edwidge Danticat, *Claire of the Sea Light* (New York: Knopf, 2013), 199. Subsequent references to this edition are included parenthetically.
74 Anissa J. Wardi, *Water and African-America Memory: An EcoCritical Perspective* (Gainesville: University Press of Florida, 2016), 3.
75 Danticat, *Create Dangerously*, 11
76 See Avery F. Gordon, *Ghostly Matters: Haunting and the Sociological Imagination* (Minneapolis: New University of Minnesota Press, 2008); Hartman, *Lose Your Mother*; and Kathleen Brogan, *Cultural Haunting: Ghosts and Ethnicity in Recent American Literature* (Charlottesville: University Press of Virginia, 1998).
77 Kathleen Brogan, *Cultural Haunting: Ghosts and Ethnicity in Recent American Literature* (Charlottesville: University Press of Virginia, 1998).
78 Ibid., 2.
79 Marisa Parham, *Haunting and Displacement in African American Literature and Culture* (New York: Routledge, 2009), 3.
80 Laurie Vickroy, *Trauma and Survival in Contemporary Literature* (Charlottesville: University of Virginia Press, 2002), 169.
81 Cathy Caruth, "Introduction: Psychoanalysis, Culture, and Trauma II," Special issue of *American Imago*, 48, 1 (1991), 5.
82 Caruth *Unclaimed Experience: Trauma, Narrative, and History* (Baltimore, MD: Johns Hopkins University Press, 1996), 7.
83 Opal Adisa Palmer, "Up Close and Personal: Edwidge Danticat on Haitian Identity and the Writer's Life," *African-American Review*, 43, 2 (Summer/Fall 2009), 348.
84 Danticat, *Create Dangerously*, 49.
85 Danticat discusses tropes of doubling, twinning, and mirror-imaging in an interview with Kima Jones, "A Conversation with Edwidge Danticat," in *Conversations with Edwidge Danticat*, ed. Maxine Lavon Montgomery, Conversations with Edwidge Danticat (Jackson: University Press of Mississippi, 2017), 169–70. As a recurring trope throughout her fictional canon, twinning functions as a decolonizing gesture in the project of self-construction on the part of diaspora subjects.

86 Danticat, *Create Dangerously*, 65.
87 Tuire Valkeakari, *Precarious Passages: The Diasporic Imagination in Contemporary Black Anglophone Fiction* (Gainesville: University Press of Florida, 2017), 195–6.
88 Danticat, *Create Dangerously*, 134; Rachel Martin, National Public Radio. Web. August 25, 2013. http://www.npr.org/2013/08/25/214857669/haitian-youth-illuminated-in-sea-light; and Tavis Smiley, "Writer Edwidge Danticat," Public Broadcasting Station. Web. October 14, 2013. http://www.pbs.org/wnet/tavissmiley/interviews/edwidge-danticat/
89 Danticat, *Create Dangerously*, 65.
90 Danticat, *Create Dangerously*, 134–5.
91 Silvia Martinez-Falquina, "Postcolonial Trauma Theory in the Contact Zone: The Strategic Representation of Grief in Edwidge Danticat's Claire of the Sea Light," *Humanities*, 4, 4 (2015), 836.
92 Cope, "We Are Your Neighbors,"102.
93 Martin, "Haitian Youth Illuminated in Sea Light," 149–50.
94 Nadège T. Clitandre, *The Haitian Diasporic Imaginary* (Charlottesville: University of Virginia Press, 2018), 1.
95 Danticat, *Create Dangerously*, 177. Instead of associating the mythical elements to African folklore, Lisa Page compares the novel's apocalyptic symbolism to those in the Judeo-Christian tradition. See "Edwidge Danticat Illuminates Haiti," *Virginia Quarterly Review*, 89, 4 (2013), 252.
96 Danticat, *Create Dangerously*, 177.

Chapter 3

1 Patricia Hill Collins, *Black Feminist Thought: Knowledge, Consciousness, and the Politics of Empowerment* (New York: Routledge, 1990), 43–66.
2 Mark Dery, ed. "Black to the Future: Interviews with Samuel R. Delany, Greg Tate, and Tricia Rose," in *Flame Wars: The Discourse of Cyberculture* (Durham, NC: Duke University Press, 1994).
3 Michelle Cliff, *Claiming an Identity They Taught Me to Despise* (Bloomsbury: Persephone Books, 1980), 8.
4 Michelle Cliff, *I Could Write This in Fire* (Minneapolis: University of Minnesota Press, 2008), 9–32.
5 Combahee River Collective, Audre Lorde and Kimberlé Crenshaw.
6 M. Jacqui Alexander, *Pedagogies of Crossing: Meditations on Feminism, Sexual Politics, Memory, and the Sacred* (Durham, NC: Duke University Press, 2005), 7.
7 Omise'eke Natasha Tinsley, "Black Atlantic, Queer Atlantic: Queer Imaginings of the Middle Passage," *GLQ: A Journal of Lesbian and Gay Studies*, 14, 2, 3 (2008), 193.

8   Lamonda Horton Stallings, *Funk the Erotic: Transaesthetics and Black Sexual Culture* (Urbana: University of Illinois Press, 2015).
9   Michelle Cliff, *Abeng* (New York: Plume, 1995), 25. Subsequent references to this edition are included parenthetically.
10 See Mae G. Henderson and E. Patrick Johnson, eds. *Black Queer Studies: A Critical Anthology*; Tinsley, "Black Atlantic, Queer Atlantic"; and Horton-Stallings, *Funk the Erotic*.
11 Horton Stallings, *Mutha Is Half a Word: Intersections of Folklore, Vernacular, Myth, and Queerness in Black Female Culture* (Columbus: Ohio State University Press, 2007), 3.
12 Hortense Spillers, "Mama's Baby, Papa's Maybe: An American Grammar Book," in *Within the Circle: An Anthology of African American Literary Criticism from the Harlem Renaissance to the Present*, ed. Angelyn Mitchell (Durham, NC: Duke University Press, 1994), 467.
13 Tuire Valkeakari, *Precarious Passages: The Diasporic Imagination in Contemporary Black Anglophone Fiction* (Gainesville: University Press of Florida, 2017), 134.
14 Carol Boyce Davies, *Black Women, Writing, and Identity: Migrations of the Subject* (New York: Routledge, 1994), 115.
15 Ibid., 115.
16 Tinsley, 209.
17 Hill Collins, *Black Feminist Thought*, 95–103.
18 Jamaica Kincaid discusses her vexed relationship with daffodils in relation to William Wordsworth and the postcolonial resistance against British colonial influence in "Garden Path Leads to Surprising Places," *The Denver Post*. Web. https://www.denverpost.com/2008/02/07/garden-path-leads-to-surprising-places/. Daffodils assume a more ambiguous role in the fiction of Edwidge Danticat as a representation of the conflicted mother–daughter dyad. In *Claire of the Sea Light*, Nozias names his daughter, Claire, after her mother, Claire Narcis, whose surname means daffodil or self-love, implying a shared identity that threatens to undermine the titular character's search for an autonomous self. Danticat's debut work of fiction, *Breath, Eyes, Memory*, opens with Sophie Caco's giving Tante Atie a daffodil on Mother's Day. Imported to Haiti from the French, the hybrid flower symbolizes issues of migration, displacement, and home.
19 Judith Butler, *Gender Trouble: Feminism and the Subversion of Identity* (New York: Routledge, 1990).
20 In a reading of *Abeng* as Black feminist bildungsroman, Caroline Rody centers her discussion of Clare's evolving subjectivity in terms of the adolescent's "developing communication with her own body." See *The Daughter's Return: African-American and Caribbean Women's Fictions of History* (Cambridge: Oxford University Press, 2001), 179. Lisa Walker labels the novel as "A Lesbian Bildungsroman," in *Looking Like What You Are: Sexual Style, Race, and Lesbian Identity*, ed. Lisa Walker (New York: New York University Press, 2001), 141.

21 Michelle Cliff and Meryl F. Swartz, "An Interview with Michelle Cliff," *Contemporary Literature*, 34, 4 (1993), 614.
22 Boyce Davies, *Black Women, Writing, and Identity*, 113–29.
23 Ibid., 123.
24 Michelle Cliff, *No Telephone to Heaven* (New York: Plume, 1987), 57. Subsequent references to this edition are included parenthetically.
25 Swartz, "An Interview with Michelle Cliff," 608.
26 Steven Shaviro, *The Cinematic Body: Theory out of Bounds* (Minneapolis: University of Minnesota Press, 1993).
27 Kate Ince, *The Body and the Screen: Female Subjectivity in Contemporary Women's Cinema* (London: Bloomsbury, 2017).
28 bell hooks, *Black Looks: Race and Representation* (Boston, MA: South End, 1992), 24.
29 Hill Collins, *Black Feminist Thought*, 151.
30 Ibid., 156.
31 The Combahee River Collective, a Black feminist lesbian organization that pointed out the failure of white feminism to address the realities of Black women, evolves out of an activist positioning. Black queer individuals played a key role in founding the US Black Lives Matter movement with its goal of addressing issues of violence and systematic racism. Recent scholarship attends to the relationship between Blackness and trans-ness as sites for political activism leading to non-gendered, gender-optional, and queer futures. C. Riley Snorton examines the relationship between Blackness and trans-ness in *Black on Both Sides: A Racial History of Trans Identity* (Minneapolis: University of Minnesota Press, 2018).
32 Spillers, "Mama's Baby, Papa's Maybe," 486–7.
33 Ibid., 480.

Chapter 4

1 Sheree Thomas, ed. *Dark Matter: A Century of Speculative Fiction from the African Diaspora* (New York: Warner Books, 2000), xiv.
2 Zora Neale Hurston, *Tell My Horse* (Berkeley, CA: Turtle Island, 1981), 206. Hurston's assertions are consistent with those of Kaiama L. Glover, who points out that the Haitian zombie differs from the figure's representation in B-grade European or Western movie productions. As Glover notes, the Haitian zombie is a victim, not a blood-thirsty, deranged predator intent on wreaking havoc on the living. See "Exploiting the Undead: The Usefulness of the Zombie in Haitian Literature," *The Journal of Haitian Studies*, 11, 12 (Fall 2005), 105–21. Amy Wilentz calls zombies a "very logical offspring of New World slavery." According to Wilentz,

because slavery in colonial Haiti was so viciously brutal, death was the only real escape and seen as a way to return to Africa or lan Guinée (which translated means Guinea). As she writes: "Suicide was the slave's only way to take control over his or her own body ... And yet, the fear of becoming a zombie might stop them from doing so ... This final rest — in green, leafy, heavenly Africa, with no sugarcane to cut and no master to appease or serve — is unavailable to the zombie. To become a zombie was the slave's worst nightmare: to be dead and still a slave, an eternal field hand." See "A Zombie Is a Slave Forever." *New York Times*. October 30, 2012.

3   Recent scholarship lends itself to theorizing the intermediacy of the postcolonial condition in relation to ghosts, ghostliness, and the spectral presence. See Homi Bhabha, *The Location of Culture* (New York: Routledge, 1994); Kathleen Brogan, *Cultural Haunting: Ghosts and Ethnicity in Recent American Literature* (Charlottesville: University Press of Virginia, 1998); and Marisa Parham, *Haunting and Displacement in African American Literature and Culture* (New York: Routledge, 2009).

4   For insight into the role of memory and forgetting as markers of cultural disarticulation leading to zombification, see Saidiya Hartman, *Lose Your Mother: A Journey along the Atlantic Slave Route* (New York: Farrar, Straus, and Giroux, 2007), 155; Drawing upon Haitian-Caribbean legend and lore, Edwidge Danticat describes the process of becoming a zombie in relation to a compulsory disremembering on the part of enslaved individuals. See *Create Dangerously: The Immigrant Artist at Work* (New York: Random House, 2010), 65.

5   Morrison asserts that Frank "Smart" Money, the troubled amnesiac war veteran in *Home*, assumed a life of his own as a ghostly apparition that attempts to take over the narrative. Alice Walker uses similar terms in reference to the fictional characters in *The Color Purple*. See the Morrison interview on Life.USAToday.com (May 8, 2012); and "Writing the *Color* Purple," in *In Search of Our Mothers' Gardens: Womanist Prose by Alice Walker*, ed. Alice Walker (New York: Harcourt, 1983), 355–60.

6   See Stephen Greenblatt, *Renaissance Self-Fashioning: From More to Shakespeare* (Chicago, IL: University of Chicago Press, 1980). Greenblatt's term is useful in its insinuations for the process of constructing an identity that unsettles raced, gendered, sexualized representations in canonical texts and visual media. My deployment of the term involves a reenvisioning of the dynamics of self-construction against a Black Atlantic geography and the implications of difference in the move toward self-identity.

7   bell hooks, *Yearning: Race, Gender, and Cultural Politics* (Boston, MA: South End, 1990), 146–7.

8   Rudyard Kipling functions as a figure for European colonialism and imperialist conquest in the British West Indies. The reference to Kipling underscores the novel's role as postcolonial critique.

9. Erna Brodber, *Myal* (Long Grove: Waveland Press, 1988), 6. Subsequent references to this edition are include parenthetically.
10. Frantz Fanon, *Black Skin, White Masks* (New York: Grove Press, 1967), 18.
11. Ibid., 100.
12. Homi Bhabha, "Of Mimicry and Man: The Ambivalence of Colonial Discourse," *Discipleship: A Special Issue on Psychoanalysis*, 28 (Spring 1984), 125–33.
13. Fanon, 109–40.
14. bell hooks, *Black Looks: Race and Representation* (Boston, MA: South End, 1992), 83.
15. Ibid., 83.
16. Jean Rhys, *Wide Sargasso Sea* (New York: W. W. Norton, 1999), 70.
17. See Sandra Gilbert and Susan Gubar, *The Madwoman in the Attic: The Woman Writer and the Nineteenth Century Literary Imagination* (New Haven, CT: Yale University Press, 1979); and Audre Lorde, "The Master's Tools Will Never Dismantle the Master's House," in *Sister Outsider: Essays and Speeches*, ed. Audre Lorde (Berkeley, CA: Crossing Press, 1984), 110–14.
18. Jean Armstrong, *Demythologizing the Romance of Conquest* (Westport, CT: Greenwood, 2000), 56.
19. Ibid., 57.
20. Jacques Derrida, "Structure, Sign and Play in the Discourse of the Human Sciences," in *Writing and Difference*, trans. Alan Bass (London: Routledge, 2001).
21. hooks, *Black Looks*, 2.
22. Brodber's deployment of the doll trope in reference to Selwyn's efforts to fashion Ella into an idealized representation of womanhood is resonant with voodoo rituals emanating from an African-Caribbean spiritual epistemology.
23. Hartman, 154–72.
24. Bhabha, 37–9.
25. Audre Lorde, *Your Silence Will Not Protect You* (UK: Silver Press, 2017), 8.
26. bell hooks, *Teaching to Transgress: Education as the Practice of Freedom* (New York: Routledge, 1994), 11.
27. Ibid.
28. Ibid.
29. Chickens figure prominently in voodoo rituals as objects of abuse. Percy and Willie are subject to zombification at the hands of Selwyn, but Ella speaks on their behalf in voicing the plight of the subaltern.
30. Audre Lorde, *Sister Outsider: Essays and Speeches* (Berkeley, CA: Crossing Press, 1984), 110–14.
31. Toni Morrison, "Home," in *The House That Race Built*, ed. Wahneema Lubiano (New York: Vintage, 1998), 3–12.
32. Ibid., 12

33 The ritual involving Mama Day's intervention in Cocoa's healing implicates whiteness and the Gaze as well as Ruby's malevolent magic in Cocoa's near-death encounter. George's ill-fated journey to the chicken coop, Cocoa's encounter with her mirrored image, and the bath scene signal an entrapment within the oppressive social structures of contemporary America and the role of Africanist healing practices in curing the psychic wounds issuing from an adherence to European culture.

34 Gloria Naylor, *Bailey's Café* (New York: Harcourt, 1992), 76. Subsequent references to this edition are included parenthetically.

35 Houston A. Baker, Jr., *Blues Ideology: Blues, Ideology, and Afro-American Literature: A Vernacular Theory* (Chicago, IL: University of Chicago Press, 1984), 13.

36 Ibid., 8.

37 Gloria Naylor, "A Conversation with Gloria Naylor," interview by Virginia Fowler, in *Conversations with Gloria Naylor*, ed. Maxine Lavon Montgomery (Jackson: University Press of Mississippi, 2004), 127.

38 Kristen Lillvis, *Post-Human Blackness and the Female Imagination* (Athens: University of Georgia Press, 2017), 8.

39 Dorothea Buehler, "Below the Surface: Female Sexuality in Gloria Naylor's '*Bailey's Café*'," *Amerikastudien/American Studies*, 56, 3 (2011), 445.

40 Naylor endows *Mama Day*'s Sapphira Wade with a similar a-temporal constituency in terms of the island foremother's role as a fluid semiotic space linked with a gendered African past.

41 Fowler, "A Conversation with Gloria Naylor," 126.

42 Angela Y. Davis, *Blues Legacies and Black Feminism* (New York: Random House, 1999), 66–90.

43 Hill Collins, *Black Feminist Thought*, 77–8.

44 Buehler, "Below the Surface," 428.

45 Simone de Beauvoir, *The Second Sex* (New York: Vintage, 1989).

46 Lara Karaian, "Policing 'Sexting': Responsibilization, Respectability, and Sexual Subjectivity in Child Protection/Crime Prevention Responses to Teenagers' Digital Sexual Expression," *Theoretical Criminology*, 18, 3 (2014), 282–99.

47 Thera Pickens, "Shoving aside the Politics of Respectability: Black Women, Reality TV, and the Ratchet Performance," *Women and Performance: A Journal of Feminist Theory*, 25 (2015), 41–58.

48 Joanne V. Gabbin, "A Laying on of Hands: Black Women Writers Exploring the Roots of Their Folk and Cultural Tradition," in *Wildwomen in the Whirlwind: Afra-American Culture and the Contemporary Literary Renaissance*, eds. Joanne Braxton and Andrea Nicola McLaughlin (New Brunswick, NJ: Rutgers University Press, 1990), 246–63.

49 See Jacques Lacan, "Some Reflections on the Ego," *The International Journal of Psycho-Analysis*, 34, 1 (1953), 11–17; and Gilbert and Gubar, *The Madwoman in the Attic*, 3–44.

50 Hortense Spillers, "Mama's Baby, Papa's Maybe: An American Grammar Book," in *Within the Circle: An Anthology of African American Literary Criticism from the Harlem Renaissance to the Present*, ed. Angelyn Mitchell (Durham, NC: Duke University Press, 1994), 480.
51 Ibid., 480.
52 bell hooks, *Yearning: Race, Gender, and Cultural Politics* (Boston, MA: South End Press, 1990), 147.
53 Ibid., 147.

Chapter 5

1 Homi Bhabha, *The Location of Culture* (New York: Routledge, 2004), 13.
2 Naomi Klein, *The Rise of Disaster Capitalism* (New York: Picador, 2007), 10.
3 Ibid., 14.
4 Ibid., 23.
5 Filmed at the Louvre Museum, *The Foreigner's Home* is a 2006 documentary that Morrison curated. The film features guest appearances by artists in conversation on the experience of social and cultural displacement. The term "foreigner's home" in relation to Paris as a space of transcultural fluidity underscores the city's historic role in attracting a multinational group of raced subject.
6 Toni Morrison, "An Interview with Toni Morrison." Interview by Nellie McKay, in *Conversations with Toni Morrison*, 147.
7 Toni Morrison, Morrison, *Tar Baby* (New York: New American Library, 1981), 46. Subsequent references to this edition are included parenthetically.
8 See Morrison's Interview with Charlie Rose. YouTube. January 19, 1998.
9 Trudier Harris, *Fiction and Folklore: The Novels of Toni Morrison* (Knoxville: University of Tennessee Press, 1991), 139.
10 bell hooks, *Black Looks: Race and Representation* (Boston, MA: South End, 1992), 373.
11 Ibid., 378.
12 Ibid., 380.
13 Toni Morrison, "Unspeakable Things Unspoken," in *Within the Circle: An Anthology of African American Literary Criticism from the Harlem Renaissance to the Present*, ed. Angelyn Mitchell (Durham, NC: Duke University Press, 1994), 370.
14 Morrison, *Playing in the Dark: Whiteness and the American Literary Imagination* (New York: Random House, 1992), 59.
15 Letitia Moffit, "Finding the Door: Vision/Revision and Stereotype in Toni Morrison's Tar Baby," *Critique*, 46, 1 (2004), 18.
16 Judylyn S. Ryan, "Contested Vision/Double Vision in Tar Baby," in *Toni Morrison: Critical and Theoretical Approaches*, ed. Nancy J. Peterson (Baltimore, MD: Johns Hopkins University Press, 1997), 70.

17 Toni Morrison, *Tar Baby* [foreword] (New York: Vintage, 1981), xiii.
18 Harris, *Fiction and Folklore*, 146.
19 Anissa J. Wardi, *Water and Memory: An Eco-critical Perspective* (Gainesville: University of Florida, 2011), 56.
20 Evelyn Jaffe Schriebert, *Race, Trauma, and Home in the Novels of Toni Morrison* (Baton Rouge: Louisiana State University Press, 2010), 137–8.
21 Harris, *Fiction and Folklore*, 147.
22 Keith Byerman, *Fingering the Jagged Grain: Tradition and Form in Recent Black Fiction* (Athens: University of Georgia Press, 2010), 215.
23 Craig Werner, *Playing the Changes: From Afro Modernism to the Jazz Impulse* (Urbana: University of Illinois Press, 1994), 111.
24 Christopher W. Clark, "What Comes to the Surface: Storms, Bodies, and Community in Jesmyn Ward's *Salvage the Bones*," *Mississippi Quarterly*, 68, 3 (2015), 350.
25 Jesmyn Ward, *Salvage the Bones* (London: Bloomsbury, 2011), 159. Subsequent references to this edition are included parenthetically.
26 See Wardi, *Water and Memory*.
27 Laura Fine, "'Make Them Know': Jesmyn Ward's *Salvage the Bones*," *The South Carolina Review*, 49, 1 (2016), 48.
28 Ibid., 48.
29 Mary Ruth Marotte, "Pregnancies, Storms, and Legacies of Loss in Jesmyn Ward's *Salvage the Bones*," in *Ten Years after Katrina: Critical Perspectives of the Storm's Effect on American Culture and Identity*, eds. Mary Ruth Marotte and Glenn Jellenik (Washington, DC: Lexington Books, 2015), 118.
30 Clark, "What Comes to the Surface," 353.
31 Marotte, "Pregnancies, Storms, and Legacies of Loss," 118.
32 Hill Collins, *Black Feminist Thought*, 66.
33 Fine, "Make Them Know," 54.
34 As a recurring symbol, gold associates the Esch's longing for Manny with the story of Medea and Jason's quest for the golden fleece.
35 I acknowledge the following sources for insight into the characteristics and numerous guises of Mama Wata whose inspiring influence continues to engage the literary and artistic imaginations of writers, visual artists, and filmmakers across the trans-Atlantic world: Karen McCarthy Brown, *Mama Lola: A Vodou Priestess in Brooklyn* (Berkeley: University of California Press, 1991; 2001); Joan Dayan, "Erzulie: A Women's History of Haiti," *Research in African Literatures*, 25, 2 (1994), 5–31; Maya Deren, *Divine Horsemen: Voodoo Gods of Haiti* (New York: Chelsea House, 1970); and Zora Neale Hurston, *Tell My Horse* (Berkeley, CA: Turtle Island, 1938; 1981).
36 The site figuring into "Love Drought" recalls the setting of Julie Dash's *Daughters of the Dust*, Gloria Naylor's *Mama Day*, and Paule Marshall's *Praisesong for the Widow*.

37 Beyonce Knowles-Carter, *Lemonade*, Columbia Records/Sony Music. DVD. All quotes are drawn from the visual album.
38 Zora Neale Hurston, *Their Eyes Were Watching God* (Urbana: University of Illinois Press, 1937), 41.
39 See Kristen Lillvis, *Posthuman Blackness and the Black Female Imagination* (Athens: University of Georgia Press, 2017).
40 Ntozake Shange, *For Colored Girls Who Have Considered Suicide When the Rainbow Is Enough*, 67.
41 Hill Collins, *Black Feminist Thought*, 69.
42 Ibid., 69.
43 See Teresa N. Washington, *Our Mothers, Our Powers, Our Texts: Manifestations of Aje in Africana Literature* (Bloomington: Indiana University Press, 2005).
44 Shange, *For Colored Girls*, xv.
45 Ibid., 48.
46 Hill Collins, *Black Feminist Thought*, 67–8.
47 The album's reliance upon Miss Hattie's recipe in the construction of the visual album recalls the narrative strategies present in a range of works in the tradition of Black women's *fiction*, including Alice Walker's *The Color Purple*, Ntozake Shange's *Sassafrass, Cypress, and Indigo*, and Julie Dash's *Daughters of the Dust*.
48 The scene brings to mind the circumstances surrounding the police shooting of unarmed Michael Brown, whose mother makes a cameo appearance, and the ensuing social unrest in Ferguson, Missouri.
49 Beyonce serves as a refiguration of Oshun, Yoruba river deity and goddess of fertility, love, and sensuality.
50 Hill Collins, *Black Feminist Thought*, 69.
51 bell hooks, "Moving beyond Pain," The bell hooks Institute. Blog. May 9, 2016. I offer a more positive reading of *Lemonade* than the one hooks advances in light of the album's engagement with speculative genre conventions and Beyonce's appropriation of a range of personae. Beyonce's reliance upon multiple and competing subjectivity undermines an assessment of female character based in essentialist constructs.
52 Toni Morrison, *Beloved* (New York: Penguin, 1988), 164. It is possible to read Baby Suggs's ad hoc sermon on self-love as an extension of the project of self-reclamation on the part of the ex-slave community and a gesture of resistance directed toward white, patriarchal authority. See Morrison, *Beloved*, 87–9.
53 hooks, "Moving beyond Pain."
54 Bhabha, *The Location of Culture*, 10.

References

Alexander, M. Jacqui. (2005), *Pedagogies of Crossing: Meditations on Feminism, Sexual Politics, Memory, and the Sacred*. Durham, NC: Duke University Press.

Alonso, Ana Maria. (2008), "Borders, Sovereignty, and Racialization," in Deborah Poole (ed.), *Companion to Latin American Anthropology*, 230–53. Oxford: Basil Blackwell.

Anatol, Gisele Liza. (2015), *The Things That Fly in the Night: Female Vampires in the Literature of the Circum-Caribbean and African Diaspora*. New Brunswick, NJ: Rutgers University Press.

Appiah, Kwame Anthony. (1991), "Is the Post- in Postmodernism the Post- in Postcolonial?" *Critical Inquiry*, 17 (2): 336–57.

Armstrong, Jean. (2000), *Demythologizing the Romance of Conquest*. Westport, CT: Greenwood.

Ashcroft, Bill, Griffith, Gareth, and Tiffin, Helen, eds. (1998), *Post-colonial Studies: The Key Concepts*. New York: Routledge.

Baker, Jr., Houston A. (1984), *Blues, Ideology and Afro-American Literature: A Vernacular Theory*. Chicago, IL: University of Chicago Press.

Baker, Jr., Houston A. (1991), *Workings of the Spirit: The Poetics of Afro-American Women's Writing*. Chicago, IL: University of Chicago Press.

Baldwin, James. (1963), *The Fire Next Time*. New York: Dell.

Barr, Marleen, ed. (2008), *Afro-Future Females: Black Writers Chart Science Fiction's Newest New Wave*. Columbus: Ohio State University Press.

Berger, James. (1999), *After the End: Representations of the Post-Apocalypse*. Minneapolis: University of Minnesota Press.

Betts, Reginald Dwayne, ed. (2015), "The Countdown to Armageddon," in *Bastards of the Reagan Era*, 3–9. New York: Four Way Books.

Bhabha, Homi. (1984), "Of Mimicry and Man: The Ambivalence of Colonial Discourse." *Discipleship: A Special Issue on Psychoanalysis* 28: 125–33.

Bhabha, Homi. (1994), *The Location of Culture*. Abingdon: Routledge.

Boyce Davies, Carol. (1994), *Black Women, Writing, and Identity: Migrations of the Subject*. New York: Routledge.

Braidotti, Rosi. (2013), *The Posthuman*. Cambridge: Polity.

Brodber, Erna. (1988), *Myal*. Long Grove, IL: Waveland Press.

Brogan, Kathleen. (1998), *Cultural Haunting: Ghosts and Ethnicity in Recent American Literature*. Charlottesville: University Press of Virginia.

Brooks, Kinetra. (2014), "The Importance of Neglected Intersections: Race and Gender in Contemporary Zombie Texts and Theories." *African American Review* 47 (4): 461–75.

Brox, Ali. (2008), "'Every Age Has the Vampire It Needs': Octavia Butler's Vampiric Vision in *Fledgling*." *Utopian Studies* 19 (3): 391–409.

Buehler, Dorothea. (2011), "Below the Surface: Female Sexuality in Gloria Naylor's *Bailey's Cafe*." *Amerikastudien/American Studies* 56 (3): 425–48.

Bustamante, Elena Clemente. (2007), "Fragments and Crossroads in Nalo Hopkinson's Brown Girl in the Ring." *Spaces of Utopia* 4: 11–30.

Butler, Judith. (2006), *Gender Trouble: Feminism and the Subversion of Identity*. New York: Routledge Classics.

Butler, Octavia. (2006), "Interviewing the Oracle: Octavia Butler." Interview by Kazembo Balagun, *The Indypendent: An Electronic Magazine*.

Butler, Octavia E. (2005), *Fledgling*. New York: Grand Central Publishing.

Byerman, Keith E. (1985), *Fingering the Jagged Grain: Tradition and Form in Recent Black Fiction*. Athens: University of Georgia Press.

Byerman, Keith. (2005), *Remembering the Past in Contemporary African American Fiction*. Chapel Hill: University of North Carolina Press.

Caruth, Cathy. (1991), "Introduction: Psychoanalysis, Culture, and Trauma, II." *American Imago* 48 (4): 417–24.

Caruth, Cathy. (1996), *Unclaimed Experience*. Baltimore, MD: Johns Hopkins University Press.

Clark, Christopher W. (2015), "What Comes to the Surface: Storms, Bodies, and Community in Jesmyn Ward's *Salvage the Bones*." *Mississippi Quarterly* 68 (3): 341–58.

Cliff, Michelle. (1995), *Abeng*. New York: Plume/Penguin.

Cliff, Michelle. (1980), *Claiming an Identity They Taught Me to Despise*. London: Persephone.

Cliff, Michelle. (2008), *If I Could Write This in Fire*. Minneapolis: University of Minneapolis Press.

Cliff, Michelle. (1987), *No Telephone to Heaven*. New York: Plume/Penguin.

Clitandre, Nadège T. (2018), *The Haitian Diasporic Imaginary*. Charlottesville: University of Virginia Press.

Commander, Michelle D. (2017), *Afro-Atlantic Flight: Speculative Returns and the Black Fantastic*. Durham, NC: Duke University Press.

Cope, Robyn. (2017), "'We Are Your Neighbors': Edwidge Danticat's New Narrative for Haiti." *Journal of Haitian Studies* 23 (1): 98–118.

Danticat, Edwidge. (2013), *Claire of the Sea Light*. New York: Knopf.

Danticat, Edwidge. (2010), *Create Dangerously: The Immigrant Artist at Work*. New York: Random House.

Danticat, Edwidge. (2013), "'Writer Edwidge Danticat' by Tavis Smiley." Accessed December 3, 2019. http://www.pbs.org/wnet/tavissmiley/interviews/edwidge-danticat/.

Davis, Angela Y. (1999), *Blues Legacies and Black Feminism*. New York: Random House.

Davis, Jonita. (2020), "How Black Women Are Reshaping Afrofuturism." *Yes!Magazine*. April 24.

de Beauvoir, Simone. (1989), *The Second Sex*. New York: Vintage.
Deren, Maya. (1983), *The Divine Horsemen: The Living Gods of Haiti*. Kingston, NY: McPherson.
Derrida, Jacques. (2001), *Writing and Difference*. Translated by Alan Bass. New York: Routledge.
Dery, Mark. (1994), "Black to the Future: Interviews with Samuel R. Delaney, Greg Tate, and Tricia Rose," in Mark Dery (ed.), *Flame Wars: The Discourse of Cyberculture*, 179–221. Durham, NC: Duke University Press.
Eshun, Kodwo. (2003), "Further Considerations on Afrofuturism." *New Centennial Review* 3 (2): 287–302.
Eshun, Kodwo. (1999), *More Brilliant than the Sun: Adventures in Science Fiction*. London: Quartet Books.
Evans, Shari. (2013), "From 'Hierarchal Behavior' to Strategic Amnesia: Structures of Memory and Forgetting in Octavia Butler's Fledgling," in Rebecca J. Holden and Nisi Shawl (eds.), *Strange Matings: Science Fiction, Feminism, and African American Voices*, 237–62. Seattle, WA: Aqueduct Press.
Fanon, Frantz. (1967), *Black Skin, White Masks*. New York: Grove Press.
Fine, Laura. (2016), "'Make Them Know': Jesmyn Ward's *Salvage the Bones*." *The South Carolina Review* 49 (1): 48–58.
Foucault, Michel. (1975), *Discipline and Punish: The Birth of the Prison*. New York: Penguin.
Fowler, Virginia. (2004), "A Conversation with Gloria Naylor," Maxine Lavon Montgomery (ed.), *Conversations with Gloria Naylor*, 123–37. Jackson: University Press of Mississippi.
Gabbin, Joanne V. (1990), "A Laying on of Hands: Black Women Exploring the Roots of Their Folk and Cultural Heritage," in Joanne Braxton and Andrea Nicola McLaughlin (eds.), *Wildwomen in the Whirlwind: Afra-American Culture and the Contemporary Literary Renaissance*, 246–63. Brunswick, NJ: Rutgers University Press.
Gates, Rob. (2006), "*Fledgling* by Octavia Butler: A Review." *Strange Horizons*. March 6. http://strangehorizons.com/non-fiction/reviews/fledgling-by-octavia-e-butler/
Gilbert, Sandra and Susan Gubar, eds. (1979), *The Madwoman in the Attic: The Woman Writer and the Nineteenth Century Literary Imagination*. New Haven, CT: Yale University Press.
Gilroy, Paul. (1993), *The Black Atlantic: Modernity and Double Consciousness*. Cambridge, MA: Harvard University Press.
Glover, Kaiama L. (2005), "Exploiting the Undead: The Usefulness of the Zombie in Haitian Literature." *The Journal of Haitian Literature* 11 (2): 105–21.
Gordon, Avery F. (2008), *Ghostly Matters: Haunting and the Sociological Imagination*. Minneapolis: New University of Minneapolis Press.
Halberstam, Judith (J. Jack) and Ira Livingston, eds. (1995), *Posthuman Bodies*. Bloomington: Indiana University Press.

Harris, Trudier. (1991), *Fiction and Folklore: The Novels of Toni Morrison*. Knoxville: University of Tennessee Press.

Hartman, Saidiya. (2007), *Lose Your Mother: A Journey along the Atlantic Slave Route*. New York: Farrar, Straus, and Giroux.

Henderson, Mae G. (2000), "Speaking in Tongues: Dialogics, Dialectics, and the Black Woman Writer's Literary Tradition," in Winston Napier (ed.), *African American Literary Theory: A Reader*, 348–68. New York: New York University Press.

Henderson, Mae G. and E. Patrick Johnson, eds. (2005), *Black Queer Studies: A Critical Anthology*. Durham, NC: Duke University Press.

Hill Collins, Patricia. (1991), *Black Feminist Thought: Knowledge, Consciousness, and the Politics of Empowerment*. New York: Routledge.

hooks, bell. (1992), *Black Looks: Race and Representation*. Boston, MA: South End.

hooks, bell. (2016), "Moving Beyond Pain." The bell hooks Institute. May 9. http://www.bellhooksinstitute.com/blog/2016/5/9/moving-beyond-pain.

hooks, bell. (1994), *Teaching to Transgress: Education as the Practice of Freedom*. New York: Routledge.

hooks, bell. (2001), *Yearning: Race, Gender, and Cultural Politics*. New York: Routledge.

Hopkinson, Nalo. (1998), *Brown Girl in the Ring*. New York: Grand Central.

Hopkinson, Nalo. (2010). "Science Fiction vs. Science Fact." TVO Channel, April 9. Accessed January 29, 2020. http://www.youtube.com/watch?v=VRNb5fUOrSA.

Horton Stallings, Lamonda. (2015), *Funk the Erotic: Transaesthetics and Black Sexual Cultures*. Urbana: University of Illinois Press.

Horton Stallings, Lamonda. (2007), *Mutha Is Half a Word: Black Performance and Cultural Criticism*. Columbus: Ohio State University Press.

Hurston, Zora Neale. (1981), *Tell My Horse*. Berkeley, CA: Turtle Island.

Hurston, Zora Neale. (1937), *Their Eyes Were Watching God*. Urbana: University of Illinois Press.

Ince, Kate. (2017), *The Body and the Screen: Female Subjectivities in Contemporary Women's Cinema*. London: Bloomsbury.

Jones, Kima. (2017), "A Conversation with Edwidge Danticat," in Maxine Lavon Montgomery (ed.), *Conversations with Edwidge Danticat*, 167–74. Jackson: University Press of Mississippi.

Karaian, Lara. (2013), "Policing 'Sexting': Responsibilization, Respectability, and Sexual Subjectivity in Child Protection, Crime Prevention Responses to Teenagers' Digital Sexual Expression." *Theoretical Criminology* 18 (3): 282–99. Web. https://journals.sagepub.com/doi/10.1177/1362480613504331

Kincaid, Jamaica. (2007), "Garden Path Leads to Surprising Places." *The Denver Post*. Web. https://www.denverpost.com/2008/02/07/garden-path-leads-to-surprising-places/

Klein, Naomi. (2007), *The Rise of Disaster Capitalism*. New York: Picador.

Lacan, Jacques. (1997), *Ecrits*. Translated by Alan Sheridan. New York: Norton.

LeSeur, Geta. (1995), *Ten Is the Age of Darkness: The Black Female Bildungsroman*. Columbia: University of Missouri Press.

Lillvis, Kristen. (2017), *Posthuman Blackness and the Black Female Imagination*. Athens: University of Georgia Press.

Lipsitz, George. (1994), *Dangerous Crossroads: Popular Music, Postmodernism, and the Poetics of Place*. London: Verso.

Lipsitz, George. (1994), "We Know What Time It Is: Race, Class, and Youth Culture in the Nineties," in Tricia Rose and Andrew Ross (eds.), *Microphone Fiends*, 17–28. New York: Routledge.

Lipsitz, George. (2011), *How Racism Takes Place*. Philadelphia, PA: Temple University Press.

Lorde, Audre. (1984), *Sister Outsider*. Berkeley, CA: Crossing.

Marotte, Mary Ruth. (2015), "Pregnancies, Storms, and Legacies of Loss in Jesmyn Ward's *Salvage the Bones*," in Mary Ruth Marotte and Glenn Jellenik (eds.), *Ten Years after Katrina: Critical Perspectives of the Storm's Effect on American Culture and Identity*, 207–19. Washington, DC: Lexington Books.

Martin, Rachel. (2017), "Haitian Youth Illuminated in 'Sea Light,'" in Maxine Lavon Montgomery (ed.), *Conversations with Edwidge Danticat*, 148–51. Jackson: University Press of Mississippi.

Martinez-Falquina, Silvia. (2015), "Postcolonial Trauma Theory in the Contact Zone: The Strategic Representation of Grief in Edwidge Danticat's *Claire of the Sea Light*." *Humanities* 4 (4): 834–60.

McCormack, Donna. (2016), "Living with Others Inside the Self: Decolonising Transplantation, Selfhood, and the Body Politic in Nalo Hopkinson's *Brown Girl in the Ring*." *Medical Humanities* 42 (4): 1–23.

Moffit, Letitia. (2004), "Finding the Door: Vision/Revision and Stereotype in Toni Morrison's *Tar Baby*." *Critique* 46 (1): 12–26.

Montgomery, Maxine Lavon. (2010), "Don't Look B(l)ack: Spectatorship and Toni Morrison's *Tar Baby*." *College Language Association Journal* LIV (1): 36–51.

Montgomery, Maxine Lavon. (2017), "Putting together the Fragments: A Conversation with Edwidge Danticat," in Maxine Lavon Montgomery (ed.), *Conversations with Edwidge Danticat*, 203–12. Jackson: University Press of Mississippi.

Morris, Susanna. (2012), "Black Girls Are from the Future: Afro-futurist Feminism in Octavia Butler's *Fledgling*." *Women's Studies Quarterly* 40 (3/4): 146–66.

Morrison, Toni. (1994), "An Interview with Toni Morrison," in Danielle Taylor Guthrie (ed.), *Conversations with Toni Morrison*. Jackson: University Press of Mississippi.

Morrison, Toni. (1987), *Beloved*. New York: Plume/Penguin.

Morrison, Toni. (1998), "Home," in Wahneema Lubiano (ed.), *The House That Race Built*, 3–12. New York: Random House.

Morrison, Toni. (1992), *Playing in the Dark: Whiteness and the Literary Imagination*. Cambridge, MA: Harvard University Press.

Morrison, Toni. (1984), "Rootedness: The Ancestor as Foundation," in Mari Evans (ed.), *Black Women Writers (1950–1980): A Critical Evaluation*, 339–45. New York: Anchor Press/Doubleday.

Morrison, Toni. (1981), *Tar Baby*. New York: Knopf.

Morrison, Toni. (2004), *Tar Baby*. Foreword. New York: Vintage, xi–xiv.

Morrison, Toni. (2017), *The Origin of Others*. Cambridge, MA: Harvard University Press.

Morrison, Toni. (1994), "Unspeakable Things Unspoken: The Afro-American Presence in American Literature," in Angelyn Mitchel (ed.), *Within the Circle: An Anthology of African American Literary Criticism from the Harlem Renaissance to the Present*, 368–98. Durham, NC: Duke University Press.

Nash, Jennifer. (2019), *Black Feminism Reimagined: After Intersectionality*. Durham, NC: Duke University Press.

Nayar, Pramod K. (2011), "Vampirism and Post-Humanism in Octavia Butler's Fledgling." *Notes on Contemporary Literature* 41 (2): 3–8.

Naylor, Gloria. (1992), *Bailey's Cafe*. New York: Harcourt.

New York Governor Andrew Cuomo Coronavirus News Conference. 2020. CSPAN. April 19. https://www.c-span.org/video/?471344-1/york-gov-cuomo-holds-coronavirus-briefing.

Obst, Anthony. (2019), "How Doomsday Rhetoric Scorched the Earth of Rap's Underground." Red Bull Music Academy Daily. March 27.

Okonkwo, Christopher N. (2008), *A Spirit of Dialogue: Incarnations of Ogbanje, the Born-to-Die, in African American Literature*. Knoxville: University of Tennessee Press.

Okorafor, Nnedi. (2015), *Binti*. New York: Tom Doherty Books.

Parham, Marisa. (2009), *Haunting and Displacement in African American Literature and Culture*. New York: Routledge.

Pickens, Thera. (2015), "Shoving aside the Politics of Respectability: Black Women, Reality T V, and the Ratchet Performance." *Women and Performance: A Journal of Feminist Theory* 25 (1): 41–58.

Porter, Russell. (1995), *Spectacular Vernaculars: Hip-Hop and the Politics of Postmodernism*. New York: State University of New York Press.

"Review of *Brown Girl in the Ring*." (1998), *Publisher's Weekly*. https://www.publishersweekly.com/978-0-446-67433-1

Rhys, Jean. (1999), *Wide Sargasso Sea*. New York: W. W. Norton.

Rody, Caroline. (2001), *The Daughter's Return: African-American and Caribbean Women's Fictions of History*. Cambridge: Oxford University Press.

Romdhani, Rebecca. (2015), "Zombies Go to Toronto: Zombifying Shame in Nalo Hopkinson's Brown Girl in the Ring." *Research in African Literatures* 46 (4): 72–89.

Rose, Tricia and Andrew Ross. (1994), *Microphone Fiends: Youth Music and Urban Culture*. New York: Routledge.

Ryan, Judylyn S. (1997), "Contested Visions/Double Vision in *Tar Baby*," in Nancy J. Peterson (ed.), *Toni Morrison: Critical and Theoretical Approaches*, 63–87. Baltimore, MD: Johns Hopkins University Press.

Salvini, Laura. (2012), "A Heart of Kindness: Nalo Hopkinson's *Brown Girl in the Ring*." *Journal of Haitian Studies* 18 (2): 180–93.

Samatar, Sophia. (2017), "Toward a Planetary Afro-futurism." *Research in African Literatures* 48 (4): 174–91.

Schreiber, Evelyn Jaffe. (2010), *Race, Trauma, and Home in the Novels of Toni Morrison*. Baton Rouge: Louisiana University Press.

Shange, Ntozake. (1977), *For Colored Girls Who Have Considered Suicide When the Rainbow Is Enuf*. New York: Bantam.

Shaviro, Steven. (1993), *The Cinematic Body*. Minneapolis: University of Minnesota Press.

Snorton, C. Riley. (2018), *Black on Both Sides*. Minneapolis: University of Minnesota Press.

Spillers, Hortense J. (1994), "Mama's Baby, Papa's Maybe: An American Grammar Book," in Angelyn Mitchel (ed.), *Within the Circle: An Anthology of African-American Literary Criticism from the Harlem Renaissance to the Present*, 454–81. Durham, NC: Duke University Press.

Strong, Melissa J. (2011), "The Limits of Newness: Hybridity in Octavia E. Butler's Fledgling." *FEMSPEC: An Interdisciplinary Feminist Journal Dedicated to Critical and Creative Work in the Realms of Science Fiction, Fantasy, Magical Realism, Surrealism, Myth, Folklore, and other Supernatural Genres* 11 (1): 27–43.

Tate, Greg and Arthur Jafa. (1992), "La Venus Negre." *Artforum* 30 (5): 90–3.

Thaler, Ingrid. (2010), *Black Atlantic Speculative Fictions: Octavia E. Butler, Jewell Gomez, and Nalo Hopkinson*. New York: Routledge.

Thomas, Sheree, ed. (2000), *Dark Matter: A Century of Speculative Fiction from the African Diaspora*. New York: Warner Books.

Tinsley, Omise'eke Natasha. (2008), "Black Atlantic, Queer Atlantic: Queer Imaginings of the Middle Passage." *GLQ: A Journal of Lesbian and Gay Studies* 14 (2/3): 191–215.

Valkeakari, Tuire. (2017), *Precarious Passages: The Diasporic Imagination in Contemporary Black Anglophone Fiction*. Gainesville: University Press of Florida.

Vickroy, Laurie. (2002), *Trauma and Survival in Contemporary Literature*. Charlottesville: University of Virginia Press.

Walker, Alice. (1983), "Writing the Color Purple," in Alice Walker (ed.), *In Search of Our Mothers' Gardens: Womanist Prose by Alice Walker*, 350–60. New York: Harcourt.

Walker, Lisa. (2001), *Looking Like What You Are: Sexual Style, Race, and Lesbian Identity*. New York: New York University Press.

Ward, Jesmyn. (2011), *Salvage the Bones*. London: Bloomsbury.

Wardi, Anissa J. (2016), *Water and African-American Memory: An EcoCritical Perspective*. Gainesville: University Press of Florida.

Warren, Calvin L. (2015), "Black Nihilism and the Politics of Hope." *CR: The New Centennial Review* 15 (1): 215–48.

Warren, Calvin L. (2018), *Ontological Terror: Blackness, Nihilism, and Emancipation.* Durham, NC: Duke University Press.

Washington, Teresa N. (2005), *Our Mothers, Our Powers, Our Texts: Manifestations of Aje in Africana Literature.* Bloomington: Indiana University Press.

Werner, Craig. (1994), *Playing the Changes: From Afro Modernism to the Jazz Impulse.* Urbana: University of Illinois Press.

White, Hayden. (1975), *Meta-History: The Historical Imagination in Nineteenth Century Europe.* Baltimore, MD: Johns Hopkins University Press.

Wilentz, Amy. (2012), "A Zombie Is a Slave Forever." [Newspaper Article]. *New York Times.* October 30.

Williams Crenshaw, Kimberlé. (1994), "Mapping the Margins: Intersectionality, Identity Politics, and Violence against Women of Color," in Rixanne Mykitiuk and Martha Albertson Fineman (eds.), *The Public Nature of Private Violence*, 93–118. New York: Routledge.

Womack, Ytasha L. (2013), *Afro-Futurism: The World of Black Sci Fi and Fantasy Culture.* Chicago, IL: Lawrence Hill Books.

Woolfolk, Lisa. (2008), *Embodying Slavery in American Culture.* Urbana: University of Illinois Press.

Yasek, Lisa. (2005), "An Afro-futurist Reading of Ralph Ellison's *Invisible Man.*" *Rethinking History: The Journal of Theory and Practice* 9 (2/3): 297–313.

Index

Abeng. See also Cliff, Michelle
   African-Caribbean dislocations 67–70
   characters and story 67–81
   futuristic concerns 74–8
   hunting expedition 78–81
   "otherness" 70–4
   queerness or trans-ness 70–4
   slavery 71–3, 78–81
absent-present 28, 30, 121
Adeyemi, Tomi 8
African-Americans 86, 140
   forms of expressivity 37
   objectification 25
African-Caribbean setting 6, 13–14, 38–9, 44, 46, 49, 62, 96, 98, 100, 102, 104–5, 144
   radical Black female subjectivity 93
   zombies 92
Africans 22, 25, 65, 67
Afro-futurism 2, 4, 7–8
Afro-Futurist Feminism 7, 34
Alexander, M. Jacqui 68
American literature 54, 125
   politics of "othering" 25
Anatol, Giselle Liza 44
Ansa, Tina McElroy 18
   Baby of the Family 18
Appiah, Kwame Anthony 10
Armstrong, Jean 98

Bailey's Café. See also Naylor, Gloria
   characters and story 105–16
   language structure 114–16
   "moon" and "stars", references in 110–11
   names, use of 112–14
   new social order 114–16
   patriarchal domination 111–12, 143
   zombies 105–9
Baker, Jr. Houston A. 36, 106–7
Berger, James 5

Betts, Reginald Dwayne 1
Beyonce, Knowles-Carter 4, 15, 117, 119, 140–50. *See also Lemonade*
Bhabha, Homi 11, 46, 95–6, 102, 118, 150
bildungsroman 13, 18–19, 21, 25, 32, 35–6, 43, 46, 62, 79
Black Atlantic subjects 3, 5–7, 10, 12, 14, 22, 34, 36, 40, 43–4, 50, 55, 57, 60
   imaginative archives 7, 75, 78, 81, 91
Black bodies 1, 12, 144
Black female/women
   conventional identity 42
   critical space 19
   empowerment 47
   futuristic visions 15
   literary and cultural production 7–8, 10, 13
   masculine control 30
   motherhood 45
   postapocalypticism 2, 4, 7, 9, 11, 43, 118
   radical subjectivity 66, 111–12
   science fiction 3, 6
   sexual ideology 18, 143
   stereotypic representations 22
   trans-Atlantic history 5
   transcultural literary tradition 18
   as writers and artists 2–3, 15, 18, 63
   zombies in literature 14
Black femininity
   body or physicality 91–2
   patriarchal domination 92–3
Black feminism 3–4, 12, 14, 21, 40, 68, 79–80, 86, 91, 111–12, 137, 143–4, 148, 150
Black girls 30, 79
   adultification 18
Black identity 7, 33, 49, 70, 87, 101, 107, 141
Blackness 7–8, 10–11, 15, 19, 22, 24–6, 29, 33, 48, 63, 67, 83–4, 88, 91, 93, 95, 100, 103, 121–3, 125–6, 128–9, 142

Index

Black Panther 9
Bones, Ebony 1–2, 15
   Behold a Pale Horse (album) 1
Book of the Goddess, The 28
border-crossing 6, 12, 21, 50, 132, 137
Boyce Davies, Carol 75, 82
Braidotti, Rosi 29
Bridewell, Lula Ann 18
   God Help the Child 18
Brodber, Erna 4, 15, 93–4, 98–100, 102–4, 114–15. *See also* Myal
Brogan, Kathleen 54
Bronte, Charlotte, *Jane Eyre* 106
Brown Girl in the Ring. *See also* Hopkinson, Nalo
   character and story 38–49
   gender identity 42–4
   healing practices 47–9
   magical realism 37
   mother–daughter relationship 45–7
   spirit world in 36–8
Brox, Ali 27
Buehler, Dorothea 109, 111
Bustamante, Elena Clemente 37, 42–3, 42–3, 47
Butler, Judith 79
Butler, Octavia E. 1–2, 4, 13, 17, 19–22, 25–6, 28–36, 43, 79, 117. *See also* Fledgling
Byerman, Keith 5, 129, 152 n.15, 167 n.22

Caribbean Nights and Days 100–1
Caruth, Cathy 54, 159 nn.81–2
cisgender 70, 88, 91, 149
Claire of the Sea Light. *See also* Danticat, Edwidge
   alien frontiers and the maroon life 59–63
   characters and story 50–62
   immigrant experience 49–53
   mother–daughter relationship 57–9
   self-reflexive encounters in 53–7
Clark, Christopher W. 131, 134
class
   contemporary challenges 4, 86, 88, 94, 123, 130–1, 142, 146, 150
   interlocking influences 3, 14, 40, 66, 82, 86, 106, 108, 122, 130, 146
   neoconservatism and new paradigms 11

Cliff, Michelle 65–6, 68–72, 77–84, 87–9. *See also* Abeng; No Telephone to Heaven
Clitandre, Nadège T. 61
colonialism 5–6, 10, 21, 25, 32, 38, 44, 48, 58–60, 66, 68–71, 74–6, 79–80, 82, 86, 89, 91–2, 94–7, 99–100, 102–4, 107, 122–3, 125–6, 128–9
Cope, Robyn 50, 60
Covid-19 11–12
crossroads 10–11, 17, 19–20, 23, 27, 35–6, 42–3, 58, 62, 68, 126
Cuomo, Andrew 12

Danticat, Edwidge 4, 13, 19, 43, 49–52, 55–8, 60–1. *See also Claire of the Sea Light*
dark matter 37, 92
Davis, Angela Y. 110
Davis, Jonita 110
Dayan, Joan "Erzulie: A Women's History of Haiti" 167 n.35
de Beauvoir, Simone 83, 111
decolonizing gesture 59, 62, 85, 93, 96, 104–5
Deren, Maya 43
Derrida, Jacques 9, 11, 28, 98
Dery, Mark 1–2, 8, 14, 65
diaspora 3, 6, 8, 28, 37, 44, 46, 51
diasporic homeland 47, 53, 58, 129
disaster capitalism 15, 117–18, 125, 129, 139, 146, 149–50
Dreaming Rivers (film) 115

Ellison, Ralph, *Invisible Man* 8, 119
Eshu Elegba 10
Eshun, Kodwo 8
Evans, Shari 27

Fanon, Frantz 5, 23, 95, 97
fantasy culture 2–4, 9, 15, 22, 24, 37
Fine, Laura 137
Fledgling. *See also* Butler, Octavia E.
   blackness in 19–23
   characters and story 19–23
   gender roles and sexuality 30–6
   mother's role 27–30
   quest for home 19, 21
   self as the other 23–7

forgetting 21, 45, 57–8, 91, 101, 109, 115, 136
Foucault, Michel 46, 126
futuristic imaginaries 3–4, 7, 18, 21, 49

Gates, Rob 27, 147
gender. *See also* Black female/women
　alternative identities 43
　bodily functions 44
　conventional notions 14, 42, 56–7, 63
　conventional role 141–2, 144–6, 150
　cosmopolitanism 12
　dominant paradigms 18
　in dominant society 109–11, 113–15, 118, 123
　futurist vision 30–1
　identity construction 4
　interlocking influences 3, 14, 40, 66, 82, 86, 106, 108, 122, 130, 146
　new social arrangement 7
　in New World Order 135
　power dynamics 30–1, 36
　self-reflexive encounters 53
　self-reflexive engagements 23, 26
　stereotypic representations 22
Gilroy, Paul 14, 65, 68

Hamilton Edith, *Mythology* 133
Hampton, Gregory 33
Harris, Trudier 123, 128–9
Hartman, Saidiya 21, 92, 101
Henderson, Mae Gwendolyn 3
heterosexual normativity 31, 53, 66, 70, 73, 87, 91, 149
Hill Collins, Patricia 40, 45
hooks, bell 9–10, 30, 83–4, 94, 97, 99, 104, 115, 124, 148–9
Hopkinson, Nalo 4, 13, 17, 19, 36–8, 40, 42–6, 49, 57, 60. *See also* Brown Girl in the Ring
Horton Stallings, Lamonda 9, 22, 43, 69, 73
Huchu, Tendai 8
Hurricane Camille 131
Hurricane Katrina 117, 130, 133, 140, 142, 145
Hurston, Zora Neale 43, 91–2, 96, 141
　Their Eyes Were Watching God 141

I Am Legend (science fiction thriller) 14
Illusion (film) 115
Ince, Kate 83
interlocking influences, race, class, gender, and sexuality 3, 14, 40, 66, 82, 86, 106, 108, 122, 130, 146

Jamaican 40, 46, 49, 67, 76, 81–2, 85, 97, 103
Johnson, Charles 5
Judeo-Christian tradition 13, 61, 103, 141

Kahiu, Wanuri 8
Karaian, Lara 111
King, Rodney, xenophobic attack 11, 154 n.37
Kirkman, Robert, *Walking Dead, The* 14
Klein, Naomi 15, 117–19, 136

Lacan, Jacques 83, 114
Lemonade. *See also* Beyonce, Knowles-Carter
　"All Night" 149
　Black female identity and sexual ideology 146–8
　Black woman's struggle for recognition 140–4
　"Daddy Lessons" 145, 147
　historical pattern of Black migration 143
　"Hold Up" 143–4
　Hurricane Katrina and domestic issues 140, 142, 145–8
　"Love Drought" 141–2
　police violence 141
　power issues and ideology of domination 140, 146, 149–50
　"Sandcastles" 149
　"Six Inch (Heels)" 143–4
　"Sorry" 147
　transgenerational masculine betrayal 145
LeSeur, Geta 17
　Ten Is the Age of Darkness 17
LGBTQ 149
Lillvis, Kristen 8, 22–3, 22–3, 28–9, 28–9, 108, 142
Lipsitz, George 10–11, 17
　Dangerous Crossroads 17

Lorde, Audre 82, 98, 103, 105
love 15, 30, 53, 56, 58, 62, 69, 103, 110, 117, 120, 124–5, 127, 134–5, 141, 144–5, 148–50
    maternal 148
    power of 62
    romantic 15, 117, 120, 134–5, 141–2, 149–50
    same-sex 53, 56
    self-love 58, 69, 149

Malcolm X 144
maleness 4, 18–19, 24, 26, 66, 88, 91, 111, 138
Marotte, Mary Ruth 133, 137
Marshall, Paule, *Praisesong for the Widow* 18
Martinez-Falquina, Silvia 60
memory 21–3, 32–3, 54, 57–8, 66, 74, 80–1, 101, 108, 115, 117–18, 121, 129, 131, 136–7, 139, 141
Middle Passage 7–8, 21–3, 42, 46, 48, 50, 60, 65, 68, 87–8, 91, 102, 121, 128, 131, 141. *See also* trans-Atlantic history
mirrors/mirroring, tropes of 23, 40, 49, 57–9, 66, 77, 97, 113–14, 121, 133, 138, 143, 149
Moffit, Letitia 126
Montgomery, Maxine Lavon 153 n.21, 159 n.69, 159 n.85
Morrison, Toni 5–6, 15, 21, 25, 69, 97, 105, 117, 119–23, 125, 127–8, 146, 149–50. *See also Tar Baby*
    Beloved 18, 69, 148
    Bluest Eye, The 101
    Paradise 26
    Playing in the Dark 13
Morris, Susanna 7, 30–1, 34
motherhood 28, 39–40, 45, 47, 65, 73, 80–1, 84, 111, 113, 127, 132–3, 135–9, 147
Mutu, Wangechi 8
Myal. See also Brodber, Erna
    characters and story 93–5
    diasporic history 101–4
    futuristic imaginary 104–5
    imperialism and patriarchal structure 98–101
    radical Black female subjectivity 93
    zombie apocalypse 94–8

Nayar, Pramod 29, 31
Naylor, Gloria 15, 93, 105–13, 115, 143. *See also Bailey's Café*
    Linden Hills 106
    Mama Day 106, 109, 115
    Women of Brewster Place, The 112
neocolonial influences 5, 10–11, 21, 25, 38, 58, 66, 71, 77, 82, 85–6, 91, 94–5, 98, 100, 102, 107, 120, 129
New World Order 10, 14, 18, 32, 78, 105, 135, 149
    global mappings 114–16
1992 Yonge Street Riot (Toronto) 4
nonhumans 29–30, 102, 105, 132, 142
No Telephone to Heaven. See also Cliff, Michelle
    Black female, relationship to home 81–4
    character and story 81–9
    forms of racism 84–6
    gender indeterminacy 88–9
    migration experiences 82–3
    "otherness" 86–8
    queerness 70–4
    racism 82–6
    slavery 71–3

Okonkwo, Christopher N. 18
Okorafor, Nnedi 9
    Binti 8, 18
"other," the 1, 24, 124, 137, 144
"othering" 22, 25, 123–5
"otherness" 24, 70, 84, 86, 101, 124

pandemics 2, 4, 12, 118, 120
Papa Legba 10, 40, 42, 46
Parham, Marisa 54
Pickens, Thera 112

queerness 9, 14, 31, 65–6, 65–6, 68–71, 73, 76–7, 77, 79–81, 87, 89, 149. *See also* sexuality

race
    autonomy 14
    contemporary political and literary discourses 18–23, 32–4, 36–7
    conventional notions 63
    interlocking influences 3, 14, 40, 66, 82, 86, 106, 108, 122, 130, 146

invisible boundary 130–1
new conservatism and paradigms 11, 18
postcolonial setting 3–5, 7, 10, 53
queerness 68–70, 72–4, 81–3, 85–6
romantic relations 120–3
self-actualization 14–15
self-reflexive engagements 25–30
transnational community 52
un-zombification 93–4, 96, 108, 109, 111
violent riots 39
Rhys, Jean 97–8
 Wide Sargasso Sea 106
Romdhani, Rebecca 44, 46
Ryan, Judylyn S. 126

Salvage the Bones. See also Ward, Jesmyn
 Black femininity 150
 characters and story 130–9
 familial and communal setting 139
 female empowerment 130–1
 Hurricane Katrina's devastating effects 130–9
 motherhood 135–9
 self and "other" 132–5
Salvini, Laura 47–8
Samatar, Sophia 8
Second World War 107, 118
sexuality 3–4, 7, 9, 14, 18–19, 30–1, 30–1, 33, 36, 39, 54, 56–7, 56–7, 111, 113, 127, 132, 137, 146. See also queerness
 interlocking influences 3, 14, 40, 66, 82, 86, 106, 108, 122, 130, 146
Shange, Ntozake 142, 144
 For Colored Girls 142
 Sassafrass, Cypress, and Indigo 18
Shaviro, Steven 83
Shock Doctrine 15, 117, 119
slavery 5–7, 14, 22, 31, 34, 38, 40, 45, 53–4, 57–8, 60, 67, 69, 71–3, 76, 78, 91, 107, 120–2, 129, 131, 136, 141–3
soucouyant 4, 14, 19, 43–4, 57, 144
Spillers, Hortense J. 3, 73, 114
storytelling 49, 53, 57, 75, 106, 140, 148
Strong, Melissa 30

Tar Baby. See also Morrison, Toni
 Black subjectivity 121–35
 characters and story 120–30
 colonizing presence 120–1
 male-female liaisons 124–5, 127–30

 maternal loss 125–7
 "othering" the "other" 123–5
Tate, Gregory 8
teaching 86, 104–5
Thomas, Sheree, *Dark Matter: A Century of Speculative Fiction from the African Diaspora* 37, 157 n.39
Tinsley, Omise'eke Natasha 14, 65, 68–9, 75
trans-Atlantic history 5–10, 21–2, 38, 40, 42–3, 45, 49–50, 52, 57–60, 75, 78, 87, 92–3, 101–2, 105–6, 108–9, 112, 130–1
trauma 5, 19–20, 32, 35, 40, 44, 51, 53–4, 56–8, 60, 62, 69, 73, 78, 80, 87, 91–3, 97, 107, 113, 116, 131, 145, 150
2010 Haiti earthquake 4, 13

un-zombification 93, 103, 105, 109, 112. See also zombie

Valkeakari, Tuire 74
vampire 4, 14, 19, 24–5, 29, 31, 35–6, 43–4, 89, 91–2
vernacular structures 6–9, 15, 36, 49, 53, 55, 63, 92, 112, 143–4, 146
 African-Caribbean 44, 92
 cultural heritage 102–3, 106–7
 Haitian-Creole 13
 West Indian 38, 43, 94
Vickroy, Laurie 54

Walcott, Derek, *Ti Jean and His Brothers* 42
Walking Dead, The (Television series) 14
Ward, Jesmyn 4, 15, 130–1, 133, 136–8, 140, 146, 150. See also *Salvage the Bones*
Warren, Calvin, L. 10
Washington, Teresa N. 143
Werner, Craig 129
whiteness 4, 7, 10–11, 15, 18, 24–6, 33, 66–7, 82–5, 88, 91, 95–7, 99–100, 103, 111, 122, 125–6, 129
Wideman, John Edgar 5
Williams Crenshaw, Kimberlé 3

Yasek, Lisa 8

zombie 14–15, 40, 44–5, 61, 83, 91–5, 98–100, 103, 105–6, 109, 111–12, 118. See also un-zombification
 colonial history 92
 in Western film and television 92

www.ingramcontent.com/pod-product-compliance
Lightning Source LLC
Chambersburg PA
CBHW061836300426
44115CB00013B/2409